DANGER ON THE ROAD: THE NEEDLESS SCOURGE

A study of obstacles to progress in road safety

Stephen Plowden
Mayer Hillman

No.627

ISBN 0-85374-235-9

Published by Policy Studies Institute, 1–2 Castle Lane, London SW1E 6DR
Printed by Bourne Offset Ltd.

Contents

LIST OF TABLES

INTRODUCTION

This study was inspired by the observation that progress in implementing road safety measures appears to lag behind knowledge of what action would be effective and would give value for money. This suggests that the main obstacles to progress are at the institutional rather than the technical level, where the term 'institutional' must be interpreted broadly to cover such questions as the prestige and status of the official bodies concerned, and the means open to individual citizens who are concerned about road safety to influence policy, as well as narrower questions of organisational structure.

It was neither possible within our resources nor necessary for our purpose to cover the whole field of road safety. We have examined the ways in which certain selected issues have been handled over the years in order to identify the problems and obstacles and to see to what extent there are institutional reasons for them. The issues selected are sufficiently numerous and diverse to illuminate the institutional points, but some that we have not examined may have at least as much potential. An obvious example is the effect of alcohol and drugs on drivers' behaviour. This is a subject of very great importance but was too large and required too much medical knowledge for us to tackle.

On some issues, we found that the amount of agreement at a technical level about what would or would not be efficacious was less than we had supposed, and we were therefore obliged to enter more deeply into technical points than we had anticipated. Although we have not attempted to make a detailed prediction of the effects of the reforms that have been examined, we are confident, on the basis of the quantified data and comparisons presented in later chapters, that it would be entirely realistic for the Government to set a target of reducing the annual number of deaths and serious casualties in road accidents by 40 per cent within eight years.

1

The arrangement of the report

A Summary of the rest of the report follows this Introduction.

Chapter I is concerned with the importance that should be attached to road safety and argues that it is even greater than the official casualty statistics and cost calculations suggest. The selected issues are then considered in the following seven chapters, each one of which ends with an attempt to bring out the institutional implications.

Chapter IX sets out what we think good institutional arrangements would be, considers how the system works at present and suggests changes to make it approximate more closely to the model described. The Appendix suggests ways in which the existing information on accidents, their costs and the other consequences of unsafe conditions on the roads could be amplified and improved.

Acknowledgements

The major sponsors of the study are the Nuffield Foundation and the Rees Jeffreys Road Fund, to whom we are extremely grateful. We would also like to acknowledge some further financial assistance from London Transport. The help we have received from very many people and organisations is acknowledged at appropriate points in the text. The references to the Department of Transport and the Transport and Road Research Laboratory, numerous though they are, do not, however, indicate the extent to which we have benefited from the information and comments they supplied. We are also grateful for comments we have received, in their personal capacities, from various members of the County Surveyors' Society and the Institution of Highways and Transportation. None of those who helped us bears any responsibility for any errors of fact in this report, nor for its conclusions and recommendations.

Finally, the authors wish to record their gratitude to the staff of PSI, especially to Clare Pattinson, Stephanie Maggin and Mari Girling who typed the drafts and the final text.

SUMMARY

The importance of road safety

In 1982 there were 255,980 road accidents in which someone was killed or injured. These resulted in 5,934 deaths, 79,739 serious casualties and 248,623 slight casualties.

In one way, these statistics may overstate the problem, since many of the injuries which fall under the official definition of 'serious' would normally be regarded as slight. In every other way they understate it. Hospital checks show that the police records on which the official statistics are based under-report slight casualties by about 35 per cent and serious casualties by about 20 per cent, although it is probably the less severe of the serious casualties that go unreported. These checks also show that there is some tendency to classify serious casualties as slight, although again it may be the least severe of the serious casualties that are misclassified in this way. In addition, there must be some injuries which are not treated in hospital at all or are not recognised in the hospital records as having their origin in a road accident, but in the absence of appropriate household surveys their numbers cannot be estimated. Fatalities are fully reported, but the official definition is narrow: for example, deaths which occur more than 30 days after an accident are excluded. The Registrar General's figures for deaths from road accidents, based on definitions which may perhaps err on the broad side, are some five per cent higher than those derived from police records.

The Department of Transport assigns costs to road casualties and accidents. The costings allow for damage-only accidents, which are not otherwise included in the statistics but are estimated to be about six times as numerous as injury accidents, which implies that there were approximately 1.5 million of them in 1982. The Department's estimate of the cost of all road accidents in 1982 was £2,370 million. This was made up of five elements: damage to vehicles and property (£900m); the value of production lost on account of death and injury (£720m); a notional sum to allow for the cost of pain, grief and suffering (£560m); police and insurance administration (£120m); ambulance costs and the cost of hospital treatment (£70).

Even apart from the fact that they are based on incomplete records of casualties, these figures err substantially on the low side. It is not clear to what extent the figures for 'pain, grief and suffering' are intended to represent the position of the bereaved, or of the family and friends of the seriously injured, as well as that of the victims themselves, but they do not do so adequately. No allowance is made for those who are involved in an accident, or who experience the shock of witnessing it, but are themselves uninjured. The extra expenses, such as help in the house, which a seriously injured person may incur, are not included and the losses experienced by people financially dependent on those killed or seriously injured are underestimated. Lost output and the cost of police and medical services are estimated on conservative assumptions. The disruption which an accident causes, for example to the owners of damaged vehicles in making arrangements for their repair and for using alternative means of transport in the meantime, or to other road users who may be diverted or delayed when an accident occurs, is not allowed for at all.

Accidents and casualties are not the only consequences of danger on the roads. Unsafe conditions disturb travel patterns. Some journeys, such as journeys on foot by old people, may be frustrated altogether; others, such as those which in good conditions would be made by bicycle, are made by means which the travellers would not otherwise have chosen. This can in turn give rise to what would otherwise be unnecessary travel by people who have to act as escorts and sometimes as chauffeurs. Such unwanted motorised travel itself causes congestion, accidents and other intrusion. Much travel still takes place by the means that would have been chosen in safer conditions, but at the cost of stress and anxiety both to the travellers themselves and to others on their behalf. In addition to travel, other activities, such as children's play and other street life, are affected in similar ways: either the activities are curtailed, or they still take place but are accompanied by anxiety.

These non-accident effects have never been costed and only sporadic attempts, none very recent, have been made to assess how widespread they are and how much resented. However, it is clearly established that traffic is a serious nuisance to many millions of people and that of the various intrusions it causes dan[ ] concern. A national survey in 1972 showed that t[ ] adults found difficulty in crossing some roads in their [ ] cent sometimes felt endangered when walking on the p[ ] beside the road; 53 per cent were sometimes worried pedestrian danger of others, especially of children or old p[ ] A statistical analysis of commuting patterns shows that in flatter parts of the country over 40 per cent of people would cycle to work if it were safe to do so. Surveys have shown an 'overwhelming desire to shop and live in situations free from disturbance and interference of traffic'.

The following sections discuss particular problems or topics in road safety in order to show what approaches have been adopted and to identify the obstacles to progress.

Motorcycling

Motorcycling is the most dangerous form of road travel. Travel by two-wheeled motor vehicles accounts for only some three per cent of vehicle mileage, but about a quarter both of fatal and of other casualties occur in accidents in which a two-wheeled motor vehicle is involved. Although most of the people injured in such accidents are the riders themselves, two-wheeled motor vehicles are also a great source of danger to other people. Per mile driven, five times as many pedestrians are killed by such vehicles as by cars. The problem essentially concerns young men: 75 per cent of rider casualties are under 24 and of these over 90 per cent are men; the accident involvement rate of riders of 18 and 19 is over six times that of riders between 30 and 50.

The main official response to the problem has been to encourage motorcyclists to be trained. Some 40 per cent of secondary schools are registered with a company financed by motorcycle trade interests which provides courses on traffic education, all of which include instruction on two-wheeled motor vehicles, as well as covering many other aspects of road safety. There are more than 650 centres at which approved motorcycle training is provided, principally aimed at people trying to acquire a licence; the courses on offer are subsidised by the trade and to some extent indirectly by the government and local authorities; arrangements to take the test are simplified for people who take it in conjunction with one of these courses. The government also gives strong moral support to motorcycle training.

There is, however, no statistical support for the belief in the efficacy of training: indeed, the evidence suggests that, by giving young motorcyclists greater confidence in their handling skills,

5

..g can sometimes lead to an increase in accident rates. Even .ne effect on rates were favourable, the widespread provision of relatively cheap training facilities and the moral support officially given to training must presumably stimulate the motorcycling habit and so cause accidents.

One way to try to reduce motorcycle accidents would be to limit the size, power and speed of the machines in use. At present the accident records do not normally give any details of the two-wheeled motor vehicles involved in accidents other than to classify them as mopeds, motor scooters and motorcycles, and the travel data required to calculate accident rates by size of machine are also lacking. There is, nevertheless, good evidence that the power of the machine has a strong influence on the accident involvement rate, especially for the more serious accidents. But although 16-year-old riders are restricted to mopeds, and holders of provisional licences to a learner motorcycle of limited power, there is effectively no limit on the weight, power and speed of the machines which holders of full licences may ride, nor has the possibility of imposing such limits ever been officially contemplated.

An alternative to stringent limits applying to all machines would be a graded driver licensing system, whereby eligibility to apply for a licence for a machine of a certain power would depend upon experience and a good record of riding less powerful machines. The merits of such a system have long been recognised, but except for the limitations placed on 16-year-olds and the holders of provisional licences, nothing has been implemented, even though the present arrangements breach what has been officially described as 'a fundamental principle of our testing system that we make the candidate perform on a vehicle as nearly as possible representative of the class for which he seeks full entitlement'.

One reason for the emphasis placed on training appears to be the doubtful argument that when accidents can be ascribed to poor behaviour on the part of road users of a particular class, the appropriate course of action is to educate road users of the class concerned. But a more fundamental reason is the belief that apart from training there is very little that the government can do to tackle the problem of motorcycle accidents. More drastic action appears to be regarded as an unacceptable infringement of liberty.

This idea would be easier to defend if motorcyclists harmed only themselves, although some degree of paternalism might be thought appropriate at least to teenagers and the principle of state intervention in the individual's own interests has also been established by the legislation on seat belts. But motorcyclists endanger other people and are also a major source of environmental intrusion: the nuisance caused by motorcycle noise is of the same order as that caused by heavy lorries. Moreover, even a stringent restriction on the machine would make little or no difference to the usefulness of the motorcycle as a mode of transport, so that the penalty for riders, except in lost excitement, would be small.

The idea that action more drastic than training would be illegitimate therefore rests on a failure to give the interests of other people due weight as against the wishes of motorcyclists. This presumably reflects the difficulty that third parties have, as compared with motorcyclists and trade interests, in bringing pressure to bear. The weak treatment of the motorcycling problem also suggests that road safety generally is given too little prestige within the Department of Transport. Motorcycling also brings out the close connection between road safety and other aspects of environmental intrusion, in this case noise, and the need for institutional arrangements that will recognise this link.

Lowering vehicle speeds

General principles suggest that the probability of an accident occurring, and the probability that when one does occur it will be severe, both increase with speed. The evidence from many countries on the effects of introducing speed limits strongly supports such reasoning. In Britain, although useful work has been done to develop means of road engineering, such as rumble strips and speed control humps, to slow vehicles down at particular points in the road network, lowering speeds is not regarded as an important element in the road safety strategy. Indeed, there is much official pressure, often in the face of local opposition, to raise what are regarded as unrealistic limits in built-up areas.

One reason for this attitude is that a comprehensive study to investigate the accidents that occurred in one area over a four-year period seemed to show that speed was not a major causative factor. But the design of this study was such that although speed which was clearly excessive for the circumstances would have been identified as a cause, the numerous subtle ways in which speed accentuates the risk of an accident would not have been. Nor did this study investigate the reasons for the degree of severity of accidents, as opposed to their occurrence.

The pressure to raise 'unrealistic' speed limits also rests on the claim that to do so leads to no deterioration and perhaps to some improvement in the accident situation. The evidence advanced in support of this claim is not very strong; nevertheless, it is quite possible that raising limits which are widely disregarded could sometimes result in a greater uniformity of speeds with less overtaking and therefore fewer accidents. But the conclusion that to raise the limit is the appropriate course of action in such circumstances follows only if it is also true that to have enforced the original speed limit would have been infeasible or too expensive.

Laws which are generally regarded as unreasonable cannot be enforced, and a reason for raising 'unrealistic' limits, and perhaps more generally for not paying attention to speed, is the belief that firmer action would be unacceptable to large sections of the public and would adversely affect their relationship with the police. Although in their capacity as residents, pedestrians and cyclists, people would welcome lower speeds, there is evidence from social surveys that a significant number of motorists are opposed to the present limits. Nevertheless, the great majority favours limits of some kind and more than half would like to see the existing speed limits more strongly enforced. It may also be that such hostility as does exist is explained, at least in part, by the failure to appreciate the connection between speed and accidents. Experience of particular schemes suggests that drivers approve of and will comply with speed limits when they can see their point, provided also that they are accompanied by measures which alter the driver's situation in such a way that driving at the required speed seems natural and appropriate.

The task of reinforcing responsible attitudes is not helped by the many influences on drivers to drive too fast and to adopt a complacent attitude towards speed even when it involves breaking the law. The background influences include car advertising and reviews of new cars by motoring correspondents, both of which put great stress on speed; the government's requirement that cars should be tested for fuel consumption at a speed of 75 mph and that the results of such tests should be published; the tolerant attitude towards speeding to be seen in the law itself and in its interpretation in the courts, combined with the very low risk of being caught or prosecuted for speeding. When actually on the road, a driver wishing to drive at a speed which he regards as reasonable may find himself under pressure from other drivers to go faster, even when he is himself driving at or even above the legal limit. The characteristics both of the vehicle and of the road are often such as to encourage speeding.

Both vehicles and roads could be designed in ways which would have the opposite effect, that of encouraging conformity with suitable speeds. To ensure compliance with the national limit, tamper-proof controls could be fitted to vehicles to prevent speeds of over 70 mph or perhaps, in order to allow some tolerance, of over 75 mph. For lower speeds, vehicles could be equipped with internal and external warning devices to alert both the driver and others when the limit was being exceeded. A more radical approach would be to use governors, which could either be switched on by the driver or activated externally, which would not merely warn of excess speed but prevent it. With microelectronic technology, warning devices and governors, at least those operated by the driver, would be reliable and very cheap.

The objection to governors that they would prevent acceleration or a temporary violation of the limit on those occasions when speed is necessary to avoid a conflict appears to be unfounded, nor could it apply at all to warning devices.

Speed control through road engineering is valuable in itself and could be much more widely used immediately. But it is likely to be most effective when used in conjunction with vehicle design. For example, the best way to enforce a general speed limit in a town might be through vehicle design, whereas humps or the radical redesign of streets could be used to enforce much lower speeds on particular streets.

A substantial programme of research and development on speed is urgently required. An independent statistical study should be made of the existing evidence from all countries on the relationships between speeds, speed limits and accidents of each degree of severity. This should be supplemented in Britain with experiments to show the effect on the number and severity of accidents of enforcing existing limits more strictly and of setting and enforcing lower limits. Other studies are required on the costs and benefits that would flow from better enforced and lower speed limits, especially on the relationship between speeds and total journey time. Public attitudes to speed control in general should be further explored, especially so as to illuminate the connection between attitudes to speed limits and beliefs about the influence of speed on accidents. Further work is also needed to see how attitudes and behaviour are affected by the means adopted to ensure or encourage compliance. Technical work to develop alerting devices and governors should be resumed and should be followed with trials among drivers to ascertain any problems in use, followed by further trials based on larger samples to ascertain the effects on fuel consumption and on accidents.

The potential of speed control as a means of reducing accidents is very great and there are other possible benefits in reducing driver stress, energy consumption and noise. But little has been done to develop its potential, and in particular to tackle the crucial problem of enforcement, and especially self-enforcement. An exception is the successful programme of research and development on speed humps, but even that took nine years between the legislation which allowed the TRRL to install humps on public highways experimentally and the issuing of regulations permitting their general use by highway authorities. All this suggests both insufficient drive from within the Department of Transport and insufficient pressure on the Department from outside. An effective pressure group commanding some technical expertise would have been able to expose the weaknesses in the arguments of those who now advocate higher speed limits and would have insisted that the necessary experiments were undertaken to clear up whatever points may still be in dispute at a technical level on the connections between speed, speed limits and accidents. The fact that no organisation now plays such a role indicates an important gap in the road safety effort.

Small-scale road engineering schemes
One way to reduce accidents is by small changes to the road or its immediate surroundings such as the conversion of straight-across junctions into staggered ones which compel drivers to slow down, the provision or improvement of pedestrian islands, the provision of median strips to ensure traffic channelisation, the use of skid-resistant surface dressings at junctions and edge-lining to improve visibility at night. The techniques to investigate accident sites in order to determine appropriate remedial measures were developed many years ago and local authorities have had mandatory responsibilities for improving the safety of the roads in their areas since local government reorganisation in 1974. It is also established that such work is extremely cost-effective, even on the basis of the current low values for the costs of accidents and without making any allowances for under-reporting. It is not unknown for particular schemes to pay for themselves several times over within a year, and a whole programme of accident investigation and prevention work is likely to achieve rates of return far higher than can be obtained from building major roads, or from most other investment whether in the transport sector or elsewhere. However, this activity has attracted far less invest-ment than these economic arguments for it would indicate.

The amounts which local authorities now spend cannot be ascertained precisely, since Accident Investigation and Prevention is not a separate heading in the forms used to apply for Transport Supplementary Grant, nor is there any other comprehensive record of counties' activities in this area. But it appears that road safety as a whole, including activities such as training, accounts for considerably less than one per cent of local authorities' transport expenditure, although this may be misleading in that some of the money put into small-scale safety schemes may be entered on the forms under another heading. It seems that there are still some counties that are not properly equipped to undertake work on accident investigation and prevention and it is doubtful whether any county is investing as much in such work as it should in view of the high rate of return.

One explanation of this is that there has been insufficient pressure from central government. The lack of systematic knowledge about what individual counties are doing is itself an indication of this. In addition, although the Department of Transport has drawn the attention of local authorities to the value of this type of work and has recommended the use of economic criteria to decide which schemes should be included in a programme of remedial measures, it has never suggested that economic criteria should be used to determine how large that programme should be. To the contrary, the discussion and examples given suggest that local authorities should devote only small sums to this type of work.

Another reason for the unduly low expenditure by county councils has been the lack of effective pressure from their own citizens. Great concern can be aroused about conditions at some particular spot, especially when some unusually sad accident occurs, but there is a lack of steady, persistent, rational pressure for a large and systematic programme of accident prevention work. The concern which a particular accident arouses can, indeed, have the unfortunate consequence that resources are diverted to that site from others which have not attracted the same attention but where remedial action is more likely to be rewarding.

Small-scale engineering schemes are at present directed only to accident reduction, rather than to making conditions safer in a way that will relieve anxiety. This can be a cause of tension between local people and the engineers specialising in remedial work, since peace of mind can be an important objective in its own right for residents. This poses the theoretical difficulty of how to allow for such a benefit in determining priorities. Another theoretical problem is that to allocate a transport budget between road safety and other areas in such a way as to maximise the total rate of return requires a method of calculating rates of return for each separate area. At present, they can be calculated for major road schemes, from which the benefits are primarily in reduced travel time, and also for these small safety-inspired schemes, but not for the other major items in a county council's transport budget, such as road maintenance and public transport investment or subsidy. If economic criteria were developed in these areas too the economic case for investing in small-scale safety schemes could be seen more clearly.

That case is, nevertheless, overwhelmingly strong. The fact that the Department of Transport has not recommended local authorities to devote very much larger sums to this work and has not used the Transport Supplementary Grant more effectively as a means of inducing them to do so suggests that the Road Safety Division does not have sufficient standing within the Department. More widely, the history of this subject demonstrates the need for, and present lack of, a strong system of relationships between the Road Safety Division, local authorities and the more concerned citizens.

Cycling
Accidents to cyclists have always been a problem, but at one time it seemed that the long-term decline in cycling itself would remove it. Thus between 1960 and 1974 cycle travel declined by 69 per cent and casualties by 60 per cent. But since then a significant revival of cycling has reversed the downward trend in casualties.

Causualties among children and teenagers are a particular cause of concern. The majority of killed or seriously injured cyclists are under 20, one third are under 15 and eight per cent are under ten. The casualty rates for child cyclists are many times higher than for adults.

In addition to casualties, unsafe conditions for cyclists have a major effect in distorting travel patterns. The calculation by a British statistician that in the flatter parts of the country over 40 per cent of journeys to work would be made by cycle in relatively safe conditions is supported by the experience of other countries. In the Netherlands, cycling is the major mode of travel, other than walking, for short journeys; in West Germany, cycling accounts for a substantial share of journeys in those towns where special efforts have been made to provide for it.

A few British towns have made provision for cyclists for many years, but apart from them investment in cycling facilities was until recently completely neglected in Britain. The transportation studies which were the approved method of urban transport planning in the 1960s and early 1970s ignored cycling altogether; the very detailed circulars issued to local authorities in the early years of the Transport Supplementary Grant system did not mention cycling; in 1975 the Department of the Environment (at that time there was no separate Department of Transport), although recognising responsibilities for providing advice, said that it could not spare resources to take positive action.

Since 1976 there has been some change in attitude. Local authorities are encouraged to consider cycling in their annual Transport Policies and Programmes; the government gives support for innovative schemes; it is clearly recognised that the key to the problem of safety lies in the provision of safe facilities rather than in other action such as training. Nevertheless, the scale of the effort is still very small. Most of the local authority schemes are very modest; the total amount of money spent by the Department on innovative schemes up until March 1984 was only £240,000; even in London, where there is a strong political commitment to cycling, it attracts only one per cent of the annual capital budget for transport or in absolute terms some £1.7 million. In general, cycling provision is seen as an aspect of traffic management rather than as a major mode of transport the potential of which is now unexploited because of unsafe conditions.

Cycling is now very much more dangerous than the modes of transport with which it competes, except for motorcycles and mopeds. The risk of a half-hearted policy of encouragement is therefore that it will lead to some transfer from other safer modes to cycling, and indeed to some new cycle travel, with a resulting increase in casualties. However, the experience of those countries where cycling is now treated as a major mode of travel shows both that cycle casualty rates lower than those now found in Britain can be achieved and that it is also possible to reduce the rates faster than cycle travel increases. Thus in Sweden bicycle travel increased by one-third between 1970 and 1982 but, since the fatality rate was reduced by more than half, the number of deaths fell by 40 per cent.

It could be argued that it is wrong to encourage cycling unless the casualty rates can be reduced to the same level as those of the major competing modes. There is no evidence either from Britain or elsewhere that so great a reduction is possible. However, this would seem to be an unduly stringent condition to justify investment in cycling facilities. The significant number of people who are prepared to cycle even in present conditions would gain from such investment; those who then took up cycling might be at greater risk as travellers than if they had continued to use their former means of transport but their health would benefit in other ways from the exercise, not least from a reduced risk of heart disease.

It has always been official policy to encourage training for child cyclists. There is some evidence that training improves children's performance in making dangerous manoeuvres, such as right turns, but the studies that have been undertaken to compare the accident records of trained and untrained children tend to suggest that any reduction in casualties is slight. The very high casualty rate for the youngest children suggests that, even if training could be greatly improved, they should be discouraged from cycling except where complete segregation is possible. Parents of older children who are prepared to accept the present risks of cycling as a lesser evil than denying their children independence are probably well advised to have their children trained and to make their permission to cycle conditional upon passing the proficiency test, but the aim of public policy should be to alter the conditions which create these agonising choices.

The main institutional question posed by cycling is why it has taken so long in Britain to recognise cycling at all and why it is still not treated seriously as a major mode of transport. This is part of a larger problem that Britain seems to have been affected more deeply than other countries by the ideas of the 1960s that the aim of transport policy was to provide for the ever increasing use of motor transport, and since then has found it harder to renounce such ideas and to formulate an alternative philosophy. Part of the explanation may lie in the fact that the Department of Transport's responsibilities for major road building are much more direct than its responsibilities for other aspects of policy. The fact that other road user organisations and similar pressure groups are more highly organised than the cyclists' lobby may also help to account for cycling's relative neglect. There is always likely to be an imbalance in the external pressures on the Department. Children, for example, for whom cycling is so important, are not in a good position to organise and lobby. There is therefore a problem for the Department to devise arrangements to ensure that the interests of people who are in a weak position to act as their own advocates are properly taken into account.

Transport policy and the volume and pattern of road traffic
The road safety problem is traditionally conceived as how to reduce the number and severity of accidents arising from a given volume and pattern of traffic. Logically, however, it would be possible to reduce accidents by encouraging the use of modes of travel which have low accident rates as well as by reducing the

rates associated with each different mode. The very great differences between the accident rates of different modes suggest that this could be a promising approach. The casualty rate per passenger mile for buses is about a quarter of that for cars and a minute fraction of the rates for pedestrians,cyclists and motor-cyclists; the rate for trains is lower still.

In addition to safety, a policy favouring public transport offers benefits environmentally and in the efficient use of road space. But such a policy has not been followed in Britain.

Between 1965 and 1977 the use of urban public transport rose substantially in five of fifteen OECD countries and remained roughly stable in four others. In the other six it declined, most of all in Britain. Central government has done little to encourage policies favourable to buses. Bus priority measures are a partial exception: they were promoted by the former Minsitry of Transport in the 1960s at a time when local authorities were mostly reluctant. Since then, useful work in developing techniques of assessment has been carried out by the TRRL; nevertheless, the principle of comprehensive bus priorities has not taken hold. Although road pricing and similar ideas have been canvassed for very many years, techniques of selective traffic restraint, which, among other advantages, could sometimes be more effective than bus priority schemes, have not been developed or implemented.

In the absence of such restraint, there is an important economic as well as social case for public transport subsidies. The influence that subsidies can have on influencing travel patterns, and hence on accidents, is illustrated by the experiment with cheap fares in London in 1981 and 1982. It has been estimated that in the year following the end of this experiment casualties were between seven and eleven per cent higher than they would have been if it had continued, and that the cost of the extra casualties and accidents, calculated at the Department's standard rates, was of the order of £20 million. In South Yorkshire, bus fares have been held constant since 1975-76. The effect on accidents has not been calculated but was presumably beneficial, since bus travel rose in South Yorkshire by three per cent in this period, whereas elsewhere it fell by 23 per cent, and motorcycling apparently declined there in the vulnerable 16-24 age group whose use of the bus increased.

The attitude of the central government to these two experiments was hostile, and to bus subsidies generally it has usually been cool. This attitude has not, however been based on any systematic method of determining what subsidies are appropriate. It is only very recently that an attempt has been made to develop economic criteria for this purpose; even though

15

accident savings are not at present included, the results suggest that the economic case for subsidies arising from passenger benefits and saved congestion is a strong one.

Railway subsidies are lower in Britain than in almost every other comparable country, and the criteria for investment in railways are systematically more stringent not only than those in use abroad but also than the criteria used in Britain to assess major road schemes. The competition to railways, both in the passenger and freight market, is less regulated in Britain than elsewhere.

Attempts to change the structure of road vehicle taxation, so that the annual licence fee would have cost less and fuel more, have indeed been made, but they fell through and have not been revived. One effect would have been to improve the competitive position of public transport and in other ways too to have reduced the volume of traffic with a consequential reduction in accidents. The system of tax concessions for company cars appears to be very much more developed in Britain than elsewhere. It influences both the level of car ownership and the choice of model and in these ways, and perhaps in other ways too, impairs the competitive position of public transport, both train and bus.

If road safety as an area of activity carried greater weight within the Department of Transport, this would have been reflected in general transport policy in the more favourable treatment of the very safe public modes of transport. But the imbalance in policy goes beyond considerations of safety. The Department of Transport has a more general responsibility to devise the legal and fiscal framework within which transport activities take place, and to set common criteria for investment in different fields of transport, in such a way as to achieve an overall optimum. The failure to do so apparently has an institutional origin in that the Department of Transport's interest in and responsibilities for the road programme are much closer and more direct than for other aspects of transport policy.

Land-use and locational planning
The volume and pattern of road traffic, and hence the number of road accidents and casualties, are affected not only by transport policy but also by land use. But although the connection between land use and transport has always been recognised, the possibilities of changing land use as a way of tackling transport problems have not been explored.

A principal reason for this has been the belief that land-use patterns can be changed either only very slowly or at great expense. But even if land use is thought of only in terms of broad patterns of settlement, these patterns change more quickly than might be thought. Between 1971 and 1981 the population of the principal metropolitan cities in England and Wales fell by 12 per cent and that of inner London by 18 per cent, while the population of rural areas as a whole rose by 10 per cent and that of the rural areas at the fringes of large cities by 16 per cent. Land use should also be thought of in terms of the number, size and location of facilities, which have an important influence on lengths of journey and means of transport. The number of retail outlets in Great Britain fell by 30 per cent between 1971 and 1980 following a substantial decline in the previous decade. This has apparently contributed to the increases in the length of shopping journeys and in the proportion of them made by car that are shown in the National Travel Survey. The same tendency for the size of facilities to increase while their number decreases has been seen for other facilities such as schools, hospitals and doctors' practices and has presumably had similar consequences for journey lengths and choice of mode.

Within any configuration of land uses, the pattern of journeys is also affected by personal decisions about where to live and where to work. About ten per cent of adults change house each year and a similar number change jobs.

A primary aim of planning should be to facilitate and encourage short journeys. Provided that it serves the traveller's purpose equally well, a short journey is preferable to him than a long one. To keep journeys short also reduces external costs, including accidents, both because mileage is reduced and because a less dangerous mode of travel is likely to be chosen - or at least a mode of travel which should be less dangerous if other appropriate policies were applied. For longer journeys, the aim of land-use and locational planning should be to increase the chance that they will be made by public transport, with its much lower accident rates, rather than by car.

In addition to the present instruments of structure planning and development control, it should be possible to use property taxation to influence locational planning, for example by encouraging small establishments. Many important facilities such as hospitals, schools, post offices, local authority offices and recreational centres are provided by the public sector; a deliberate policy of providing 'small and many' rather than 'large and few' could be adopted. The quality of the physical environment, and in particular the nuisance of traffic, which is largely a function of policy, has an important influence on decisions to move house.

Notwithstanding some important exceptions, such as the generally hostile attitude of planning authorities to hypermarkets, planning now tends to be based on contrary principles of dispersion and low density. This leads to relatively long journeys of a pattern difficult to accommodate by means other than car. There seems to be a divergence between British and continental practice in this respect; on the continent, higher densities are favoured and new settlements tend to be planned with close access to railways.

The present trends in land use are unfortunate in a number of ways that go beyond road safety or transport planning, including the loss of countryside and the decline of the inner city, and a major study of ways of changing them is required. One implication for the road safety effort is that any system of incentives to reduce road accidents should take account of all reductions, however achieved, rather than being related only to conventional methods of accident investigation and prevention, highly important though that work is.

The design of residential areas

A quarter to a third of casualties in built-up areas arise from accidents on residential streets. For particular kinds of casualty the proportion is much higher. Old people and children account for the majority of pedestrian casualties, and it is probable that most of the accidents in which they are injured take place in their own neighbourhoods. The problems of the frustration of travel and of other activities, and of anxiety about danger on the roads, are also largely connected with conditions very near where people live.

The Department of the Environment is concerned with road safety in new housing areas in connection with its responsibilities for housing policy, and the TRRL has also studied accidents in housing estates and in residential streets. In general, however, pedestrian policy in residential areas as elsewhere has been regarded as a problem for local authorities, with which neither the Department of Transport nor its Road Safety Division in particular need be much concerned. Presumably as a consequence, the possibilities of using physical design in a bold way to improve safety in residential streets and the local neighbourhood have been very little explored in Britain.

This neglect is unfortunate, since although in most aspects of road safety the British record is good by international standards, in pedestrian safety Britain is some way behind the leaders. This is illustrated by the following table, taken from the OECD publication Traffic Safety of Children, which relates to 1979. The units are pedestrian deaths per million population.

18

All pedestrians		Pedestrians aged 0-14 years	
Netherlands	18.7	Sweden	9.7
Sweden	21.4	Finland	13.3
Norway	23.8	Netherlands	18.3
Japan	24.9	Spain	21.1
Denmark	28.2	Denmark	24.6
Finland	31.9	Japan	25.4
Spain	34.2	France	25.9
United States	37.4	Norway	26.3
Canada	37.6	United States	28.1
United Kingdom	39.0	United Kingdom	32.6
France	39.3	Canada	34.3
Belgium	50.4	Belgium	35.5
Switzerland	51.0	Switzerland	38.6
West Germany	51.5	West Germany	40.7
Ireland	67.4	Ireland	48.5

In the Netherlands and Scandinavia, new residential areas are designed on the principle of the subordination of motor traffic to pedestrians and the environment. Very low speeds are enforced through physical design, and it is accepted, at least in the more advanced practice, that parking spaces can be provided at some distance from dwellings, thereby giving residents a virtually traffic-free immediate environment (allowance has to be made for various service and emergency vehicles) at the cost of some inconvenience in access. Bold steps have also been taken to reconstruct existing streets on the same principle of the subordination of traffic. Thus in the Dutch woonerven, features such as rough road surfaces, 'pinch-points' which narrow the road to the width of a single vehicle, ramps at intersections, trees and other planting, have been used to enforce very low speeds. The popularity of woonerven is shown by the fact that since September 1976, when the law authorising them took effect, about 350 Dutch municipalities, or half the total number, have introduced woonerven and there are now some 2,700 such schemes.

Sweden was the first country to study child pedestrian accident seriously, and to realise that, because of the difficulty young children have in absorbing training, safe design is the key to the problem. The very low child pedestrian accident rate in Sweden shown in the table suggests that their approach has been successful; what is perhaps even more impressive is how that rate has declined over the years. By the early 1980s it was about one-third what it had been in 1965.

In Britain, there have been experiments, inspired partly by safety and partly by visual and architectural considerations, to break away from the traditional layout of residential estates, characterised by wide roads, gentle curves and generous distances between roads and frontages. But although vehicle speeds appear to be somewhat lower in estates built to an innovative design, with narrow and somewhat tortuous roads, mean speeds can still be 25 km/h or higher. Whether the accident rate is lower in such estates than in ones of traditional design it is too early to say, but more than half the residents say that they find safety a problem. The principle of allowing some distance between parking spaces and houses is accepted only for estates built to unusually high densities; otherwise the Department of the Environment recommends, principally as a counter to vandalism, that parking spaces should be provided as close to individual dwellings as possible. Although schemes to exclude through traffic from existing residential streets are often accompanied by measuures to improve the behaviour of the remaining traffic, there have been few if any bolder experiments along the lines of a woonerf.

It is clear that a bold programme of works is required in Britain, which should include the extensive use of speed humps as well as experiments and demonstration projects of a more fundamental kind, including the creation of traffic-free areas. At the institutional level, this subject shows that there is a need for the Road Safety Division, or any equivalent central government road safety agency, to be involved even in matters where the executive action not only rests with local authorities but could be regarded as a function of their town planning or even their housing responsibilities rather than as a matter of highways and transport. Since the benefits of excluding traffic from residential areas, or allowing it entry only when it is kept subordinate, are environmental as well in safety, this subject also shows the need for institutional arrangements which would allow danger to be seen as one aspect, albeit the most important, of the general intrusion of traffic.

Institutions

Although other organisations, such as the police, have an important role to play, the main responsibilities for preventive action in road safety lie with the Department of Transport and local authorities. In both their fields the message of previous sections is the same. The conventional measures which rely on reducing accident rates are all now covered but have not been pursued with enough vigour. The possibility of tackling the problem by restraining traffic and encouraging the use of safer modes of transport has scarcely been recognised at a!l.

This shows that road safety is not accorded the importance in policy making that it deserves; the ultimate reason for that is a lack of pressure from the public. This is not due to indifference. Concern is widespread, but it is diffuse and many of the people most affected are poorly placed to organise and to represent their own interests. For these reasons, and also because road safety often seems to be a forbidding technical subject, concern has not been translated into pressure. At the local level, many organisations exist, particularly in the form of environmental societies, which would be well suited to take up the cause of road safety in their areas; the problem is to mobilise this potential. At the national level, a lobby to campaign for road safety in the way that the motoring organisations, freight user groups and trade associations represent their own interests, has been lacking.

This fundamental institutional weakness is accentuated and made more difficult to cure by others, especially the low standing of road safety within the Department of Transport and the weak and uncertain relationship between the Department's Road Safety Division and local authorities.

One way to enhance the prestige of road safety at the level of central government would be to create a separate government department for it. The countries that have adopted that approach include Japan and Sweden, whose records in road safety, in terms both of the rate of improvement and of the low casualty levels now achieved, are among the best in the world. Nevertheless, it is an artificial step to separate road safety from transport. It would be better, if feasible, to keep the responsibility for road safety within the Department of Transport but to enhance its standing there.

The Minister now responsible for road safety in the Department of Transport also has many other heavy responsibilities, including the trunk road programme, local roads, the bus industry, local public transport, rural transport, privatisation of HGV testing, transport for disabled people, a Channel Link and general responsibility for the Department's work in connection with the European Communities and the promotion of transport exports. A first step would be to free that Minister from all other responsibilities except those for environmental intrusion, with which road safety is indissolubly linked. But a mere rearrangement of responsibilities is unlikely to be sufficient: road safety is always likely to be something of a poor relation so long as the Department continues to have its present range of functions.

The function that should be shed, or at least substantially reduced, by a transfer to county councils, is that of a road building authority. The demands on the time of Ministers and senior civil servants that arise from this function inevitably limit the attention they can pay to other things. The fact that this responsibility is more direct than the Department's other responsibilities, which are regulatory and supervisory, distorts the approach to national transport policy, as is most obvious in the different criteria now applied to investment in road and rail. Local transport planning is also seriously distorted, since there are now in effect two transport budgets in each county. One, under the control of the county council, can be spent on any transport purpose as the needs and rates of return indicate. The other, under the control of the Department, can be spent only on roads, and a limited set of roads at that, even though the return from such investment may be much lower than that from other transport expenditure. This division, which must lead to some misallocation of resources, can no longer be justified by the traditional distinction between national and local traffic; the Department's responsibilities to safeguard the needs of longer distance traffic and to ensure coherence between the plans of neighbouring counties could be discharged by means of reserve powers and do not require the existence of a separate 'national' road building authority. The present arrangement costs £9.5 million a year in duplicated administration. It also creates friction between the Department of Transport and people such as the environmental movement who should be its natural allies in promoting road safety.

Whatever steps are taken to strengthen the road safety lobby, there are always likely to be interests which are poorly represented by pressure groups. The Department should recognise this imbalance and correct for it by creating an internal division whose function would be to act as advocates for those people, such as children, who are not able to represent their own interests, and to scrutinise all departmental policy on their behalf. For example, this division would submit replies to the Department's consultation documents as if it was an outside organisation.

The relationship between the Road Safety Division of the Department of Transport and local authorities should be such that, although the initiative to take safety properly into account in local transport planning, and in related fields of town planning and housing policy, is left with the local authorities, they are given every encouragement and incentive to do so. We recommend a system of financial incentives, quite separate from the present arrangements for Transport Supplementary Grant and Transport

Policies and Programmes. The Department of Transport would pay local highway authorites for any reduction in casualties on their roads in one year as compared with the previous year. The sum paid for each casualty saved would vary according to its severity; it would be a fixed proportion, perhaps a half, of the value officially calculated for a casualty of each degree. Payment would be automatic; there would be no obligation on the local authority to demonstrate that the reductions were due to its own efforts rather than to national action, but it might be desirable to make any payment conditional upon the achievement of some minimum reduction, for example of four per cent.

This system of incentives would stimulate local authorities not only in their own field of activity but also to work with the road safety lobby to press for stronger action at a national level, for example in motorcycle licensing, drink-and-drive laws, etc. It would also give local citizens an extra reason as ratepayers as well as road users to take an interest in road safety.

We also recommend that the NHS should automatically charge local highway authorities for treating casualties which occur on their roads. This is not to suggest that highway authorities are culpable in a legal or moral sense for how other people behave on their roads; nevertheless, it is better that the bill should fall on county councils which, if only in the longer term, can do something to reduce accident risks than on the NHS which can do nothing.

These new financial arrangements should be accompanied by the provision of much fuller information about the road safety activities of local authorities which would encourage them to emulate each other and would also enable local citizens to bring effective and rational pressure to bear on their own authorities. Each county council should publish an annual report on the work, cost and achievements of its accident investigation and prevention unit. In order to ensure comparability between counties, the central government should give guidance on points of statistical analysis, the values to be attached to accident savings and the non-accident benefits such as reduced anxiety, and the treatment of overheads in the calculation of the unit's costs. In addition, the Department of Transport should publish much fuller information than it does at present on road accidents and casualties in different counties. This could be done by means of a companion volume to the present annual publication Road Accidents Great Britain which, in addition to tables, would contain articles describing interesting innovations and achievements in different counties and relevant foreign experience as well.

These reforms should stimulate local environmental societies and similar local groups to take more interest in road safety. A greater effort put into road safety generally, and stronger policies on speed limits and pedestrian crossings in particular, would also largely remove the tensions between them and their local authorities which now inhibit a close working partnership.

There remains the question of the absence of a road safety pressure group at the national level. Such a body is needed to lobby the Department of Transport and Parliament, to campaign in the media, to put pressure on the Advertising Standards Authority, and so on, just as other pressure groups do in their own fields. In addition, it could promote road safety among environmental societies and similar local groups and provide them with technical advice and support. None of the older established organisations now plays quite this role, nor could do so without substantial changes in its present scope and perhaps even in its constitution. The most important institutional development in road safety in recent years has been the foundation of PACTS (the Parliamentary Advisory Council for Transport Safety). PACTS was formally launched in July 1982, although it had already been operating on an ad hoc basis for about a year before that. So far, its main activities have been to inform members of Parliament and to press for legislative action; with greater resources it could both intensify such activities and take on others. To provide the resources that would enable PACTS to expand is the most important priority; we believe that there is also room for another pressure group, working as an ally of PACTS but separate from it. The great strength of PACTS is that a wide range of organisations is represented on it and its pronouncements therefore carry great weight, but this could also prove to be a handicap in tackling matters which are thought to be contentious, such as speed or traffic restraint. A smaller body without outside links might be better placed to press for action in such fields.

A problem whether in increasing support for PACTS or in founding a new organisation is that there is little commercial interest in road safety. Nevertheless, there are some sections of industry, such as insurance, the bicycle industry, the public transport industry and its suppliers, to which the cause might appeal, and it should also be possible for the Department of Transport, and perhaps also other government departments, such as the Department of Health and Social Security, to provide some financial help to outside organisations without jeopardising their independence. The cause of road safety should find wider backing, too, once it is realised how large the prize is and how easily it could be grasped.

I.   THE IMPORTANCE OF ROAD SAFETY

Danger on the roads causes accidents and casualties, and the fear of accidents also affects people's lives in a great variety of ways. To give a comprehensive account of the importance of road safety would be a vast undertaking which is not attempted here. But one inspiration of this study was that the official treatment of road safety, in the form of the road accident statistics and the money valuations attached to casualties and accidents, fails to bring out its full importance. The aim of this chapter, therefore, is to state briefly what the official treatment is and to give the principal grounds for the claim that it does not do justice to the subject.

The official treatment of accidents
Accident numbers
Road accidents and casualties are reported in the annual publication Road Accidents Great Britain, which is based on police records. Table I.1 which shows trends in road casualties over the last 20 years, and Tables I.2 and I.3, which give further details for the year 1982, are taken from this publication.

To interpret these statistics requires an understanding of the definitions involved. To be included in the police records, an accident must involve a personal injury. Thus accidents in which an animal is hurt or killed but not a human being, or in which there is damage to vehicles or property but no casualty, are excluded. Personal injury accidents are included only if they take place on the public highway: those taking place on private roads, in shop unloading areas, industrial premises, garages, vehicle workshops, etc. are therefore excluded except insofar as some may be recorded in error. Deaths occurring on the public highway from natural causes, such as a heart attack, are excluded, as are homicides and suicides. Accidents to pedestrians which occur on the public highway or an adjacent footpath without any vehicle being involved do not qualify. But if a pedestrian has to move quickly to avoid a vehicle, or trips against a parked vehicle, such casualties would be included(1).

Casualties are classified as fatal, serious and slight. Accidents are also classified in these categories according to the severity of the casualty suffered by the injured person or, for an accident in which more than one person is hurt, by the most severely injured person. For a death from a road accident to count as a fatality in the statistics, it must occur within thirty days of the accident. A serious injury is one for which a person is detained in hospital as an 'in-patient', or any of the following injuries whether or not he is detained in hospital: fractures, concussion, internal injuries, crushings, severe cuts and lacerations, severe general shock requiring medical treatment, injuries causing death 30 or more days after the accident. A slight injury is an injury of a minor character such as a sprain, bruise or cut judged not be be severe, or slight shock requiring roadside attention. A person who is merely shaken but who has no other injury and does not receive or appear to need medical treatment is not counted as a casualty.

The evaluation of casualties and accidents

As an indication of the importance to society of road accidents and casualties, money values have been assigned to a casualty and accident of each severity. These values are then applied to the accident statistics to give the total cost to society of the road accidents that occur each year.

According to this procedure, the cost of a casualty is made up of three elements: lost production; medical and ambulance costs; and a notional sum to allow for the subjective effects of pain, grief and suffering. The values currently attached to each of these elements are shown in Table I.4.

Some of the costs arising from road accidents involving personal injury cannot be assigned to the individual casualties. These are damage to road vehicles and other property, police costs and the costs to insurance companies of administering claims. The values officially allotted to those costs are shown in Table I.5.

Although damage-only accidents are not included in the police records nor, in consequence, in the annual road accident statistics, an allowance is made for them for costing purposes. According to a study of insurance records carried out many years ago(2) but checked roughly since(3), the ratio of damage-only accidents to personal-injury accidents is estimated to be about six to one. The average cost of a damage-only accident in 1982 was estimated at £490, made up of the cost of damage to vehicles and other property (about 90 per cent) and the cost of insurance administration and police(4).

On this basis, the total cost of road accidents in Great Britain in 1982 was officially estimated to be £2,375 million; the breakdown of this figure into its main components is given in Table I.6.

The adequacy of the official treatment of accidents
<u>Numbers of accidents and casualties</u>

It has been seen that the definitions on which the official statistics are based systematically exclude some incidents which might in ordinary speech be counted as road accidents.   Whether accidents involving conventional road vehicles which occur off the public highway are in this category is debatable.   They are not the responsibility of any highway authority, but they are a consequence of society's dependence on a transport system based on motor vehicles, and some of the policies which could be employed to reduce accidents on the public highway might reduce the number of these other accidents too.   Presumably their number is relatively small.

Views will differ about the importance of the omission of animal casualties. Apart from the question of animal rights, to kill or injure an animal can be an upsetting experience for the driver and other people present and the loss of a pet can be a source of grief to its owner. We know of no estimates of the numbers of animals killed or hurt in road accidents. However, to see cats, dogs, birds and, in the country, wild animals, dead on the roads is not an uncommon experience.

It is questionable whether the omission of pedestrian-only accidents should be thought of as a gap in the statistics or not. To the extent that some might be prevented by public policy, for example by the better maintenance of kerbs or footpaths, there would be a strong theoretical argument for including them.   It clearly would be desirable to include damage-only accidents in the statistics, but the practical difficulty of over-burdening the police precludes it. In 1982 they amounted to some 1.5 million.

In addition to these cases where the definitions used exclude some accidents which it would be theoretically desirable to include, the rules for classifying the casualties that are in the record may be misleading. Some of the people who die more than thirty days after the occurrence of a road accident should properly be counted as fatalities: for example a young, healthy person who dies after two months without ever having recovered

27

consciousness. On the other hand, there may be some deaths included under the thirty-day rule for which the accident was only part of the cause and which would have taken place at that time, or very soon after, in any event. In 1980, the figure for deaths from road accidents in the Registrar General's records was 10 per cent higher than the figure in Road Accidents Great Britain, although five per cent seems to be a more typical figure(5). The Registrar General's statistics include deaths from road accidents occurring off the public highway as well as those occurring more than thirty days after the accident.

It is generally accepted that the 'serious casualty' category is much too wide. A TRRL study of road accidents treated at an accident hospital in Berkshire in 1974 to 1976 showed that two-thirds of the casualties counted as serious by the police definition would be only counted as moderate in the AIS (Abbreviated Injury Scale), which is an internationally recognised clinical classification(6). The problem with having such a wide category is not so much that it overstates or understates the gravity of the problem - in this case it may well overstate it - but that it obscures important differences. It is difficult, and perhaps makes little sense, to attribute an average value to a range of injuries which include some which most people would describe as slight and others which are more to be feared than death itself. Apart from allotting values, the use of such a wide category makes it hard even to interpret the trends. A drop in the total number of serious injuries, if it were accompanied by a shift towards the upper end of the range, might not necessarily indicate an improvement, and a rise might not indicate a deterioration.

If the present definitions are accepted, there is still a major problem in making sure that the records are complete and the classifications correctly applied. Two studies have been carried out using hospital records to check on the completeness of the police records, one in 1970 at the Birmingham Accident Hospital and the other in the years 1974 to 1976 at an accident hospital in Berkshire. In both studies it was found that fatal accidents were fully reported (i.e. all fatalities from road accidents shown in the hospital records had also been included in the police records), but that there was considerable under-reporting of serious casualties and even more of slight. Thus in Birmingham, 18 per cent of the serious casualties treated by the hospital and 35 per cent of the slight casualties were not included at all in the police records; the corresponding figures for Berkshire were 21 per cent and 34 per cent. It was found in both hospitals that the degree of under-reporting varied by class of road user and was most marked for cyclists. The majority of serious casualties among cyclists and a large majority of slight ones go unreported, as is shown in Tables I.7 and I.8.

The Birmingham study also contained a check on the accuracy of the classification in the police records of those casualties that were included: the hospital investigators made their own classifications, but using the same definitions as those used by the police, of the casualties treated. (Since there is some judgement involved in applying the definitions, it cannot be said that a disagreement necessarily implies an error. Nevertheless, the hospital classifications were made by trained medical staff in conditions much more favourable than those in which the police are obliged to work; they should therefore be preferable.) There was no disagreement about the classification of fatalities, but as Table I.9 shows, the hospital staff were more inclined than the police to classify a non-fatal injury as serious rather than slight. Presumably most of the injuries classified by the police as slight but by the hospital as serious would be at the lower end of the 'serious' range, so this mis-classification may be less important than it appears at first sight.

The hospital studies do not reveal the full extent of under-reporting. Some casualties arising from road accidents which are treated in hospital may not be recognised in the hospital records as being due to road accidents: this is particularly likely to happen if the person is not brought to hospital immediately, for example, because the injury only becomes apparent some time after the accident occurs. By definition, some slight injuries are not treated in hospital at all; possibly some people whose injuries are severe enough to merit a stay in hospital do not go to one, not even as out-patients.

In spite of difficulties of completeness and interpretation, it is of some interest to see how the national figures would be increased by adjusting them for the degree of under-reporting and mis-classification found in the Birmingham study. Table I.10 shows that the difference is substantial.

Costings
To the extent that the accident statistics themselves are inadequate or incomplete, whether for reasons of unsatisfactory definitions, under-reporting or mis-classification, the corresponding cost figures must also be too low. But even if the accident records were perfect, important questions arise about whether the costs officially allotted to casualties and accidents do justice to the gravity of the problem.

<u>Conceptual questions</u>. The most fundamental question of all is whether the attempt to evaluate casualties and accidents, especially their more human and subjective consequences, in money terms is correct in principle. Some people would hold that to do so is logically or morally wrong.

The difficulty with this position is that, in a decision-making context, some kind of money evaluation seems unavoidable. No society could spend its entire wealth on safety. The line must be drawn somewhere, and any decision as to where to draw it implies a judgement that the extra lives and injuries that would be saved by spending more on safety would not justify the resources required. If money judgements have to be made at all, it is better that they should be explicit than implicit. Some rational discussion of what the values should be then becomes possible, whereas with implicit judgements it is often hard even to calculate what the implied values are, still more to justify them. It is also hard to see how particular decisions concerning safety can be made in a rational and consistent way unless explicit values have been determined in advance. This is true even of relatively simple decisions which, apart from their cost, involve no considerations other than safety, such as the decision whether to install a crash barrier at a hazardous point on a road. For a more complex decision, such as determining a speed limit, which may affect safety, energy conservation, noise and time spent travelling, the difficulty is still greater.

How should the explicit values be arrived at? In our view they should be political judgements, decided on by the appropriate Minister after full public and parliamentary debate. This view differs from that of most cost-benefit economists which is that the values should be those of the people affected. In their view, if one could ascertain, by studying people's behaviour in risk-taking situations or by skilfully designed social surveys, how much people would be prepared to pay to achieve a specified reduction in the risk of losing their lives while (for example) driving a car, those are the values that should be accepted when deciding how much to spend on making car travel safer.

The idea that such an approach can avoid the need for political judgement seems to us to be mistaken on at least two grounds. It rests on the assumption that the value to society of some particular benefit is the same as its value to the people directly concerned. This assumption, which is itself a political judgement, is not necessarily correct. Some people may put a much higher value on the avoidance of a certain risk than others because they are more timorous, but society might not accept their

30

different valuations. The strict economic approach also leaves out moral considerations, but society ought to have more concern about some citizens, or some situations, than about others. Thus, a high degree of safety from traffic in one's everyday environment might perhaps be regarded as a citizen's right; at least society has a strong obligation to ensure it for those people, such as the very young and very old, who are not always physically or mentally capable of coping with the hazards that now confront them. Society's obligation to those who take up dangerous sports, or who choose to travel by means which are known to be relatively dangerous for reasons of their own pleasure or convenience, is less strong.

It does not follow that studies to ascertain how people value safety and what they would be prepared to pay to improve it are pointless. Sound political judgement must be based on an understanding of how accidents and danger affect people's lives, otherwise it is not judgement at all but mere guesswork. To know how much the people affected would value a diminution of risk adds to such an understanding. But although such studies provide valuable material for political judgement they are not a substitute for it. Perhaps it can be said that elected representatives should normally accept the values of those directly affected, to the extent that their values can be ascertained, but should be prepared to depart from them when there are over-riding reasons to do so.

The main criticisms that can be made of the Department's costings do not depend on the view that is taken on this philosophical problem. There is, in fact, no dispute that the official cost estimates are too low. The Department of Transport has always been at pains to point out that because not all considerations are included, and some are costed conservatively, the estimates must be taken as minima(2). However, in our view the degree of understatement is greater than is often recognised.

Lost output. It was seen in Table I.6 that 30 per cent of the total costs of accidents, as officially estimated for 1982, were accounted for by lost output, and that most of this was attributed to output lost because of road deaths. The value of lost output is estimated by reference to the costs of employing someone: it consists of the present value of a person's likely future earnings together with that of the other salary-related expenses, such as national insurance contributions, paid by the employer. The value of the lost output of a non-working housewife, who does not receive an income from the work done for her household, is taken to be equivalent to the income of a working woman of the same age.

31

It is apparent that this procedure takes no account of other output for which no income is received. The obvious example would be the work done as housewives by women who also work, but much other housework is also unpaid, as is help to neighbours, voluntary work etc. To measure the output of a paid employee by the cost borne by the employer must also lead to an under-estimate, since the employer should be making some surplus, and so should the firm's customers, from each employee's activities.

The material loss experienced by the dependants of someone who is killed in an accident, or who suffers a severe drop in earnings because of an incapacitating injury, should sometimes be valued at more than the reduction in income involved. A sharp fall in income may require all sorts of changes to be made to a family's life style, perhaps involving moving house, a change of school etc. (The assumption that a loss of £10,000 to one person or family is worth the same as a loss of £1 to 10,000 people simplifies economic analysis, but is not correct as the existence of insurance shows.)

Pain, grief and suffering. The subjective elements of pain, grief and suffering accounted for 24 per cent of the official cost estimate of road accidents in 1982. Although the cost per fatality under this heading was ten times that of the cost per serious injury, the vastly greater number of serious injuries meant that in total they accounted for more than fatalities.

The values attached to these considerations are highly notional and were not in fact derived from any direct attempt to consider what society or its members might be willing to pay to avoid their occurrence. When the first official attempts to give money values to casualties were made in 1967(3), output lost because of a death on the roads was costed not as the value of a person's production over the rest of his life, but as that value less the cost of his own future consumption: the figure sought was the net value of a person's contribution to the economy after taking account of the cost of his own support. This procedure, which was later changed on the grounds that if someone's life were saved he would still be alive to enjoy his consumption, had the effect of ascribing a negative value to some people's lives - for example, old people who no longer produced but who continued to consume. Clearly, however, society places a value on saving such lives. Subjective costs were therefore estimated in such a way that any deficit in the production-less-consumption figure was eliminated, even for that category of person for whom such a deficit was largest. £5000 was the amount required at that time to eliminate the largest deficit, so it was chosen as the value of the subjective losses arising in any fatality, regardless of the victim's age or circumstances. At that time, a value of £200 was arbitrarily allotted to each serious casualty; in 1971 this sum was, equally arbitrarily, raised to £500 and at the same time a value of £10 was ascribed to the subjective costs of a slight casualty(8). Following the recommendations of the Leitch Committee(9) in 1977, all subjective costs were raised by 50 per cent. The present values are therefore the 1971 values raised by 50 per cent and adjusted each year to allow for inflation and for the increase in Gross Domestic Product.

There is no reason to think that values derived in this way - as makeweights arbitrarily adjusted - bear any relation to those of the subjective considerations with which they have been linked. It must first be recognised that there are many different people whose feelings are affected by a fatality other than the victim himself. There are his friends and relations who are bereaved; the other people involved in the accident who may suffer shock, trauma and feelings of guilt, whether any blame attaches to them or not; witnesses of the accident who may also suffer similarly; all those who are affected by the sadness, depression and guilt of the bereaved and of people involved as participants or witnesses. Non-fatal accidents have similar repercussions.

The victim in a fatal accident may or may not be affected by pain, grief and suffering. If death is instantaneous, as in a road accident it often is (65 per cent of the fatalities in the Berkshire study were dead on arrival at the hospital), or if the person never recovers consciousness, he presumably is not. Even if he is, it would seem desirable to distinguish this cost from that of the curtailment of life and its activities. Almost everyone would place a value on a reduction of the risk that his or her life might be abruptly curtailed in an accident.

People who are injured but not fatally so presumably usually do experience physical pain and sometimes mental pain as well. Some of them will also have to face a restriction of their activities and capabilities which may be permanent. Although the distinction is less clear-cut than in the case of fatalities, it would seem desirable to distinguish once again between the experience of suffering and the reduced capacity to pursue or enjoy activities.

Following another recommendation of the Leitch Committee, the Department of Transport has commissioned a study of the values people attach to reductions in the risks of road accidents. We understand that initial results suggest much higher values than those now ascribed to pain, grief and suffering. It seems that the method is designed to find out what value people would attach to a reduction in the risk of becoming a victim, and may not therefore, even if otherwise sound and successful, help to evaluate the losses of the bereaved and of others involved or affected less directly. Work on bereavement and loss has shown that the psychic effects can be very severe, especially when the loss is unexpected(10).

Medical and ambulance. Since these costs account for only three per cent of the total, even gross errors in estimating them might not have a substantial effect. It is, however, noteworthy that the estimates are based on the cost of supplying medical services. At a time when demand exceeds supply and facilities cannot be expanded to correct the imbalance, the true costs are those of the potential users of medical services who are obliged to wait or go without because of the need to deal with road casualties. These opportunity costs would be higher than the bill to the NHS. For this reason, and because of the under-reporting already noted, the official estimates of medical costs are likely to be low.

Damage to vehicles and property. This is the largest single item in the annual cost of road accidents as officially calculated, amounting in 1982 to £903 million or 38 per cent of the total. The breakdown of this figure by severity of accident is shown below:

	£m
Fatal accidents	8
Serious accidents	78
Slight accidents	151
Damage-only accidents	666

It has been seen that serious and slight casualties are under-reported by some 28 or 29 per cent in the police records on which the national figures are based. It is reasonable to suppose that serious and slight accidents are also under-reported, although probably not to the same extent. If 25 per cent of serious and slight accidents are unreported, and if on average they involve as much damage to vehicles and property as those that are reported, the bill for damage in 1982 should be increased by £70 million: a figure which should, however, be treated as an upper estimate(11). In addition, as has been noted, the estimates of the numbers of damage-only accidents do not take account of those which were not reported to insurance companies, although they do allow for those that were reported without any claim being made. In 1975 the Department of Transport undertook a household survey on the cost of damage in road accidents. In this survey, it was found that in 36 per cent of incidents involving privately insured vehicles no claims had been made to insurance companies(12). It is not stated in how many cases where no claim was made the incident was reported to the insurers, but presumably such reports would be rare. One would expect it to be the cheaper accidents that go unreported. On the assumption that the reported accidents accounted for 90 per cent of the cost of damage in damage-only accidents, then the 1982 bill should be increased by £74 million.

Insurance administration and police. The cost of these two items in 1982 was officially estimated at £124 million, of which over 80 per cent was for insurance administration.

The same point of principle applies to police as to medical costs. At a time when police resources are inadequate to cope with the calls on them and cannot easily be increased, the right way to estimate the cost of dealing with accidents is by reference to the value of the other tasks that have to be foregone. This should be higher than the costs of employing police and equipment on which the official estimate is based.

The unestimated costs of disruption. Apart from major adjustments in life style that may be forced upon a severely injured person and his family, or on the dependants of a person killed in an accident, almost every accident involves temporary disruptions and consequent rearrangements which are not allowed for in the figures. Sometimes a financial outlay will be involved, and almost always time and trouble. For example, if a car is damaged there is not only the repair bill to consider. The car has to be taken to and collected from the garage; alternative travel arrangements have to be made; the insurance company has to be contacted and forms filled in and so on. If someone is off work and a temporary replacement is required, that person has be be recruited and instructed. If someone is hurt, other people may be involved in accompanying them to hospital or to the doctor and in subsequent visits. Accidents involve delay to the travellers immediately concerned and sometimes to many other road users as well. The number of reported and unreported road accidents, including those in which no one is hurt, considerably exceeds two million a year. The total disruption caused must be formidable.

Distortion and anxiety.
Accidents are the most conspicuous but not the only consequence of danger on the roads. Some travel, particularly of the most vulnerable people, the young, the old and the disabled, is deterred

altogether, which implies a curtailment of activities. Other journeys are made which would otherwise be unnecessary: in particular, journeys to accompany those people who, in present conditions, cannot venture out alone. In between the two extremes of frustrated and unwanted journeys, danger distorts travellers' behaviour in a variety of ways, particularly in the choice of mode. Danger causes stress and anxiety both to travellers and to others on their behalf. It also deters and distorts other activities, such as children's play, street life generally and the informal social contacts which arise therefrom. When such activities still take place, they also become a source of anxiety.

These effects have not been officially regarded as part of the road safety problem and there has therefore been no systematic attempt to establish how prevalent they are and how much importance people attach to them. Perhaps the only fully satisfactory study would be a comparison between the way that people live in towns free from the danger of traffic and in others, which would require a major demonstration project to create virtually traffic-free towns or, at least, large districts. Nevertheless, various studies and surveys allow something to be said about the scale and importance of these problems.

Moving about on foot is a difficulty for many old people, for 41 per cent of the pensioners interviewed in one survey. Many of them suffered from a physical condition which would have made walking hard for them even in ideal conditions, but a quarter of those who were fit mentioned external hazards which also clearly exacerbated the difficulties of those who were not completely fit. Inadequate or poorly maintained pavements were the major single source of difficulty, but the speed and volume of traffic, an insufficient number of pedestrian crossings and other problems with traffic were also frequently mentioned. About one in six of the pensioners disliked some aspect of travel by car; a fear of accidents and the speed of traffic were the most commonly reported worries(13).

Danger has a very substantial influence on children's travel. A large national survey in 1972 found that two-thirds of the youngest school children in each household walked to school and, of these, half were accompanied by an older person, usually because of the traffic(14). In a survey of mothers in the Outer Metropolitan Area of London it was found that half of the primary school children were accompanied to school; 60 per cent of the mothers concerned gave traffic danger as the reason and others gave reasons such as 'child too young' which might not have applied in better traffic conditions(15). Another survey in five different areas of the country in 1971 showed that even in places where most children of junior school age had bicycles, (and presumably the level of cycle ownership is itself partly a function of conditions for cycling) scarcely any of them cycled to school(16). The 1975/76 National Travel Survey showed that in towns generally only one per cent of journeys to school of children aged five to ten, and eight per cent of those of children aged eleven to sixteen, were by bicycle(17). In a study by the TRRL of the journey to school by secondary school children in Berkshire and Surrey, it was found that although those who cycled were more satisfied with their journey than those who travelled on a school bus or by public transport, only 11 per cent did in fact cycle(18). A study carried out in Nottingham in 1974 by Social and Community Planning Research showed that only four per cent of school children (primary and secondary) cycled to school. When the parents of the others were asked why their children did not, 34 per cent said that the roads were too dangerous. The survey showed that these parents very much resented having to impose this restriction. Other parents gave reasons which might not have applied in safer conditions - for example that the children were too young or did not own bicycles(19).

Children's travel for social and leisure purposes is also affected by the lack of safety on the roads. Restrictions on crossing main roads, on travelling by themselves and on the use of bicycles, even when owned, are common among children of junior school age (seven to eleven). Even though adults may compensate for these restrictions by accompanying children on journeys for leisure purposes, there is some evidence that they lead to some curtailment of activities(20), apart from any adverse effect that the need to be accompanied may have on a child's growth towards independence.

The need to accompany someone else can act as a serious restriction on the life of the person who acts as escort. In addition to the time taken in travel, the fact that many journeys, for example those to and from school, have to be made at a particular time of day imposes a severe constraint on the activities in which the escort can participate. The 1975/76 National Travel Survey found that in households where there were children under fifteen, 16 per cent of all the trips made by housewives, and 27 per cent of the trips they made as car drivers, were to escort others(21). There may be many reasons for escorting, but the only survey evidence that we have seen on the subject, which is to do with journeys to school by children at primary school, suggests that traffic danger is the principal one(22). Apart from the inconvenience to the escort, when such trips are made by car they add to general congestion, danger and environmental intrusion.

Danger can affect the travel behaviour even of active and healthy adults. The most obvious and probably the most marked effect is to discourage cycling. Survey evidence suggests that danger is the chief deterrent to cycling and powerful support comes from an analysis of journeys to work carried out by J.A. Waldman, a statistician then at the Department of Transport(23). The analysis was confined to journeys made by people who lived and worked in the same town; it thus excluded the longer commuting journeys. The 1966 Census of Population showed that the percentage of such journeys made by bicycle varied between towns from zero to over 50 per cent; the object of the study was to account for this variation. It was found that the main deterrents to cycling were hilliness, danger and rainfall, in that order, and that the effect of all other factors was slight. Thus 'a highly dangerous town which is otherwise average with respect to other factors would have a two per cent level of cycling as opposed to 20 per cent if it were safe'. The expected level of cycling in a flat but dangerous town was six per cent and in a flat and safe town 43 per cent. The term 'safe' as used in the study is relative only; conditions for cyclists could have been substantially improved even in the safest of the towns studied.

Dutch experience suggests that these findings are of the right order of magnitude. Climatic conditions in the Netherlands are similar to those in England, the terrain is flat and cycling is substantially safer (see Chapter V below). Table I.11, derived from the Dutch National Travel Survey, shows that cycling is the main mode of mechanical transport for short trips and a significant one for trips of up to ten kilometres.

Anxiety about pedestrian danger is extremely widespread. In the 1972 national survey on traffic and the environment mentioned above, 69 per cent of the adults interviewed claimed to be bothered by pedestrian danger and 27 per cent said they were bothered 'quite a lot' or 'very much'. As Table I.12 shows, none of the strictly 'environmental' nuisances of traffic, such as noise and fumes, attracted the same number of complaints. When respondents were asked to compare the various nuisances more directly, by saying which ones on a list bothered them most, 'difficulty and danger in walking or crossing roads' again headed the list (Table I.13). Two-thirds of the sample found difficulty in crossing some roads in their area, 29 per cent said that they sometimes felt endangered when walking on the pavement or beside the road and 53 per cent said that they were sometimes worried about the pedestrian safety of others, especially children and old people(24).

There seems to be no systematic data about the anxiety associated with other forms of travel. Everyday observation suggests that cycling and motorcycling can both be a source of great worry, especially to parents, as can playing in the streets. The stress of long-distance car travel and the worry it can cause are thought by British Rail to be significant enough to be featured in their advertisements.

Several of the surveys conducted by Social and Community Planning Research have tried to establish what importance people place on the freedom from traffic in their streets vis-a-vis other aspects of travel and urban life. Sometimes danger is separately identified and sometimes traffic is treated as a single nuisance. In the Nottingham study referred to above, people were asked to imagine that they had decided to move to another area and to consider how important each of ten different features would be in choosing that area. They were first asked to rate each feature separately on a five-point scale of importance, and then to consider the features together and to place them in order of importance. The results are shown in Table I.14. The ranking is influenced by the fact that some of the features listed, in particular access to work and school, would not be of interest to all households. It is perhaps fair to comment that listing 'safety from road traffic' and 'peace and quiet' separately may have had the effect of splitting the votes, so to speak, of those who would be primarily concerned when choosing a new area to avoid the general nuisance of traffic.

A study undertaken in 1972 in urban areas of England and Wales with the specific intention of ascertaining the importance attached to traffic disturbance found 'an overwhelming desire to shop and live in situations free from disturbance and interference of traffic'(25). Many people were prepared to accept some extra time on the journey to work for the sake of an improved residential environment or on the journey to shop for the sake of an improved shopping environment. Very few would contemplate sacrificing environmental quality to gain travel time(26).

In the other major survey on road traffic and the environment carried out by SCPR in the same year, which has already been mentioned, various questions were asked on the acceptability of traffic restraint. As Table I.15 shows, the statements that people have a right not to be bothered by traffic, that cars should be banned from city centres and that many more residential roads should be closed to traffic commanded the support of most people.

Survey results always attract some doubt on the grounds that the questions are hypothetical. However the great success of pedestrianised shopping streets, originally opposed by the shop-keepers for fear of loss of custom, and the welcome given to the TRRL's experimental programme of speed-control humps on residential streets(27) support the surveys. So does the experience, some of which is described in Chapter VIII of those countries which have been bolder than Britain in policies of traffic restraint in residential neighbourhoods.

Freedom from the intrusion and, above all, the danger of traffic is highly prized. Its absence causes widespread frustration, trouble and anxiety.

Implications for the road safety effort
It has been shown that road safety has wider implications and plays a greater part in people's lives than the official treatment, as exemplified in the statistics and cost estimates of Road Accidents Great Britain, brings out. Some of the information which is needed both to monitor the more factual aspects of the problem and to assess its importance is now lacking: Appendix A contains suggestions for supplying it. Meanwhile, it is important in any practical decision-making context to bear in mind that the current cost estimates are much too low and that any attempt to use them to assess how much effort to put into road safety, or whether some particular measure is justified or not, will tend to understate what should be done. In addition, the fact that the current values relate only to casualties and accidents, and take no account of the other ways in which unsafe conditions impinge on people's lives, may lead to a distortion of priorities within road safety. In particular, the importance of creating safe conditions in residential streets and local neighbourhoods, where young, old and disabled people, who are the most vulnerable members of the community, spend so much of their time, may not be fully recognised.

At another level, the existence of such large gaps in our knowledge itself suggests that road safety is not accorded very high priority. The scant attention that has been given to ascertaining the value of safety contrasts strongly with the numerous studies on the value of travel time. It is significant that it was only at the suggestion of an outside body, the Leitch Committee, that the work now in progress on the evaluation of risk was undertaken. This is not a criticism of the road safety professionals at the Department of Transport and the TRRL, but it is an indication of the relatively low prestige attached to their work by colleagues and Ministers.

References

(1) The form on which police record the details of an accident is known as Stats 19 and the accompanying instructions as Stats 20. The account in this and the following paragraphs is taken from the 1980 edition of Stats 20, published by the Statistics Division of the Department of Transport, supplemented by information from that Division and by the definitions given in Road Accidents Great Britain 1982.

(2) R.F.F. Dawson, Cost of Road Accidents in Great Britain, RRL Report LR 79, 1967. The insurance records analysed in this study related to 1963.

(3) Road Accidents Great Britain 1974, paragraphs 43 to 47.

(4) Department of Transport Highways Economics Note No. 1, July 1982.

(5) Road Accidents Great Britain 1980, page xi.

(6) L.A. Hobbs, E. Grattan, J.A. Hobbs, Classification of Injury Severity by Length of Stay in Hospital, TRRL Laboratory Report 871, 1979.

(7) J.P. Bull and B.J. Roberts, 'Road Accident Statistics - A Comparison of Police and Hospital Information'. Accident Analysis and Prevention, Volume 5, 1973.

(8) R.F.F. Dawson. Current costs of road accidents in Great Britain, RRL Report LR 396, 1971.

(9) Report of the Advisory Committee on Trunk Road Assessment, HMSO, 1977.

(10) Colin Murray Parkes, Bereavement: Studies of Grief in Adult Life, Tavistock Publications 1972, Chapter 9.

(11) Some of the unreported accidents are likely to have resulted in very low damage costs: for example, accidents in which only a cyclist was involved. It is also possible that some of the unreported injury accidents are implicitly allowed for in the procedure by which damage-only accidents are estimated, in which case their costs are under-estimated rather than excluded altogether.

(12) As ref. 3.

(13) Mayer Hillman, Irwin Henderson and Anne Whalley, Transport Realities and Planning Policy, Political and Economic Planning, December 1976, pages 53 to 56.

(14) Jean Morton-Williams, Barry Hedges, Evelyn Fernando, Road Traffic and the Environment, Social and Community Planning Reseach, 1978.

(15) Mayer Hillman, Irwin Henderson and Anne Whalley, op.cit., pages 68 and 87.

(16) Ibid., page 26.

(17) National Travel Survey 1975/76, special tabulations.

(18) J.P. Rigby and P.J. Hyde, Journeys to School: A Survey of Secondary Schools in Berkshire and Surrey, TRRL Laboratory Report 776, especially Tables 9 and 37.

(19) Gillian Courtenay, Greater Nottingham Problems and Preferences, Social and Community Planning Research, 1974, page 23 and diagram opposite page six, supplemented by tabulations supplied by Nottinghamshire County Council.

(20) Mayer Hillman, Irwin Henderson and Anne Whalley, op.cit., pages 28 to 31.

(21) As ref. 17.

(22) Mayer Hillman, Irwin Henderson and Anne Whalley, op.cit., page 87. As noted earlier, 60 per cent of the mothers who escorted their children to the primary school gave traffic danger as a reason and some gave reasons, such that their children were unreliable or too young, which might not have applied in safer conditions.

(23) J.A. Waldman, Cycling in Towns: A Quantitative Investigation, LTR1, Working Paper 3, Department of Transport, December 1977.

(24) Jean Morton-Williams, Barry Hedges and Evelyn Fernando, op.cit., pages 50 and 51.

(25) Gerald Hoinville and Patricia Prescott-Clarke. Traffic Disturbance and Amenity Values, Social and Community Planning Research, December 1972, page 8.

(26) Ibid, pages 8, 10, 12.

(27) R. Sumner, J. Burton and I. Baguley, Speed Control Humps in Cuddesdon Way, Cowley, Oxford, TRRL Supplementary Report 350, 1978. R. Sumner and C. Baguley, Speed Control Humps - Further Public Trials, TRRL Laboratory Report 1017, 1981.

Table I.1   Road casualties in Great Britain by year and severity

Year	Killed (number)	Seriously injured	Slightly injured (thousands)	All casualties (thousands) (thousands)
1963	6922	88	261	356
1964	7820	95	282	385
1965	7952	98	292	398
1966	7985	100	285	392
1967	7319	94	269	370
1968	6810	89	254	349
1969	7365	91	255	353
1970	7499	93	262	363
1971	7699	91	253	352
1972	7763	91	261	360
1973	7406	89	257	354
1974	6883	82	236	325
1975	6366	77	241	325
1976	6570	80	254	340
1977	6614	82	260	348
1978	6831	83	260	350
1979	6352	81	248	335
1980	6010	79	243	329
1981	5846	78	241	325
1982	5934	80	249	334

Sources: Annual editions of Road Accidents Great Britain.

Table I.2   Road casualties in 1982 by severity and class of road user

Class of road user	Severity of casualty							
	Killed		Seriously injured		Slightly injured		All casualties	
	No.	%	No.	%	No.	%	No.	%
Pedestrians	1,869	31	17,094	21	42,456	17	61,419	18
Pedal cyclists	294	5	5,673	7	22,170	9	28,137	8
Riders and passengers of two-wheeled motor vehicles	1,090	18	21,597	27	49,233	19	71,920	22
Car occupants	2,443	41	31,542	40	115,903	47	149,888	45
All others	238	4	3,833	5	18,861	8	22,932	7
All road users	5,934	100	79,739	100	248,623	100	334,296	100

Note: The category "all others" is made up of bus and coach drivers and passengers and van and lorry drivers and passengers, together with a small number of people whose classification as road user was not recorded.

Source: Road Accidents Great Britain 1982.

44

Table I.3   Casualties and accidents in 1982 by severity

	Casualties	Accidents
Fatal	5,934	5,447
Serious	79,739	66,139
Slight	248,623	184,394
Total	334,296	255,980

Source: Road Accidents Great Britain 1982.

Table I.4   Average costs officially imputed to road casualties by severity

Units: £s at 1982 prices

Element of cost	Severity of casualty		
	Fatal	Serious	Slight
Lost output	102,240	1,300	20
Pain, grief and suffering	38,860	3,890	80
Medical and ambulance	140	780	40
Total	141,240	5,970	140

Source: Department of Transport.

45

Table I.5   Average costs of road accidents involving personal injury, other than the costs of the casualties themselves, by severity

Units: £s at 1982 prices

	Severity of accident		
Element of cost	Fatal	Serious	Slight
Damage to vehicles and property	1,480	1,190	820
Police and insurance administration	250	200	160
Total	1,730	1,390	980

Source: Department of Transport.

Table I.6   Costs of road accidents in Great Britain in 1982

Units: percentages

	Severity of casualty			
Elements of cost	Fatal	Serious	Slight	Total
Lost output	26	4	*	30
Pain, grief and suffering	10	13	1	24
Medical and ambulance	*	3	*	3
All costs related to numbers of casualties	35	20	1	57
Damage to vehicles and property				38
Insurance administration and police				5
Total				100
				£2,375m

* Less than 0.5 per cent
Sources: Tables I.3, I.4 and I.5 above and Department of Transport Highways Economics Note No. 1, October, 1983.

Table I.7   Coverage of casualties in the police records, analysed by severity and by class of road user: Birmingham 1970

Units: percentages

| | Severity of casualty | | | |
Class of road user	Fatal	Serious	Slight	All casualties
Pedestrians	100	91	80	85
Cyclists	100	35	19	24
Riders or passengers of 2-wheeled motor vehicles	100	72	63	67
Car drivers	100	93	71	77
Others	100	90	70	75
All road users	100	82	65	71

Note: The figure in each cell is the number of casualties shown in the police records expressed as a percentage of the number shown in the hospital records.

Source: J.P. Bull and B.J. Roberts(7).

Table I.8   Coverage of casualties in the police records, analysed by severity and by class of road user: Berkshire 1974 to 1976

Units: percentages

| | Severity of casualty | | | |
Class of road user	Fatal	Serious	Slight	All casualties
Pedestrians	100	82	60	73
Cyclists	100	41	29	34
Motorcyclists	100	73	54	64
Vehicle occupants	100	91	82	86
All road users	100	79	66	72

Note: See note to Table I.7.
Source: L.A. Hobbs, E. Grattan and J.A. Hobbs(6).

Table I.9   Comparison of police and hospital classifications for
               non-fatal casualties: Birmingham 1970

Units: casualties

| Police classification | Hospital classification | | Total of police records |
	Serious	Slight	
Serious	255	7	262
Slight	42	528	570
Not recorded	64	289	353
Total of hospital records	361	824	1,185

Source: J.P. Bull and B.J. Roberts, 1973(7)

Table I.10   Serious and slight road casualties in Great Britain in
               1982, adjusted and unadjusted figures

Severity of casualty	Unadjusted figures (thousands)	Adjustment ratio	Adjusted figures (thousands)
Serious	80	$\frac{361}{262}$	110
Slight	249	$\frac{824}{570}$	360

Source: Unadjusted figures, Road Accidents Great Britain 1982.
           Adjustment ratios, Table I.9 above.

Table I.11   The importance of cycling in the Netherlands in 1978
Units: percentages

Journey length (kms)	Journey purpose					
	To and from work		Shopping		Social	
	(a)	(b)	(a)	(b)	(a)	(b)
Less than 1.0	40	77	29	76	27	64
1.0 < 2.5	53	59	41	59	36	48
2.5 < 3.7	41	42	32	36	29	32
3.7 < 5.0	33	33	24	26	22	23
5.0 < 7.5	23	23	15	15	16	16
7.5 < 10.0	15	15	9	9	9	9
10.0 < 15.0	9	9	7	7	6	6
15.0 and over	2	2	1	1	1	1
All journey lengths	26	28	29	41	17	20

(a)   all journeys
(b)   all journeys except those made on foot
Notes: 1. The survey covered people aged twelve years and over.
         2. The use of cycles has increased in the Netherlands since 1978.
Source: Dutch National Travel Survey 1978.

Table I.12   Features of traffic found disturbing

Units: per cent of adults

Type of disturbance	Bothered at all	Bothered very much or quite a lot
Pedestrian danger	69	27
Noise at home	49	9
Noise outside	54	16
Fumes at home	7	3
Fumes outside	47	23
Dust and dirt	36	15
Vibration	27	8
Parking	21	12

Source: Jean   Morton-Williams,   Barry   Hedges   and   Evelyn Fernando,(14).

Table I.13   Ranking of disturbances

Units: per cent of adults

Type of disturbance	Ranked first	Ranked first or second
Pedestrian danger	29	45
Noise and vibration	12	30
Parking (visual aspects)	13	26
Dust and dirt	9	27
Fumes	9	26

Note: The base of the percentages includes those adults, 29 per cent of the total, who did not rank the items because they were not bothered by any of them.

Source: Jean   Morton-Williams,   Barry   Hedges   and   Evelyn Fernando,(14).

Table I.14   The relative importance of different features when choosing a new area to live in

Feature	Average points allotted	% of respondents ranking it first
Good shops nearby	3.68	19
Safety from road traffic	3.59	19
Peace and quiet	3.29	14
Plenty of open space	3.29	5
Easy access to country recreation	2.90	2
Easy access to town recreation	2.86	2
Availability of jobs locally	2.84	14
A short journey to work	2.76	5
Easy access to schools and colleges	2.74	9
Friends and relatives nearby	2.66	9

Source: Gillian Courtenay,(19).

Table I.15   Views on traffic and restraint

Statement	Comp-letely agree	In-clined to agree	In-clined to disagree	Comp-letely disagree	Don't know
Cars ought to be banned from town centres	33	29	18	17	3
Many more residential roads should be closed to traffic	21	30	27	18	4
People have a right not to be bothered by traffic	30	32	22	11	5
Traffic jams and delays to motorists are a more serious problem than disturbances like noise or fumes	28	23	24	19	7

Source: Special tabulations from Social and Community Planning Research survey,(14).

II MOTORCYCLING

The scale of the accident problem

The danger from two-wheeled motor vehicles, both to their users and to others, is summarised by the fact that in 1981 25 per cent of all road casualties and 24 per cent of fatalities occurred in accidents which involved them, although they accounted for less than three per cent of the mileage travelled by motor vehicles.

These hazards are not new. In 1930, 1,832 riders and passengers of two-wheeled motor vehicles were killed on the roads of Great Britain, the highest number ever recorded. Casualties fell sharply during the war years but rose again after 1945 as motor-cycling itself revived. Both travel and casualties reached a peak in the year 1960 and, as Table II.1 shows, both of them declined until 1972 and then once more started to rise. Travel, in vehicle kilometres, has more than doubled since 1972 and casualties to riders and passengers have increased by 61 per cent.

In interpreting these figures, it must be borne in mind that there is a substantial degree of under-reporting of slight and even of serious casualties suffered by users of two-wheeled motor vehicles (see Tables I.7 and I.8). In addition, hospital studies have shown that a serious casualty to a motorcyclist is more likely to lead to a severe or very severe disability than one affecting another road user(1).

When a two-wheeled motor vehicle is involved in an accident, other people may be hurt as well as the rider or passenger. Table II.2 gives a breakdown of the road users that were involved in 1981: apart from riders and passengers, pedestrians predominate. The risk to pedestrians is illustrated by Table II.3, which shows the numbers of pedestrians killed and injured in 1981 after being hit by bicycles, cars and two-wheeled motor vehicles respectively, expressed as rates per hundred million vehicle kilometres travelled by each type of vehicle. It will be seen that two-wheeled motor vehicles are several times more dangerous for pedestrians than either bicycles or cars and that the contrast is especially marked for fatalities.

Most accidents to two-wheeled motor vehicles are associated with young riders; 53 per cent of rider casualties in 1981 were under twenty and 75 per cent were under twenty-four. Over 90 per cent of those under twenty-four were men. Travel by two-wheeled motor vehicles is .very much an activity for young men, but this only partly accounts for the concentration of accidents among them: mile for mile, young riders are more likely to be involved in accidents than older ones, and male riders than female. Accidents involving a young rider or a male rider are also more likely than others to cause injuries, and especially fatal injuries, to other people. These points are shown in Table II.4 which compares rates for casualties (where the rider himself is the victim) with rates for accidents (where the rider or someone else, including his passenger, may be a victim) of riders of different ages. But the danger from two-wheeled motor vehicles is not entirely accounted for by the age of their riders. Table II.5 shows the accident involvement rates of car drivers. At every age, their rates are lower.

One would expect the type and size of machine used to have an influence on the risk of accidents. The police accident report form does not classify two-wheeled motor vehicles by engine size but it does distinguish between motorcycles, scooters and mopeds. In 1968, when a special analysis was made, the fatal and serious casualty rates for riders and passengers, per hundred million kilometres travelled, were motorcycles 469, scooters 348, mopeds 174(2). The Department of Transport's estimates of casualty rates for mopeds and motorcycles in 1982 are shown in Table II.6. For slight casualties, the difference between the two rates is not very marked, but the fatality rate for motorcycles is almost four times that for mopeds. When a motorcycle is involved, it is also more likely that other road users will be hurt. The risk of a fatal injury to another road user is especially high: an accident involving a motorcycle is more than four times as likely than one involving a moped to result in the death of someone other than a rider or passenger of a two-wheeled motor vehicle(3).

We have not found any systematic evidence on the degree to which motorcycling causes anxiety on behalf of the motorcyclists or intimidates other road users, but everyday experience and articles in the press suggest that these must be common effects. As will be seen below, the noise of motorcycles is widely disliked; possibly some of this dislike is accounted for by the fears aroused rather than by the decibels themselves.

The response to the problem

The main emphasis in the official response to the problem of motorcycle accidents over the years has been put on rider training, which is discussed below. However, there have also been a number of other initiatives, some particularly concerned with motorcycling and others more general. Among the general measures are the introduction in 1960 of annual tests of roadworthiness for ten-year-old vehicles, including motorcycles; in 1968 such testing was extended to three-year-old vehicles. The drink-and-drive regulations of the 1967 Road Safety Act, which apply to motorcycle riders as well as to drivers of other motor vehicles, are generally considered to be among the most effective road safety legislation ever introduced, at least in their initial impact. Small-scale road engineering schemes, discussed in another chapter of this report, are an extremely effective and cost-effective way of reducing road accidents, and users of two-wheeled motor vehicles are among the beneficiaries.

Among the more particular measures, a continuing strand of action concerns the age and other attributes governing eligibility to ride machines of different types. In 1960, a limitation was placed for the first time on the size of machine that could be ridden by a provisional licence-holder. Unless a side-car was attached, the maximum permitted engine capacity was set at 250 cc. In December 1971, regulations were introduced debarring 16-year-olds from riding motorcycles: they could ride only mopeds, which at that time were defined as machines equipped with pedals and with a maximum engine capacity of 50 cc. To pass the moped test was not a qualification to ride any larger machine. Legislation which came into effect in August 1977 changed the definition of the moped. The point of the change was to eliminate the fast "super mopeds" which had been developed since 1971. Thenceforward, to qualify as a moped a machine had to have a maximum design speed not exceeding 30 mph, a kerbside weight not exceeding 250kg and, as before, an engine capacity not exceeding 50 cc. However, machines registered before August 1977 which satisfy the former definition still count as mopeds.

The 1981 Transport Act introduced the concept of a learner motorcycle. This is defined as a machine the engine capacity of which does not exceed 125 cc, the power output 9 kilowatts and the power-to-weight ratio 100 kilowatts per metric tonne. These limits are intended to prevent too rapid acceleration and to restrict top speed to some 65 to 70 mph. A provisional motorcycle licence now entitles its holder to ride only a learner motorcycle or, in the case of a machine first used before January 1982, a motorcycle which has the same maximum engine capacity as the learner motorcycle but does not meet all its other specifications.

Another field of action concerns the machines themselves and riders' equipment. In the autumn of 1973, regulations came into effect making it compulsory for riders of two-wheeled motor vehicles and their passengers to wear helmets. Since 1973, the Transport and Road Research Laboratory has been concerned with the development of an Experimental Safety Motorcycle. Among the features of the motorcycle examined and developed have been anti-locking brakes to reduce skidding; sintered metal disc brake pads to improve braking performance, in wet conditions especially; chest pads and leg protectors to reduce the severity of injury when an accident occurs; a digital display speedometer, designed to be visible to the rider without distracting his attention; and the design, positioning and use of lamps to make the motorcycle more conspicuous. Work on conspicuity has also been concerned with the rider's clothing: for example, the effect of wearing a fluorescent jacket. Improved brake performance and sintered brake pads, or their equivalent, will soon become obligatory on new machines, but otherwise this programme has not so far borne fruit in policy. Nevertheless, various changes in the characteristics of motorcycles permitted on public roads have been made over the years through the medium of the Construction and Use Regulations. These affect such features as brakes, lights, tyres, the material from which fuel tanks may be constructed, the positioning of fittings.

Motorcycles have often featured in the Department of Transport's road safety publicity. The introduction of the law on safety helmets was preceded by intensive advertising campaigns to encourage people to wear helmets voluntarily. A number of television advertising campaigns have been mounted since 1976 to encourage motorists to look out for motorcycles, especially at junctions.

The emphasis put on training

The importance that has always been officially attached to training motorcyclists can be illustrated from official documents spanning a long period. In 1957 the Committee on Road Safety of the Ministry of Transport and Civil Aviation investigated the minimum age for motorcyclists and related matters. Its report stated that 'we felt strongly that adequate motorcycle training would be the most valuable feature of all in reducing the accident rate for motor cyclists ...'(4).

In 1967, a major report on road safety in general, after pointing out the high risks associated with motorcycles, went on to say that 'only a limited amount can be done to build more safety into them'; that more motorcycle training was 'vital'; and that

56

since training was very unlikely ever to be a paying proposition it would have to be sponsored, presumably by local authorities(5).

In 1977 at a time when it had become clear that the decline in motorcycle casualties that had started in 1965 had been reversed, a meeting was held at the Department of Transport with representatives from local authority associations, the police and other interested bodies. The remarks made by the Chairman, the Under-Secretary at the Department in charge of road safety, in opening the discussion were reported as follows:

'The recent rise in the popularity of motorcycling had brought an increase in the number of casualties among riders. The size of this increase was beginning to cause concern to the public, and the Department of Transport was considering what action could be taken to deal with the problem. There was some scope for improving safety by better conspicuity and by making other drivers more aware of the need to look out for two-wheelers, but the main area where improvement was needed was in training motorcycle riders. The meeting was arranged to hear views about how this could be achieved'.

A committee was then set up whose terms of reference were 'to consider the provision and development of training for motorcycle riders and to make recommendations'. These terms of reference were interpreted broadly so that matters such as licensing could be covered, but clearly they precluded any attempt to examine the whole field of motorcycle safety and preventive action. The Committee, believing firmly in the value of training, although acknowledging that quantitative support for this belief was lacking, directed most of its efforts towards examining ways of increasing the number of riders, particularly young riders, coming forward for training(7). Although its ideas were not accepted in full, they are the basis of the provisions on motorcyclists in the 1981 Transport Act (see below).

In March 1983, the Parliamentary Under-Secretary of State for Transport, Mrs. Chalker, spoke at the launch of the British School of Motoring's Road Safety Campaign for Secondary Schools, as part of which the display motorcyclist Dave Taylor was to tour secondary schools giving a display ride followed by a talk on road safety. After presenting Mr. Taylor with a cheque on behalf of the Department of Transport for £1,000 towards the running costs of the campaign, Mrs. Chalker made a short speech on the value of education in road safety generally, concluding with the following remarks on the value of training for motorcyclists(8)

57

'Motorcycling, a popular form of transport with many young people, is, however, far more dangerous than any other. Over half the motorcyclists killed or seriously injured are teenagers.

I know many learner motorcyclists feel that training is dull and boring. Dave Taylor has proved that this isn't so. A trained biker who has learned to handle a machine properly is less likely to be involved in an accident, and can enjoy biking to the full.'

Apart from statements and moral support, the government has encouraged training both by legislation and in other ways. It has been seen that the 1981 Transport Act limited holders of provisional licences to using less powerful machines. This was partly because the modern 250 cc machine was regarded as 'just too fast and powerful for the average learner'[9] but in addition it was felt that this restriction would act as an incentive to learners to seek training in order to pass the test and therefore become eligible to ride more powerful machines[10].

The other measures concerning motorcyclists in the Act were entirely concerned to encourage training. The motorcycle driving test was divided into two parts. The second part, which is little changed from the previous test, consists of a road test conducted by an official Driving Examiner. But a new first part, which is an off-the-road rest concerned with handling skills, was introduced in the hope that learners would be encouraged to take training in order to improve their chances of passing the test. As a further inducement, part one of the test can be taken in conjunction with a course of training at an authorised training centre where it can be administered by a member of the staff, whereas a candidate who did not take a course would have to make his own arrangements to be tested by a Driving Examiner.

The Act also introduced a limit on the duration of the motorcycle provisional licence, which now lapses after two years and cannot be renewed until a year has passed. It is hoped that the necessity of passing a test in order to be able to continue riding will again act as an incentive to take training.

For many years, the great majority of training centres available to the general public were provided under a scheme run jointly by the RAC and ACU (Auto-Cycle Union). This scheme was started in 1947 and by 1979 provided some 360 centres, out of a national total of some 470[11]. Although this particular scheme has now closed down, the number of training centres has continued to grow and by early 1983 there were over 650 sites available nationwide(12). About half of them are run by STEP Management Services Ltd., a company set up by motorcycle industry and trade interests in 1974, and other organisations, including RoSPA, are also involved. Some centres are run by local authorities, who may also help in other ways, e.g. by helping to find sites.

STEP Management Services Ltd. are also concerned with traffic education in schools. Their courses all include instruction on two-wheeled motor vehicles, although also covering many other aspects of road safety. At present, approximately 2,500 secondary schools in the United Kingdom(13) out of a total of some 6,000 are registered with STEP, which has also been instrumental in having Traffic Education accepted as a CSE examination subject. In addition to courses for pupils, STEP organises courses for school teachers which include instruction on moped riding.

The Ministry of Transport first gave financial help to the RAC/ACU scheme in 1961(14) and this help continued until the final year of the scheme's operation in 1982/83. In that year, the Department of Transport also gave £100,000 to the British Motorcycle Safety Foundation, the body through which STEP receives its funds from the motorcycle trade and which also helps to support RoSPA's motorcycle training activities(15). It may be that some of the Department's grant of £420,000 to RoSPA in 1982/83(16) also found its way into motorcycle training and education, although if so it would only have been a small proportion. The Department has also run publicity campaigns, using motorcycling magazines, other press, cinema, posters and television, urging new motorcyclists to seek training(17).

The value of training

Is training in fact an effective way of reducing motorcycle accidents? It was not until 1971 that a formal study to answer this question was undertaken at the University of Salford. This compared the accident rates of a sample of motorcyclists who had been through the RAC/ACU training scheme with a sample of others who had not. It was found that the accident rate of those who had been trained was higher and that the difference was statistically significant at the 99.9 per cent level. The authors of the report mention that 'in a few areas training appeared to effect a positive change in performance' and that 17-year-old riders in particular may have benefited, and they warn that 'it is not possible to infer from this research that attendance at a training scheme may result in inferior riding ability since the predicted performance of the individual rider cannot be determined'(19). Nevertheless they point out some possible adverse effects of training. It may encourage poorer riders, who would otherwise have given up motorcycling riding, to continue; it may also improve handling skills at the expense of the other aptitudes required to cope with other road users; and it may lead to over-confidence and a false sense of security(20).

It is also possible that the people who decided to take the RAC/ACU scheme were the poorer, more accident-prone riders; the Salford study provides some support for that hypothesis(21). Moreover, research can only assess particular training schemes, not training in general, and it could therefore be said that the Salford study shows, at most, only that the particular training provided by the RAC/ACU schemes was defective. The TRRL has indeed claimed to have found some deficiencies in them(22). However, a study in Buckinghamshire and others in the United States (none of which we have examined) apparently came to similar conclusions with respect to the methods of training they studied(23). A Canadian study found no difference in accident likelihood among trained and untrained motorcyclists after the effect of other variables such as sex, age and driving experience, had been allowed for. It did find that trained motorcyclists were significantly less likely to commit a traffic violation, although this difference could not necessarily be ascribed to the training programme rather than to the attitudes which influenced riders to seek formal training in the first place(24).

If the cause of motorcycle accidents was a lack of handling skills, the fact that training did not produce safer motorcyclists would be surprising, since it should be possible to impart such skills in a course. But if the cause lies in attitudes and a lack of maturity, it is not surprising, since a short course is hardly likely to alter personality features and, in virtue of the fact that it should indeed lead to an improvement in skills, may even reduce caution. The marked difference in accident rates between young and old riders and between men and women (see Table II.4) suggests that inappropriate attitudes are likely to be more important as a cause of accidents than a lack of skill. This is supported by a study of the motivation of young motorcyclists undertaken at the Tavistock Institute in the late 1960's. It was found that they could be divided into two groups: the 'addicts' and the 'young transport' motorcyclists. The addict was '... likely to be a highly skilled driver in a technical sense. He knows his machine extremely well, knows exactly what to expect of it and exactly how to handle it under various conditions.' But addicts were also likely to be aggressive, reckless and accident-prone; there was even a feeling that 'you're not really a motorcyclist until you have had an accident'(25). Those concerned with the STEP scheme have expressed some disquiet that, because many participants take the training courses

60

in order to pass part one of the test, there is a pressure to concentrate on teaching off-the-road handling skills rather than competence on the road(26). But even if this pressure could be relaxed, by changes in the nature of the part one test, it is difficult to see that six two-hour lessons, which is what the STEP Silver Star course comprises, could do much to change attitudes, especially if the trainees are attending the course only because it makes it easier for them to overcome the obstacle of the test rather than from their own wish to become better riders. It may be that for school children on the CSE course there are greater opportunities for influencing attitudes and behaviour as well as imparting technical skills; we know of no research on this point.

Even if motorcycle training of some kind did help to reduce the accident rates for a given distance travelled, the influence that it may have in increasing accidents through encouraging the motorcycling habit must also be considered. It seems unlikely that the effects of exposure to motorcycle training in schools, the large-scale provision of subsidised facilities and official propaganda in favour of training are confined to persuading young people who would have been motorcyclists in any event to become trained. Some are likely to take up motorcycling who in other circumstances would have rejected the idea if it had even occurred to them. Parents also are likely to receive the idea that, providing riders are trained, motorcycling is a safe and acceptable form of travel for young people and will therefore be less inclined to oppose it. It was seen in Table II.1 that travel by motorcycle more than doubled in the ten years between 1972 and 1982. There are likely to be many causes for this, including, for example, the decline in availability and rise in price of public transport, but it would be surprising if the great efforts made to promote motorcycling were not among them.

Neglected alternatives
Limits on the machine
An obvious approach to tackling the motorcycle accident problem would be to limit the size, power and speed of the machines that can be used on the public highway. This field of action has been exploited only to the extent that 16-year-old riders and holders of provisional licences, who were at one time not subject to any special rules concerning the type of machines they might ride, are now confined to mopeds and to learner machines respectively. The possibility that similar limits could be applied to the machines ridden by experienced riders holding full licences seems never to have been contemplated, unless one counts the fact that part of the definition of a motorcycle is that its unladen weight should not

61

exceed eight hundred-weight(27).

The very great influence of machine size is immediately apparent from Table II.7, taken from an article by a member of the Road Research Laboratory (as it then was) analysing a survey conducted by the government's Social Survey in 1958. Since that time, technical developments have enabled machines with relatively small engines to attain speeds for which larger engines would formerly have been necessary. It is therefore unlikely that this analysis would show quite as strong a pattern if repeated today. But that would mean only that engine capacity is a less good proxy for all the dangerous characteristics of a motorcycle than it used to be, not that the influence of the machine as a factor in accidents is any less than it was. Nevertheless, data from various more recent sources support these findings and suggest that engine capacity is still a reasonable proxy for powerfulness and danger. Insurance premiums for any given age group are higher for larger machines(28). The size of the premium partly reflects the cost of the motorcycle and of repairs to it, but data provided to us by an insurance company specializing in motorcycle insurance show that the same trend holds for third party insurance. Another leading company in this field has provided us data on the incidence of claims met. It is substantially higher for machines in the 100-225 cc range than for those in the 0-100 cc range and higher again in the 225-350 cc range. This result applies to each of fourteen rider age groups and to both comprehensive and non-comprehensive policies. Over the 350 cc size there is still a tendency for the incidence of claims to rise with engine size but the pattern is less definite(29). The Department of Transport has claimed, on the basis of a statistical anlaysis, that when a limit was placed on the maximum speed of mopeds, the effect was to bring about a substantial reduction in moped accidents(30). A detailed investig-ation by the TRRL of 425 motorcycle accidents occurring in an area of Buckinghamshire and Berkshire in 1974 showed a relation-ship between speed of travel and severity of casualty(31). In Japan, research in 1974 showed that although only 2.1 per cent of motorcycles in use were over 700 cc, they accounted for 21.5 per cent of motorcycle fatalities(32).

For regulatory purposes, it is not sufficient to specify the size of machine in terms of engine capacity alone. Other features relating to acceleration and speed have also to be taken into account, as indeed they are in the definition of both mopeds and learner motorcycles. The present specification of the learner motorcycle can, however, be criticised on the grounds that it permits too high a speed, approaching 70 mph. The data that have been quoted strongly suggest that if all riders were limited to

62

machines similar to learner machines, but preferably somewhat less powerful and with lower top speeds, the number and severity of motorcycle accidents would be greatly reduced.

Such a restriction might impose some penalty on the use of a motorcycle for long trips and for purposes such as holidays and expeditions. For everyday purposes such as journeys to work or college and social trips, motorcycling would still be just as convenient, if less exciting. Tables II.8 and II.9, taken from the 1978/79 National Travel Survey, show that the shorter everyday journeys vastly predominate. Even for the larger machines (250 cc or over) only 23 per cent of journeys exceed 10 miles in length and only 10 per cent exceed 15 miles. Holidays and day trips account for a minute proportion of journeys.

A reduction in accidents, and presumably in intimidation and anxiety, would not be the only social gains that would follow from a restriction on the size of motorcycles. Motorcycles are second only to heavy lorries in the amount of noise nuisance they cause. In 1972, when motorcycle travel was at its lowest point, a survey of the adult population of England found that 26 per cent were bothered when at home indoors by noise from motorcycles and 15 per cent were bothered quite a lot or very much(35). In 1980, a survey of the adult population of Great Britain found that 21 per cent of them said that motorcycles were 'particularly bothersome' to them when they were indoors at home(34). If this percentage also applies to children, then over eleven million people are bothered - almost nine people for each two-wheeled motor vehicle on the road. Small motorcycles can cause as much annoyance as large ones, especially when they are poorly maintained or have been tampered with. But they need not be noisy, whereas to construct a powerful, quiet motorcycle is an extremely difficult technical problem (35, 36), a fact which is reflected in the noise limits set for new machines, shown in Table II.10. If the problem were solved, that might only add to the hazards.

It would be too optimistic to suppose that if large motor-cycles were banned, the young men who would have ridden them would exhibit accident rates on the smaller machines no higher than those of their contemporaries now riding those machines. No doubt it is the more reckless riders who are attracted to the more dangerous machines. Nevertheless, the machine must help to stimulate reckless attitudes, and some dangerous behaviour, such as 'doing a ton', would be physically impossible on a low-powered machine.

A graded licensing system
An alternative to limiting all riders to less powerful machines

63

would be to institute a graded rider licensing system. The essence of such a system is that motorcycles are divided into categories for rider licensing purposes and that more stringent conditions apply to obtaining a licence for the higher (more dangerous) categories than for the lower ones. This is not only a matter of the test becoming harder in the higher categories; the rules for eligibility to take the test would also be more stringent. These rules might be related to age only, but since experience affects the accident rates as well as age, it would be better to relate them to experience as well. Thus no one would be allowed to take the test for a motorcycle in grade N+1 until he had held a licence, with a clean record, for machines of grade N for a certain length of time.

Our reason for discussing this possibility is not that we are in doubt about the arguments in favour of limiting virtually all riders to less powerful machines. In our opinion, only the police and certain riders in the armed forces should be allowed to ride powerful motorcycles on the public highway. The problem - small as it appears to be - of people who use motorcycles for long expeditions and take a lot of equipment with them might perhaps be tackled by developing a permanent motorcycle combination; it does not, in our view, justify the use of a more powerful two-wheeler. But the purpose of this report is not to make recommendations on particular road safety measures, but to examine institutional obstacles to progress. In this context, it is of particular interest to examine the reasons why a graded licensing system has not been introduced (except in the embryonic form represented by restricting 16-year-olds to mopeds and provisional licence holders to learner machines) since its potential usefulness has always been acknowledged.

The 1957 Report on the Minimum Age for Motorcyclists which has already been mentioned refers twice to the idea of graded licensing. In paragraph 37 the report states:

'Expert opinion among motor cyclists favours a progressive approach to the larger machine by way of the lightweight, and we consider that an attempt should be made, by introducing different age limits for different classes of machine, to influence the younger rider to progress by stages. Thus, in our view, the best approach to the problem of the minimum age lies in replacing the present sharply cut division between those who may, and may not, ride motor cycles, by a progression of steps permitting a rider to ride different types of machine, at successive ages.'

In paragraph 39, it states:

'Although strongly advocating that all motor cyclists should have experience in riding lightweight machines before riding the larger machines, we can see no practicable means whereby such a progression could be enforced among riders of all ages.'

The idea of grading has international approval as well. For example, it was a principal theme of a report on the safety of two-wheelers published by OECD in 1978(37). In Japan, a partially graded system was introduced during the 1970s, apparently in response to statistical studies which showed that risks increased with the engine size and speed of the machine used. Two-wheeled motor vehicles are divided into four categories for rider licensing purposes: under 50 cc, 50 to 125, 125 to 400, 400 to 750. At the government's request, the industry has entered into a voluntary agreement not to market machines of over 750 cc in Japan, although they are still manufactured for export(38). The conditions for obtaining a licence become harder with increasing engine size. It is recommended that candidates to ride a machine of over 400 cc should already have a licence for a less powerful machine, but that is not a condition for eligibility(39).

In France, a cyclomoteur, roughly equivalent to a moped, can be ridden at the age of 14 without a licence or test. A velomoteur, a machine with an engine not exceeding 80 cc and a maximum speed not exceeding 75 km/h, can be ridden at 16, but riders are required to take both a theoretical exam and a practical test. Larger motorcycles can be ridden at 18. They are divided into two categories, split at 400 cc, and the tests for the higher category are harder, but there is no obligation to have held a licence for a less powerful machine before taking the test for a more powerful one(40).

Neither the Japanese nor the French, therefore, require motorcyclists to progress upwards through the grades, although both systems to some extent encourage such a progression. But they do at least ensure that motorcyclists cannot ride machines much more powerful than the one on which they passed their tests. In 1979, the Report of the Advisory Committee on Motorcycle Rider Training stated that '... it is a fundamental principle of our testing system that we make the candidate perform on a vehicle as nearly as possible representative of the class for which he seeks full entitlement ...'(41). In fact, the British system does not at all comply with this principle. A candidate who has passed the test on a learner machine is thereby entitled to ride one of unlimited power.

Other safety features

It was seen above that little of the TRRL's work to design safer motorcycles has borne fruit in legislation, although sintered brake pads will soon be compulsory. Among the other promising devices are anti-lock brakes, which would reduce stopping distances and the incidence of skidding in wet conditions. The development work was completed at the TRRL in 1979. It is estimated that to fit such brakes to both wheels would add about £100 to the cost of a motorcycle and that about 10 per cent of accidents involving motorcycles might be saved; this estimate presumably assumes that riders would not take advantage of the increased intrinsic safety of their machines by driving less safely in wet weather. No doubt because of the extra cost, no manufacturer has yet fitted such brakes voluntarily, although commercial development work is in progress, and international cooperation would be required to make them compulsory(42).

Another feature developed at the TRRL is a chest pad which restrains the rider when he is thrown forwards in a crash, thus both altering his trajectory and very greatly reducing his speed at impact and his impact energy. It is estimated that this feature would have some beneficial effect in 30 per cent of the accidents which now result in rider fatalities and would also help in a substantial number of severe accidents. No international agreement would be necessary for the UK to introduce Construction and Use Regulations requiring chest pads to be fitted on new motorcycles, or on new motorcycles of specified types, for example the larger machines. Work on chest pads started at the TRRL in the early 1970s; by 1979 their technical feasibility had been successfully demonstrated. The cost per machine has not been estimated but it would be significant. The work has now been dropped, however, because of problems of consumer acceptability(43).

Altering the choice of travel mode

The measures that have been discussed would make motorcycling safer by reducing the accident rate for a given distance travelled and they might also have some incidental effect on reducing that distance. The problem can also be tackled by measures which would explicitly be directed towards changing the use made of transport modes. Although cycling is dangerous, it is substantially less so, both to the rider and to other road users, than motorcycling. A positive policy to make cycling safer and to provide appropriate facilities on a large scale should attract some motorcyclists. It was suggested above that the large and rapid increase in motorcycling must be partly accounted for by the decline of local public transport. The experience of South Yorkshire, where bus fares were unchanged, and therefore fell substantially in real terms between 1976 and 1982, appears to support this suggestion. Between 1972 and 1981 motorcycle ownership remained little changed overall and use among the 15-24 age group apparently declined(44). The encouragement of cycling and the revival of public transport are both to be desired on other grounds in addition to that of reducing motorcycle travel.

The 1979 working party discussed whether financial incentives, in the form of reduced premiums for motorcyclists who take training, could be used as a safety measure, but concluded that insurance companies would be unlikely to agree in the absence of statistical data that training reduced accidents(45). We have not, however, seen any discussion of the use of taxation as an incentive, although it is an instrument within the control of the government whereas insurance premiums are not. A respectable use of taxation is to reduce the gap between the total costs arising from the use of a mode of transport and that part of the total which is borne by the user himself. The current annual tax for motorcycles varies with engine size as follows: not exceeding 150 cc, £8.50; 150-250 cc, £17.00; over 250 cc, £34. We have not investigated this, but prima facie there would be plenty of room to increase these fees without any risk that motorcyclists would then be paying more than the social costs of motorcycling warrant.

The suggestion that the age of eligibility to hold a car driving licence should be reduced has sometimes been mooted, on the grounds that four-wheeled motorised travel is safer than two-wheeled; and that if they became accustomed to driving a car first, some young people might skip the motorcycle stage altogether. In view of the great difference in costs between the two modes, however, it is doubtful whether there would be much diversion, and any reduction in the age of eligibility to drive a car would also presumably stimulate extra car driving. Table II.5 showed that the accident rates for young car drivers are extremely high, albeit substantially lower than those for motorcyclists of the same age. The alternative of raising the age at which motorcycles (as opposed to mopeds) can be ridden has also been suggested. At one of the consultation meetings with interested parties chaired by the Parliamentary Secretary of the Department of Transport (then Mr. Kenneth Clarke) after the receipt of the report of the Advisory Committee on Motorcycle Rider Training, it is reported(46) that there was 'no dissent' from a suggestion that the minimum age for motorcyclists could be raised to 18 years. Nevertheless, this suggestion was not taken up.

French practice suggests another way in which the driver licensing system might be used to encourage the use of safer four-

67

wheeled transport rather than two-wheeled. It is possible to drive a car in France without a driving licence, and at the same age (fourteen) as one can ride a moped, provided that the car is no more powerful than a moped. Hence a market has developed in 'voiturettes', cars with 50 cc engines and maximum speeds of approximately 50 km/h. The first such car was produced in 1973 and there are now some seventeen manufacturers whose annual sales were estimated at 13,000 in 1979 and 18,000 in 1980(47). We do not advocate that anyone should be able to drive a car, even such a small one, indefinitely without a licence, nor that the minimum age for riding or driving any kind of motor vehicle should be as low as fourteen. But it does seem sensible that the conditions of eligibility should depend on the power of the vehicle rather than upon the number of wheels; indeed, less stringent conditions should apply to a four-wheeled vehicle of a given engine size and maximum speed than to the equivalent two-wheeled machine. This way of encouraging young people to skip the motorcycle stage should help to avoid the difficulty of the high accident rate of young male car drivers. The low speed of the voiturette should reduce the chance of an accident occurring; its lightness should reduce the damage it inflicts on other road users when an accident does occur. The financial disincentives would also be reduced. The prices of voiturettes ranged from £1300 to £2000 in 1981(47). After the costs of insurance and protective clothing for motorcyclists have been taken into account, the total running cost would not always be more than that of a powerful motorcycle. Different rates of vehicle excise duty could help to reduce the ramaining gap.

Implications for the road safety effort

This account of the attempts made over the last 25 years to deal with the very grave problem of motorcycle accidents has revealed a paradoxical situation. The major effort has been put into a policy, the encouragement of rider training, which has not been shown to be effective and which could even, especially if it has led to an increase in the use of motorcycles, have been counter-productive. Meanwhile, other policies which, on the evidence, really could make a substantial impact on the problem have been partly or wholly neglected. The examination of this paradox may throw light on institutional obstacles in road safety more generally.

One reason why it may not always have been easy to see what the most promising paths were has been a shortage of data. There are, for example, no data which would allow the accident rates of people who have been through the major training scheme now on offer, the STEP scheme, to be compared with the rates of some

control group. It can always be argued, therefore, that the
disappointing results from studies of other training schemes do not
apply to the scheme now on offer. The size of the motorcycle is
not recorded on the police accident form (STATS 19), nor does this
form give any information on driver characteristics other than age
and sex. It is therefore not even possible to say how many
motorcycle accidents are accounted for by different cross-categor-
ies of rider and machine. Although such data would be of some
value on their own, they could be misleading without information
on the extent of exposure to risk, as measured by distance
travelled, for each such cross-category. But exposure data are also
lacking.

But to say this only raises the further question of why data
necessary to describe the problem are not collected on a continuous basis. It would be very easy to amplify the information given
on the STATS 19 form without imposing any extra trouble on the
police. The police would only have to record the vehicle registration number on the number plate and the number on the driver's
licence. Full details on the vehicle (make, model, age, engine
power) and on the rider or driver (age, sex, type of licence and
length of time held) could be obtained at leisure from the Driver
and Vehicle Licensing Centre at Swansea. It is unfortunate that
the DVLC does not at present have any records relating to part one
of the motorcycle test, which means that riders who become
involved in accidents cannot be classified according to what
training, if any, they have undergone, but it should be possible to
modify the system in order to provide that information also.

To obtain exposure data, i.e. annual mileages, for similar
categories of rider and machine requires a survey such as that
conducted by the Social Survey in 1958; Social and Community
Planning Research has been engaged in a similar exercise more
recently, but the results are not yet published. This is a straightforward exercise, insofar as surveys ever are straightforward.

Road accidents accounted for 36 per cent of all deaths and 76
per cent of accidental deaths among people in the 15-24 age group
in 1980(48); the great majority of these young people died in
motorcycle accidents. It is hard to imagine that if a similar
scourge were to occur in any other field of activity, society would
not equip itself with the fundamental data required to describe and
monitor the problem.

The faith pinned on motorcycle rider training may be to some
extent derived from a more general argument purporting to show
the importance of traffic education. The argument is, roughly,
that as 95 per cent of road accidents involve human error,
education is required in order to produce more skilful and careful

road users. In the particular case of motorcycle accidents, the argument has been put as follows in a publication of STEP(49).

> 'With accident figures - especially among young motor-cyclists - at such a frighteningly high level, the company's formation in April 1974 was a direct response to the need for traffic education in schools. As the number of deaths and injuries rose, it became increasingly apparent that inexper-ience was the prime cause of so many road accidents. Only sustained education could resolve such a situation; and only a hand-picked body of road safety and education experts could be sufficiently qualified to provide it.'

One difficulty is that education may not in practice remove the errors. But there are two other reasons why it is wrong to argue that where human error is the cause the remedy must lie in education. The first is that education is not the only way to change attitudes and, through them, behaviour, especially since the problem is not so much to inculcate quite new attitudes as to reinforce the responsible attitudes that almost everyone has. Attitudes are affected by many features in the rider's or driver's environment, including his vehicle, the road, the behaviour of other drivers and so on, all of which can be influenced by policy. The second is that accidents caused by human error may be tackled without any change in skills or attitudes by policies which make accidents less likely to occur or less likely to give rise to death or injury when they do occur. Pedestrianisation and the compulsory wearing of seat belts are examples. Human beings are not changed but their circumstances are.

To train road users, and young people in particular, seems such an obviously desirable and helpful thing to do that a reluct-ance to query it or to check its efficacy would be very under-standable, particularly after so much had been committed to it over many years.

But the impression that the documents give is that the most important reason for clinging to education as the main means of attack on the problem of motorcycle accidents was the belief that there were no other means - none at least that the government could employ. This point of view was expressed very clearly by the representatives of the Association of Metropolitan Authorities at a meeting in 1980 following the Report of the Advisory Committee on Motorcycle Rider Training(50).

> 'The AMA were in favour of compulsory training of new motorcyclists stressing that, although the road safety value

70

of training could not be proven, examination and education were the only means at the Government's disposal to deal with the problem.'

But, as the foregoing discussion has shown, there are several other lines of attack which appear very promising. It seems that it has been thought that, whatever their technical merit, they were somehow politically non-starters. Presumably this was what the authors of the 1957 Report on the Minimum Age for Motor Cyclists had in mind when they said (see page 64 above) that strongly as they advocated that all motorcyclists should have experience in riding lightweight machines before riding the larger ones, they could see no practicable means whereby such a progression could be enforced among riders of all ages. As it stands, this is a puzzling remark, since there would seem to be no practical difficulty in stating or enforcing a rule that only someone who had held a licence for one type of motorcycle for a given number of years would be eligible to take the test for a machine of the next most powerful type. It seems likely that the Committee's difficulty was political rather than practical; they disliked the idea of imposing any restrictions on adults.

This reluctance would be easier to understand if motorcyclists were a threat only to themselves, although the argument that society would then have no right to intervene was rejected when seat belt wearing became compulsory. Even when the rider is the only casualty, other people are affected, for example the NHS and its other actual or would-be patients. Moreover, some degree of paternalism is appropriate in relation to teenage road users. But since in fact motorcycles are a threat and annoyance to millions of other people, scruples about restricting them are quite misplaced; it should be a central task of transport policy to ensure that the nuisance which one class of road user can impose on everyone else is kept within reasonable bounds.

It seems that the problem has not been seen so broadly. When introducing the meeting held in June 1977 to launch the Advisory Committee on Motorcycle Rider Training, the Under-Secretary in charge of road safety described the problem as the 'increase in casualties among riders' (see page 15 above). He did not mention casualties to others, intimidation or noise. Had the problem been stated in all its fulness, perhaps more fundamental solutions would have been examined.

The failure to relate noise, or other environmental matters, to road safety, or indeed to give them much prominence at all in transport planning, is a serious weakness which is raised again in later chapters. There must be occasions when some policy which would contribute to safety, to the reduction of noise and fumes and to conservation cannot be justified when each of these benefits is taken separately, but is very worthwhile if they are all considered together. However, in the case of motorcycles, road safety by itself would be sufficient to justify the measures which have been regarded as non-starters, but without which the problem remains insoluble.

One reason why the Department has adopted such a limited view both of the problem and of possible solutions has to do with the kind of people which it involves in the consultation process. Motorcyclists, motorcycle trade interests and people professionally concerned with motorcycle training are heavily involved; people whose lives are adversely affected by motorcyclists are not. Thus the members of the Advisory Committee on Motorcycle Training consisted, besides officials, of nominees of the police, the Accident Offices Association, the various local authority associations, the Greater London Road Safety Unit, the British Motorcyclists' Federation, the Motor Agents Association, the Motorcycle Association, the National Association of Cycle and Motorcycle Traders Ltd., the RAC/ACU motorcycle training scheme, RoSPA (the Royal Society for the Prevention of Accidents) and STEP Management Services Ltd. Pedestrians, cyclists, old or disabled people, environmentalists and hospital casualty departments were not represented. If they had been, it is more likely that the Committee would have entertained the ideas that training might be counterproductive; that the larger and faster motorcycles should be prohibited; or that travellers should be encouraged to use safer and less intrusive means of transport in preference to motorcycles.

There is a problem in involving interests such as pedestrians, cyclists and environmentalists in the conventional consultation process, especially when it requires participation in a working party, since their organisations, unlike trade associations, rarely have funds or full-time staff. Some interests may not have representative groups at all: children are an obvious example. It is therefore of great importance to supplement the conventional consultation process by social surveys which will ensure that all interests, including the less vocal and less organised, are properly represented. The conventional process is likely to be most misleading, and social surveys most necessary, when issues of what is or is not acceptable to the public arise. Although some social surveys have been undertaken, as is evident from the material quoted in this chapter and in Chapter I, it does not seem that much use has been made of the findings in policy formulation.

In conclusion, the failure to adopt, or even to consider, the most promising ways of reducing the number of motorcycle accidents reflects the low importance placed on road accidents generally, the failure to relate accidents to wider issues of danger and environmental intrusion and the inadequate attention given to those issues in their own right. An excessive concern for the rights of motorcyclists has been coupled with an almost complete disregard for the interests of the many more people who are adversely affected by motorcycling. One reason for this imbalance is that the Department of Transport's methods of sounding public opinion are systematically biased towards trade and user interests to the neglect of third parties.

References

(1) E. Grattan and J.A. Hobbs, Permanent Disability in Road Traffic Accident Casualties. TRRL Laboratory Report 924, 1980. This report also refers to an earlier study in Birmingham which showed a similar result: W. Gissane, J.P. Bull and Barbara Roberts, 'Sequelae of road injuries', Injury, 1970 Volume 1, pages 195-203.

(2) Road Accidents Great Britain 1968.

(3) Calculation from a special tabulation of the 1981 road accident figures provided by the Department of Transport.

(4) Report on the Minimum Age for Motor Cyclists, Ministry of Transport and Civil Aviation, HMSO, 1957, para. 54.

(5) Road Safety - A Fresh Approach, HMSO, 1967, Cmnd 3339.

(6) Note of meeting to discuss motorcycle rider training held at the Department of Transport, 2 Marsham Street on 17 June 1977, supplied by Department of Transport.

(7) Report of the Advisory Committee on Motorcycle Rider Training, Department of Transport, October 1979, especially paras. 18 to 21 and 64.

(8) Department of Transport Press Notice No. 104, 28 March 1983.

(9) Transport Act 1981 Motorcycle Safety, Note by the Department of Transport issued July 1982.

(10) Report of the Advisory Committee on Motorcycle Rider Training, op.cit., especially para. 40.

(11) Ibid., para 11.

(12) Department of Transport's Minutes of Evidence to the House of Commons Transport Committee Inquiry on Road Safety, 22 March 1983, HMSO 1983, page 20.

(13) Communication from STEP Management Services Ltd.

(14) Report of the Working Party on the Training of Learner Motorcyclists, Ministry of Transport, 1966, para. 20.

(15) Hansard, House of Commons 20 December, 1983, column 417.

(16) Ibid.
(17) Report of the Advisory Committee on Motorcycle Rider Training, op.cit., para. 16.
(18) Stanley Raymond and Susan Tatum, An evaluation of the effectiveness of the RAC/ACU Motor Cycle Training Scheme - A final report, Road Safety Research Unit, Department of Civil Engineering, University of Salford, 1977, Tables 10 to 13.
(19) Ibid., page 123.
(20) Ibid., pages 40, 98, 123, 124.
(21) Ibid., page 34.
(22) Transport and Road Research Laboratory's Minutes of Evidence to the House of Commons Transport Committee, 3 May, 1983, HMSO 1983, page 107.
(23) Mentioned, but with no further detail, on the same page in the TRRL's evidence.
(24) Brian A. Jonah, Nancy E. Dawson and Barry W.E. Bragg, 'Are Formally Trained Motorcyclists Safer?', Accident Analysis and Prevention, Vol. 14, No. 4, 1982.
(25) Isobel Menzies, Some Social and Psychological Aspects of Road Safety, Centre for Applied Social Research, The Tavistock Institute of Human Relations, 1968, especially pages 56 to 63.
(26) Andrew Clayton, 'Trainers, Trainees and Tests', Traffic Education, Autumn 1982.
(27) C.M. Brand, 'Transport Act 1981: New Provision for Motorcycles', New Law Journal, August 6, 1981.
(28) See, for example, the list of premium rates published in The Guardian, 26.11.79.
(29) Private communications from insurance companies.
(30) Department of Transport's Minutes of Evidence to the House of Commons Transport Committee Inquiry on Road Safety, 22 March, 1983, HMSO, 1983, page 38.
(31) J. Whitaker, A survey of motorcycle accidents, TRRL Laboratory Report 913, 1980, page 23 and Figure 12.
(32) Carol Calvert, Jean Walters, John Bolland, Nick Marler, Erik Skovfoged, The Evaluation of Motorcycle Driver Training, University of Wales Institute of Science and Technology, June 1982, page 111.
(33) Jean Morton-Williams, Barry Hedges and Evelyn Fernando, Road Traffic and the Environment, SCPR, 1978, page 35.
(34) C.J. Baughan, B. Hedges and J. Field, A national survey of lorry nuisance, TRRL Supplementary Report 774, Table 4.
(35) Proposed Motorcycle Noise Emission Regulations, Background Document EPA 550/9-77-203, US Environmental Protection

Agency, November 1977, especially Section 5.

(36)   Alan Baker, 'Control of Motorcycle Noise', Noise and Vibration Bulletin, April 1982.

(37)   Safety of Two-Wheelers, OECD, Paris, 1978. See preface, page 10 and elsewhere.

(38)   Bernard Mamontoff 'La Securite Routiere au Japon', Transport, Environnement, Circulation No. 38, January/February 1980.

(39)   K. Russam, Motorcycle training and licensing in Japan, TRRL Laboratory Report 916, page 2.

(40)   Communication from the Service National des Examens du Permis de Conduire.

(41)   Report of the Advisory Committee on Motorcycle Rider Training, op.cit., para. 55.

(42)   Anti-lock braking for motorcycles, TRRL Leaflet LF 591 (Issue 3), April 1979, supplemented by information from Vehicle Standards and Engineering Division, Department of Transport.

(43)   The motorcycle chest pad, TRRL Leaflet LF 863, April 1979, supplemented by information from Vehicle Standards and Engineering Division, Department of Transport.

(44)   Subsidised Public Transport and the Demand for Travel, the South Yorkshire Example, Summary, Transport Studies Group, Oxford University, February 1983.

(45)   Report of the Advisory Committee on Motorcycle Rider Training, op.cit., para. 60.

(46)   Note of a meeting held at 11.30 hours on Friday, 29 February 1980, at the House of Commons to discuss motorcycle safety, copy supplied by the Department of Transport. This meeting was attended by representatives of the local authority associations. At the meeting which immediately preceded it, held on 25 February 1980, Dr Bull on behalf of the BMA and Mr Dave Taylor had suggested that either the minimum age for car drivers should be lowered to 16 or the minimum age for motorcyclists should be raised to 18 'in the hope that this would persuade more young people to drive rather than ride - the only sure way of reducing motorcycle accidents'. None of the minutes from this series of meetings mentions opposition to the idea of raising the minimum age for motorcyclists to 18.

(47)   Ligier (of Vichy, France), Dossier de Presse.

(48)   Road Accidents Great Britain 1980, Table 24.

(49)   The story of STEP and Star Rider, STEP Management Services Ltd., 1981.

(50)   As ref. 46.

Table II.1   Two-wheeled motor vehicles: casualties and travel 1960-1982

Year	Fatal	Casualties Serious	Slight	All severities	Index 1960=100	Travel Billion kms	Index 1960=100
1960	1,743	27,330	70,169	99,242	100	9.98	100
1962	1,323	24,256	61,034	86,613	87	8.66	87
1964	1,445	25,920	63,918	91,283	92	7.55	76
1966	1,134	21,582	50,527	73,243	74	5.97	60
1968	877	17,114	40,188	58,179	59	4.70	47
1970	761	15,378	33,508	49,647	50	3.88	39
1972	729	13,380	29,525	43,634	44	3.75	38
1974	796	13,905	32,133	46,834	47	4.21	42
1976	990	18,861	47,775	67,626	68	6.12	61
1978	1,163	20,339	48,231	69,733	70	6.66	67
1980	1,163	21,534	48,141	70,838	71	7.54	76
1981	1,131	21,198	46,800	69,129	69	7.47	75
1982	1,090	21,597	49,233	71,920	72	7.97	80

Note: Casualty figures refer to riders and passengers of mopeds, motor scooters and motorcycles, including combinations.

Source: Annual of Road Accidents Great Britain, Transport Statistics Great Britain, and Highway Statistics.

Table II.2 Casualties in 1981 in accidents involving two-wheeled motor vehicles, analysed by severity and by class of road user

| Class of road user | Severity of casualty | | | | | | All casualties | |
| | Fatal | | Serious | | Slight | | | |
	No.	%	No.	%	No.	%	No.	%
Rider of 2-wheeled motor vehicle	983	70	18,833	78	41,729	75	61,545	75
Passenger on 2-wheeled motor vehicle	148	10	2,365	10	5,071	9	7,584	9
Pedestrian	221	16	2,103	9	4,625	8	6,949	9
Cyclist	21	1	363	1	1,219	2	1,603	2
All others	40	3	616	3	3,317	6	3,973	5
All road users	1,413	100	24,280	100	55,961	100	81,654	100

Note: Over 98% of the pedestrians who became casualties were hit by a two-wheeled motor vehicle.

Source: Department of Transport, special tabulations of the 1981 road accident statistics.

Table II.3   Casualty rates for pedestrians hit by road vehicles in 1981

Units: Pedestrian casualties per hundred million vehicle kilometres

| | Severity of casualty | | |
Vehicle hitting pedestrian	Fatal	Fatal or serious	All casualties
Bicycle	0.15	4.56	15.73
Car	0.57	5.46	20.10
2-wheeled motor vehicle	2.91	27.70	91.62

Sources: Road Accidents Great Britain, 1981, Table 18. Transport Statistics Great Britain, 1971-1981, Table 2.2.

Table II.4   Casualty rates and accident involvement rates per hundred million vehicle kilometres travelled for riders of two-wheeled motor vehicles, 1979

| Age of rider (both sexes) | Fatal casualties and accidents | | All casualties and accidents | |
	Casualty rate	Accident involvement rate	Casualty rate	Accident involvement rate
16-17	15	22	1,200	1,410
18-19	39	59	2,000	2,350
20-29	14	21	700	860
30-39	9	12	610	720
40-49	4	6	330	390
50-59	6	6	320	370
60 and over	12	12	450	530
All ages	15	21	860	1,020
Males	16	23	870	1,040
Females	5	6	770	850

Sources: Road Accidents Great Britain 1980, Table E and Road Accidents Great Britain 1981, Table J. The information on distance travelled on which these tables were based came from the 1978/79 National Travel Survey.

Table II.5   Accident involvement rates for car drivers, per hundred million vehicle kilometres travelled, 1979

Age of driver	Fatal accidents		All accidents	
	Males	Females	Males	Females
17-18	10.7	3.8	400	320
19	8.7	3.5	340	220
20-24	5.1	2.6	210	190
25-29	3.1	2.1	140	160
30-39	2.0	1.6	100	130
40-49	1.8	1.4	90	110
50-59	1.7	2.0	80	120
60 and over	3.2	3.6	120	140
All ages	2.7	2.0	120	140

Source: Road Accidents Great Britain 1981, Table K. The information on distance travelled on which this table is based comes from the 1978/79 National Travel Survey.

Table II.6   Casualties to riders and passengers of mopeds and motorcycles in 1982 per hundred million vehicle kilometres

Severity of casualty	Mopeds	Motorcycles
Fatal	4.2	16
Serious	176	298
Slight	510	649

Notes: The differences between the rates of the two types of machine are slightly exaggerated by the methods of estimation used.

Sources: Road Accidents Great Britain 1982, Table G.

Table II.7   Motorcycles involved in fatal and serious accidents per million miles travelled, analysed by age of rider and size of machine

Engine capacity in cc	Rider's age in years					
	16-20	20-24	25-29	30-39	40-49	50 and over
Up to 60	1.8	1.1	1.7	1.2	0.9	1.8
61-150	4.7	3.1	2.6	1.8	1.8	2.8
151-250	6.2	4.4	2.8	2.8	2.7	3.2
251-350	8.5	5.1	3.3	3.3	2.9	3.9
Over 350	10.9	8.3	5.6	6.6	7.9	7.7

Note: These figures show the rates after adjustments had been made to eliminate the effect of inexperience.

Source: J. M. Munden, 'The Variation of Motorcycle Accident Rates with Age of Rider and Size and Age of Machine', International Road Safety and Traffic Review, Vol. X11, No. 1, Winter 1964, Figure 2. The analysis is based on fieldwork conducted in England and Wales in 1958.

Table II.8   Journeys made as rider of a two-wheeled motor vehicle analysed by length of journey and size of machine

Units: cumulative percentages

Length of journey	Engine size			
	Not over 50 cc (Moped)	51 to 250 cc	Over 250 cc	All 2-wheele motor vehicle
Under 2 miles	23	26	14	24
Under 3 miles	45	43	28	41
Under 5 miles	72	64	51	64
Under 10 miles	94	88	77	88
Under 15 miles	98	95	90	95
Under 25 miles	99	98	98	98
All journeys	100	100	100	100

Source: 1978/79 National Travel Survey

Table II.9   Journeys made as rider of a two-wheeled motor vehicle analysed by purpose of journey and size of machine

Units: percentages

| Length of journey | Engine size | | | |
	Not over 50 cc (Moped)	51 to 250 cc	Over 250 cc	All 2-wheeled motor vehicles
To or from work or education	61	49	41	51
In course of work	4	5	5	5
Shopping and personal business	15	20	22	19
Social and recreational	17	20	24	20
Escort	-	*	6	1
Holidays and day trips		2	5	2
Other	1	*	-	*
All journeys	100	100	100	100

* less than 0.5 per cent
Source: 1978/79 National Travel Survey

Table II.10   EEC noise limits for new vehicles

	Noise limit on standard test in dB(A)
Cars	80
Motorcycles	
not over 80 cc	78
81-125	80
126-350	83
351-500	85
501 or over	86

Source: P. M. Nelson, Some notes on the disturbance caused by motorcycles, TRRL Supplementary Report 569, 1980.

III LOWERING VEHICLE SPEEDS

A large amount of evidence from all over the world is available to support the view that if vehicle speeds were lower than at present, both the number and severity of road accidents would be reduced. Conversely, if speeds were allowed to rise above their present level, and no effective counter-measures were taken, accidents would increase in number and severity. Nevertheless, speed reduction has attracted comparatively little attention from the Department of Transport and some of the other main organisations concerned with road safety; on the contrary, much emphasis has been put on the need to raise various 30 mph speed limits which are regarded as unrealistic. One important reason for the official attitude has been the difficulty of enforcing speed limits, but developments in technology can be exploited to reduce this problem. For these reasons, speed seems a particularly useful case study. In addition, it raises important questions of public attitudes and of the connections between road safety, fuel conservation and environmental protection.

Evidence of the influence of speed on accidents
There are strong grounds for concluding that accidents are less likely to occur when vehicles are travelling at lower than at higher speeds. Lower speeds allow more time and space to take evasive action following commonplace errors of judgement, whether by pedestrians - children acting impulsively or old people being forgetful - or by drivers.

Studies have shown that the error in estimating time and distance required for overtaking increases with speed and that two thirds of drivers make serious misjudgements; and, in general, safe stopping distances increase with gross vehicle weight[1,2]. At higher speeds, too, mechanical failure or burst tyres are more frequent and less easy to cope with[3].

82

The Highway Code shows that, in comparison with cars being driven at 30 mph, the shortest stopping distance for vehicles being driven at 70 mph is about four times greater. Even at 30 mph , a car will cover a sixth of a mile during the 20 seconds or so that it can take an old person to cross a road: this can often be a curving road which does not allow adequate sight lines along its length.

Likewise, a basic law of physics points to the fact that accidents are likely to be less serious at lower speeds, given that energy has to be dissipated on impact and that this energy is proportional to the square of the speed of the vehicle.

Numerous studies over the years, both in this country and abroad, have found near overwhelming evidence of the link between speed and accidents. Even in 1970, a review of the evidence up to that date concluded that 'attempts to formulate alternative explanations' (of the association of speed with accidents), 'different in each case, are too dependent on coincidence to be acceptable(4).' Much more evidence has accumulated since then, largely arising from the lower speed limits introduced in many countries in response to the energy crisis. Some examples of the effect on road accidents of imposed or lowered limits taken from before-and-after surveys are shown in Table III.I. For the sake of simplicity, we have limited the information in the table to changes in the level of accidents without describing the methods used in determining the changes; and we have omitted various other findings where there is a possibility that they overlap with some of those shown in the table. It can be seen that substantial reductions in accidents have been consistently recorded both in rural and urban areas in all countries where such limits have been introduced.

There is plentiful other evidence of the relationship between speed and the severity of an accident. Table III.2 shows that the ratio of fatalities to all injuries in road accidents in rural areas, subject to higher speed limits, is generally much higher than the equivalent in urban areas, subject to lower limits.

As can be seen, the risks in rural areas are particularly high for pedestrians and cyclists. Indeed, one study has shown that if a pedestrian is struck by a vehicle travelling at 34 mph, there is a 1 in 2 chance of death, whereas when the vehicle is travelling at over 40 mph, the chance is increased to 9 in 10(5); another one showed that in injury accidents, adult and especially child pedestrians were far more likely to be killed when vehicle speeds at impact were estimated to have exceeded 25 mph than at lower speeds(6).

It will be seen in Chapter VIII that even when it would appear to be quite unreasonable to expect pedestrians, especially children or the old, to be alert and careful, the need for their behaviour to improve has been stressed, rather than for the speeds of the vehicles that threaten them to be reduced. Training and conspicuity have been stressed more than speed reduction as accident avoidance measures; and methods of limiting the severity of an accident when it occurs, by the better protection of vehicle occupants, have also been emphasised more strongly than the need for lower speeds, although secondary measures do nothing for the other road users involved. They may indeed increase the dangers, especially to pedestrians and cyclists, if drivers feel emboldened to take more risks.

The official attitude to speed control

The emphasis placed by the Department of Transport and others concerned with road safety on the control of speed has been much less than might have been expected in the light of this evidence. A report of the Department's Road Safety Division issued in 1974 made no reference to lowering speeds in the seven basic options set out in its accident reduction strategy(7). There are many circumstances in which lower speeds would seem to be the obvious method of reducing risk where the Department has put the emphasis on action which is likely to be much less fruitful.

If, nevertheless, there have been important innovations, such as speed humps, which are discussed below, it is also true that the Department of Transport has attached great weight to raising the 30 mph limit in situations where it is regarded as unrealistically low; one of the criteria for determining that a limit is unrealistically low is the extent to which it is disregarded by 15 per cent of drivers(8). Britain, in common with many other countries, imposed emergency speed limits in response to the 1973 energy crisis. But the British controls were relaxed, whereas several other countries maintained the limits partly because of their contribution to accident reduction. Among these countries were the United States where the national limit is 55 mph and New Zealand where it is 50 mph.

A similar attitude is shown by many other organisations concerned with transport planning. Both the AA and the RAC, in evidence to the House of Commons Transport Committee in 1983, suggested raising the motorway limit on the grounds that the present limit 'serves no real purpose'(9). Although speed limits and enforcement were specifically listed by the Committee among the topics on which it wished comment to be focussed, the majority of the 50 or so bodies which submitted memoranda did not mention this subject(10). In its recent evidence to this Committee, the Association of Chief Police Officers called for a revision of speed limits which were described as being 'in a mess' and urged it to consider raising the limit on motorways to 80 mph on grounds of realism(11).

Apart from problems of possible public hostility to lower or more strictly enforced speed limits, which are discussed below, there are three main sources of evidence on which the Department of Transport appears to have relied to justify the relatively low emphasis it places on keeping speeds down.

The first is a comprehensive study by the TRRL to try to reveal the causes of all the accidents that took place in a large area of south-east Berkshire between 1970 and 1974(12). This study covered 2,130 accidents. Trained investigators visited the site of each accident and also visited and questioned people who had been involved in it. Hence judgements were made as to its cause or causes. This on-the-spot study is open to question on several counts. It was not a representative sample and, more importantly, did not address the question of what factors contributed to the severity of accidents. Since speed affects the severity of accidents as well as their number, and to change a fatal or serious accident into a slight one would be more advantageous than reducing the number of slight accidents, this is a serious limitation.

There is also an important difference between a study of this kind, where causes were assigned by subjective judgement and majority opinions of the investigators - which sometimes did not coincide - and studies such as those cited in Table III.1 which are based on a before-and-after survey or on some similar comparison of traffic situations with different speeds. When speed is clearly and substantially excessive, which may of course include many occasions when it is lower than the legal limit, it is indeed likely that trained investigators will identify it as a cause. But very often the effect of speed is to amplify, perhaps only slightly, other dangers inherent in the traffic situation; it seems less likely that this effect would be identified, although over a long period slight increases in risk will lead to the occurrence of more accidents. Nor would it be easy to take account of the fact that, if lower speeds had obtained, the whole traffic pattern might have differed in ways which would have led to fewer hazardous situations arising. For example, one effect of substantially lower speeds might be that fewer or shorter journeys were made. But even if the pattern of journeys were unaltered, in terms of origins and destinations, timing and type of vehicle used, one would expect headways to differ systematically as a result of a general reduction in speeds. The actual distance between vehicles decreases, but so does the distance which ought to be kept in the interests of safety. There is evidence that at lower traffic speeds the ratios of actual to desirable headways increase(13).

The TRRL investigation concluded that 2,211 drivers were primarily or partially at fault for the accident in which they were involved. The list of driver faults, which are not mutually exclusive, includes the following:

Errors of Perception
Looked, failed to see	367
Distraction	337
Lack of attention/alertness	152
Interpretation	125
Misjudged speed/distance	109

Errors of Skill
Inexperience	215
Lack of judgement	116
Wrong action/decision	50

Errors in Manner of Execution
Lack of Care	905
Too fast	450
Failed to look	183
Wrong path	175
Improper overtaking	146
Too close	75
Difficult manoeuvre	70
Irresponsible/reckless	61

Impairment
Alcohol present	463
Fatigue	159
Drugs present	87

Thus, although only 450 drivers were judged to be going too fast (although this is itself 20 per cent of the drivers who were found to be at fault), these findings do not rule out, but indeed lend credence to the hypothesis that if traffic speeds had been lower then:

a)   some of the conflict situations would not have arisen;
b)   in some of those that would still have arisen, it would have been possible for the drivers to take evasive action in order to avoid the accident;
c)   some of the accidents would have been less serious.

Similar points could be made about the accidents where no driver was considered to be at fault, but either a pedestrian was held to be responsible or the accident was attributed to environmental factors. These judgements may be quite correct; nevertheless, if lower traffic speeds had obtained some of the accidents might have been avoided and others have been less severe.

The second source referred to in support of the contention that only minor emphasis can be attached to speed as a contributory factor is evidence of the apparent effect of raising 'unrealistic' speed limits.

This evidence is not wholly convincing. Table III.3 shows that where limits have been raised, the effects have varied, in some instances apparently producing a rise and in others a fall in accidents. One simple reason for this may be that where new speed limits have little or no effect on vehicle speeds, they have no effect on accidents, whereas those that do have a marked effect in reducing the higher speeds lead to the substantial accident reductions shown in Table III.1. Another reason for the disparity in a few of the instances may be explained by statistical invalidity owing to less than rigorous control being maintained for weather, traffic levels and composition, or extent of police presence before and after the limits were imposed. It is also difficult to compare the significance of the changes in some instances as there is no record of changes in the severity of accidents, which could be crucial.

Nevertheless, it may well be that to raise speed limits which are disregarded could sometimes lead to an improvement in the accident situation. It is known that accidents are related to the variability in speeds, which leads to dangerous manoeuvres such as overtaking, as well as to the average speed of the traffic. If raising the 30 mph limit led to some increase in the speed of the drivers who had previously complied with it so that there was less difference between their speeds and those of the drivers who had not, and therefore a reduced need or opportunity for the faster drivers to overtake, the situation might well become safer. But the conclusion that raising the speed limit is the right course of action in such circumstances follows only on the assumption that other possible remedies would have been inapplicable or less effective: in particular, that it would not have been feasible, or only at undue expense, to have enforced the original 30 mph limit.

The third source is a study made at the TRRL of the potential of various measures for reducing road accidents, which concluded that by the more appropriate use of speed limits it would be possible to save five per cent of the accidents that occur in Britain(14). However, it is clear from the more detailed description of the study given in an earlier paper(15) that the conclusion should have been that by the more appropriate use of speed limits on rural roads (on which only about one quarter of all accidents occur), it would be possible to save five per cent of the accidents that occur in Britain; it is also clear that this percentage saving would be higher for serious accidents and even higher for fatal ones. The estimate also assumes that there would be a substantial degree of non-compliance with any new speed limit. Another estimate in the same study, based on a different set of data, was that a higher degree of enforcement and police presence could lead to a further five per cent saving in accidents. This estimate, however, relates only to what might be achieved by a better deployment of the present police staff, perhaps slightly increased, using their present methods(16). It is not a guide to what might be achieved by devoting substantially more resources to enforcement or by the application of new techniques.

Public opinion

An argument used in defence of raising speed limits which are ignored by a significant number of motorists and against any reduction in limits is that there is little point in setting limits at a level 'which do not command general support(17)'. It would be difficult to disagree with this sentiment, but what is the evidence about public attitudes to speed limits and their enforcement, and if there is hostility to the idea of lower limits and stricter enforcement, on what is it based?

There is little doubt that in their capacity as residents, pedestrians and cyclists, people would welcome lower speeds. Efforts to raise 'unrealistic' speed limits often encounter fierce local opposition. A survey of people's attitudes to a range of environmental issues recorded 37 per cent of respondents considering that people drive too fast down their road(18); and surveys inquiring into pensioners' concerns when getting about on foot and crossing roads and into the grounds cited by mothers for accompanying their children to and from school recorded traffic volume and speed as very influential(19). A TRRL survey of the public response to the installation of road humps found that two thirds of the residents along the roads near those with the humps thought that traffic was travelling too fast on their roads, and even of the residents of the roads with the humps, one in five still considered that traffic was travelling too fast, and that the risk of accident whilst crossing it was high or very high(20).

But it is drivers whose compliance is required, and there is survey evidence to suggest that a stronger policy on speed limits would be opposed by a significant number of motorists. A national survey conducted in 1976 among 950 motorists found that 12 per cent were not in favour of a speed limit at all while many more thought that particular speed limits should be raised. For example, 17 per cent suggested in reply to an open-ended question that some 30 mph limits could be raised to 40 mph and doubtless more would have agreed with that proposition if it had been explicitly put to them. Most motorists displayed a tolerant attitude to driving 10 mph faster than the limit set for any given road and in particular to driving at 40 mph in a 30 mph area. Nevertheless, this survey and others show that the great majority of motorists approve of speed limits in principle and recognise that there would be chaos without them(21). A recent very large national survey of motorists found that 54 per cent agreed and 40 per cent disagreed with the statement that 'speed limits should be enforced more strongly'(22). Moreover, insofar as there is opposition to speed limits or their enforcement, the survey evidence suggests (although more work is required on this point) that ignorance of the causal connections between speed and accidents may account for it. Thus, the 1976 survey showed that 10 per cent of motorists thought that if all speed limits were obeyed at all times there would be no reduction in the number of accidents(23). Similarly, one of the conclusions of an earlier, smaller study of male motorists' attitudes to speed restrictions and their enforcement was that 'male motorists are not generally convinced of a significant relationship between breaking a speed limit and accident causality'(24). Although in our opinion this wording is rather stronger than the survey findings warrant, nevertheless it would not be surprising if many motorists were unaware of the relationship between speed and accidents, which would in turn make them sceptical about the value of speed limits.

Useful evidence on motorists' attitudes also comes from the surveys that have accompanied various measures of speed control. The celebrated experiment with linked traffic lights in Slough in the mid-1950s, which is described further below, was approved by most motorists in spite of the increase in delays(25). The more recent experiments with speed humps also found favour with the majority of the motorists affected. In Cuddesdon Way, Cowley, the humps imposed a minute's delay on motorists driving the whole length of the road; nevertheless 84 per cent of motorists thought that they served a useful purpose and 73 per cent that they should be retained. The views of motorists who did not live on the estate, and who therefore did not stand to gain in their capacity as residents, did not differ significantly from those of the rest.

This evidence suggests that motorists will approve and respect particular methods of enforcing low speeds if they think that there is a good reason for them, provided also that the measures alter the drivers' environment in such a way as to encourage compliance. We return to these points below.

The pressure on drivers to drive too fast
Even drivers who approve of speed limits and would wish to see them more strictly enforced feel the temptation to speed on

occasion. There are many outside pressures which tend to reinforce a complacent attitude towards fast driving even when it
involves law breaking.

Background propaganda
It is commonplace for the facility to drive at or above the legal
limit to be presented by manufacturers in their advertising and by
the motoring correspondents of national newspapers as a highly
desirable characteristic of a car. Here are some of many
examples:

> 'The (SAAB owners) enjoy the sports car sensation of corner-
> ing at high speeds, with the car sticking to the road like tar,
> and the body feeling like it's moulded around them'(26).
> 'This (the particular car) can reach 70 mph at just under half
> the engine's maximum revolution'(27).
> 'Toyota brings in power car for the young ...' introduces its
> 122 mph Corolla ... 'part of campaign to make the products
> of Japan's largest car manufacturer more attractive to the
> increasing number of young drivers demanding performance
> versions of popular family cars'(28).

Almost invariably, cars capable of being driven at particularly high
speeds, well in excess of the legal limit, are extolled:

> '... the 112 mph Turbo (Metro) could be another winner'(29);
> '... the 136 mph Rover Vitesse taking pride of place ...'(30);
> '... a cause for celebration ...' referring to a model of the
> Rolls Royce that can reach 145 mph'(31);
> 'New 164 mph Jaguar ...' road version of the Jaguar with the
> 'Successful track record. .. enabling it to accelerate from 0
> to 60 mph in 5.8 secs'(32), and 'Gilding the 155 mph Lily - ...
> something extra for the driver not satisfied with a maximum
> of say 155 mph'(33);
> '... the 928S (Porsche) has all the performance you could wish
> for - top speed of 160 mph ...'(34).

The language used in commenting on the speeds at which it is
possible to drive in different circumstances reflects a similar view
of the relevance of the maximum speed limit to 'real' driving:

> 'trundling along at 70 ...'(35)
> '... sweeping up to 110 mph ...'(36)
> '... stricter enforcement of harsher (sic) speed limits ...' (in
> Japan) for which regret is expressed(37).

When such language is used in advertisements, it might be expected to earn the disapproval of the Advertising Standards Authority. But in the view of the ASA, it does not contravene its existing code of practice and the impetus for a stricter code would need to come from either the government or the Society of Motor Manufacturers and Traders(38). To our knowledge neither of these two parties has expressed a desire for such a code to be drawn up. Moreover, in further justifying their inactivity on this, the ASA has pointed out that the government itself requires publication of fuel consumption figures for vehicles travelling at a speed, 75 mph, which exceeds the limit for any public highway in Britain. This requirement does indeed seem to constitute an official invitation to motorists not to take the national limit too seriously.

Vehicle design and performance

Associated with the highlighting of speed in the description of most new vehicles is the wide availability of fast vehicles. In 1966, about half of the private cars registered for the first time had engine sizes above 1200cc whereas by the early 1980s, this proportion was three quarters(39). Motor manufacturers have responded to, and perhaps stimulated, car owners' preferences for this type of car. They have designed engines capable of accelerating to a high speed in an ever shorter period of time, and of being driven at ever rising speeds well in excess of the maximum legal limit permitted in Britain.

As a result, the performance of standard family cars available today is comparable with that of the most expensive ones available ten or fifteen years ago. The number of seconds it takes to reach 60 mph among the same models of top selling cars has been reduced by about half a second per annum, and the mean maximum speed has been increased by between one and two miles per hour per annum in recent years(40). The average maximum speed of the 16 cars used by 'a panel of everyday motorists' is now more than 50 per cent in excess of the legal limit(41).

Tax concessions on company cars, which are discussed in Chapter VI, must affect the choice of model as well as the number of cars owned. The probable effect is to encourage manufacturers to pay more attention to performance than to the more homely virtues of economy and durability. In addition, it is easy to see how a trend towards high performance cars could be self-reinforcing. Motorists who may not be particularly concerned about speed and acceleration in their own right may not wish to drive cars substantially inferior in these respects to the general run of cars on the road, since they would then be placed at a competitive disadvantage in many traffic situations and would find themselves constantly being overtaken by other motorists or otherwise under pressure from them. If low-performance cars are also relatively light, which they commonly are, their occupants may also feel vulnerable in case of an accident with another vehicle. There would be good reasons for such fears, since when vehicles of different mass collide, the lighter vehicle and its occupants are indeed much more likely to sustain serious damage and injury. For example, in head-on collisions where two vehicles are involved, the proportion of fatalities is seven times higher among occupants of vehicles whose weight is only half that of the other vehicle(42), and life expectancy has been calculated to be reduced on average by 3 months simply by switching from a car weighing 1800 kg to one weighing 900 kg(43).

Roads and other drivers
The design of roads is often such as to encourage rather than to control excessive speeds. On motorways for example, even people driving vehicles of relatively low performance may find that they constantly have to check themselves in order to keep within the limit. On country lanes there can be an incompatibility between a road's surface and its geometry: the surface encourages drivers to travel at speeds which the narrowness of the road and restricted lines of sight make unsafe. On minor roads in towns and villages, where speeds should not be much above walking pace, again the geometry and surface often encourage much higher speeds.

It is a common experience that drivers who wish to drive slowly in some particular situation, and even those who merely want to comply with the limit, find themselves under pressure from other drivers. In the 1976 national survey of motorists referred to above, 28 per cent mentioned as one reason for their own speeding that 'I have to keep up with other traffic on the road' and 46 per cent mentioned this as a reason for speeding by others(44).

The law and its enforcement
Surveys have established that most drivers do not know the speed limit for the road on which they are travelling(45), that their subjective estimates of the speeds at which they are travelling are not always adequate for safe driving(46), and that they are at the limit of their visual capabilities in a number of key driving situations(47). They do not allow sufficient gap between themselves and the vehicle in front of them: in fact, of all accidents involving at least two vehicles, well over a quarter occur when they are all travelling in the same direction(48).

Drivers' judgement of their own competence is excessive, too: one study recorded that, of those convicted of causing death or dangerous driving, or of driving while under the influence of drink, 40 per cent thought that they were better drivers than most, and almost all of the remainder that they were as good as most(49).

Many found speeding are unaware of their offence and, in any case, do not consider it particularly serious or likely to cause an accident(50). Only 18 per cent of respondents to a TRRL survey claimed that they personally always obeyed speed limits(51), and two-thirds of young male drivers in a MORI poll claimed that they regularly drive at over 70 mph; a fifth of them that they do so regularly on motorways; and a quarter that they have driven at over 100 mph(52).

Thus, a further factor influencing the level of compliance with a speed limit relates to drivers' attitudes, and particularly their perceptions of the consequences of exceeding it. This has a number of facets stemming from judgements about the likelihood of being caught breaking the law and of then being prosecuted, and from concern about the actual penalty. A TRRL study found that the main motivating force leading drivers to moderate their speed is the fear of being apprehended. It was concluded that 'only by making them feel more at risk in this respect is there a likelihood of changing their behaviour'(53).

Although it appears that many drivers overrate the risk of being caught(54), statistics show that the risk is low, that it is known to be low, and that if a driver is caught the typical penalty is unlikely to induce greater respect for this law for more than a short time.

How low the risk is at present is illustrated by the fact that, although well over 300,000 drivers, the great majority of whom are motorists, are found guilty of speeding offences in England and Wales each year - of all motoring offences that come before the courts, that of speeding is by far the most common - and some 170,000 for careless driving, these figures represent respectively only about one conviction for every 70,000 and 120,000 journeys made. Calculated on a distance base, the figure for speeding offences is equivalent to one prosecution for every 700,000 kms travelled, that is an average of about once in a lifetime of motoring(55). However, surveys concerned with establishing the extent of compliance with mandatory speed limits consistently reveal that a substantial proportion of drivers are breaking the law at any one time. For instance, the 1983 National Speed Survey found 12 per cent of cars and two-wheeled motor vehicles exceeding the limit on dual carriageways and 40 per cent exceeding the limit on motorways, including 14 per cent exceeding 80 mph. The survey also found that the mean speed of lorries on dual carriageways (which at the time were subject to a limit of 40 mph) and on motorways was 48 mph and 58 mph respectively, and that 89 per cent and 39 per cent respectively were exceeding the limit(56). In all instances these proportions exceeded the equivalents recorded in earlier comparable National Surveys. A recent survey of vehicular speeds in residential areas recorded that the legal limit was exceeded by 50 per cent of the vehicles on 50 per cent of the roads and by 15 per cent of the vehicles on 85 per cent of the roads.

Police argue that limits cannot be enforced because of the sheer number of drivers breaking the law. Indeed, one reason for the exceedingly low rate of conviction for what is known to be an extremely common occurrence is the fact that the police fear that unwelcome enforcement would lose them public support. They are generally unprepared to institute proceedings against motorists unless the speed limit is being exceeded by a margin of at least 10 mph. The police also support the rule that particular speed limits should be raised if they are broken by more than 15 per cent of drivers.

In addition to the laxity with which the law on speeding is enforced, there is further evidence of what could be construed as a tolerant interpretation of the law on convictions for this type of offence. Guidelines laid down by the Magistrates Association include recommendations for speeding offences that, where a fine is applicable, the charge should be £1.50 per mile an hour in excess of the limit(57). On this scale the maximum fines of £500 on motorways and £100 on ordinary roads apply when vehicles exceed 90 mph in an area subject to a 30 mph limit and 300 mph on a motorway. And the government's concessionary attitude can be seen in the penalty points system covering this type of offence: given no other traffic offences incurring loss of points, the offending driver is automatically disqualified from driving only if he is successfully prosecuted for speeding four times over a period of three years. In view of the very low risk of being caught speeding once, it will be very surprising if many drivers are disqualified for speeding even under this new system. It is significant, too, that the disqualification will last only six months if the driver has not been disqualified in the previous three years.

In recent years, of those found guilty of a speeding offence nearly all have had their licences endorsed and have paid a small fine - in 1981 this averaged £30. Only one per cent were disqualified from driving, with the average period of disqualification being less than six months(58).

Further evidence of the concessionary attitudes of those who set or apply the law with regard to speed limits can be seen in the criteria laid down for determining an appropriate new limit: one of these, the 85 percentile rule, relates to the extent to which the existing limit is observed. The other is the injury accident rate along the route in question; the use of this rule implies that accidents have to happen before corrective action is taken. For instance, in urban areas, the value chosen is two injury accidents per million vehicle miles(59). Such a criterion would be inadmissible in determining the acceptable level of safety on the railways.

There will always be a need for punishments for drivers who break the law on speed and the present system of sanctions is clearly unsatisfactory. But the key to the problem of ensuring reasonable speeds does not lie here. It lies in action which will reduce the existing pressures on people to drive too fast and will augment instead those features in a driver's situation which reinforce the responsible attitudes which almost everyone has. The next section considers the record and potential of existing methods of enforcement.

Present methods of enforcement and their efficacy
Visual signs
The simplest device is the advisory or exhortatory sign, either reminding drivers of the limit, or recommending a safe speed along a dangerous stretch of road. Such signs are cheap: for instance, the cost of erecting 'Watch your speed' notices on 60 roads in one area was about half the cost of one injury accident for urban roads(60).

However, recent studies have revealed that signs are not very effective. A TRRL study of the effects on speeds of the most commonly used advisory sign for motorways of 50 mph found that one in ten drivers complied with the advice; when the signals were modified so as to remedy this, there was only a small improvement(61). Sussex police found that their experimental use on selected roads in the county led to a reduction in mean speed of from 4 to 11 per cent; at the same time observance was raised by higher levels of police activity without which it was judged the limits would have been less well observed(62).

Police activity
Nearly 20 years ago research showed that police patrols aided by kerbside radar speedometers were very effective in encouraging conformity with the 30 mph speed limits; a reduction of 25 per cent in the number of road accidents was recorded(63). Other demonstration projects have shown that decreases in speed of 7-10 per cent could be achieved simply by the presence of a police patrol car(64).

In spite of these successes in influencing the behaviour of drivers, surveys made in many countries show that there is a significant fall-off in effect with distance from the check points. One study showed the effect to be reduced by half for every 900 metres beyond the police car(65), and another that the effect had evaporated 5 kms beyond it(66). A Swedish report recorded that when police speed detection devices were widely publicised as having been taken out of service, there was a marked increase in speeds(67). Several studies have confirmed that, within a few days of the departure of police cars, drivers revert to their former speeds(68).

A further difficulty with this method of encouraging compliance with speed limits is that under the Construction and Use Regulations, speedometers are allowed a 10 per cent error. In addition, the electronic equipment required to prosecute offending drivers is so inaccurate that the police have to allow a margin of tolerance before taking action. The more sophisticated electronic devices for identifying vehicles which break the speed limit or cross the red phase of traffic signals are now being used in West Germany and in the United States. They have been shown to be highly cost-effective and can be linked to police stations providing photographs of the vehicle, its registration plate and, if required, the driver. Their cost is one-fifteenth that of a one-man police patrol car and they can handle 900 violations an hour as against five for the one-man car(69). But as far as we are aware, there are no plans for their introduction in Britain, perhaps because that would be interpreted as a further symbol of the advent of 'Big Brother', or because of a fear that it would lead to clogging up Magistrates Courts.

The road environment
The marking of roads with horizontal lines, on slip roads leading off motorways, and on approaches to roundabouts, is a cheap and effective method to slow drivers down by creating an optical illusion through the exponential decrease in the spacing of the lines(70). A variation of this device is the 'rumble strip' which alerts drivers instead by creating an unusual noise inside the vehicle. Clearly, rumble strips can be used only sparingly, otherwise drivers would become accustomed to them and would no longer slow down.

One well proven device aimed at encouraging better observance of limits has been the use of linked fixed time traffic signals. They were first used in a traffic management exercise in the mid-1950s. It was very effective, for drivers soon learned that there was little point in exceeding the limit set, since to do so only led to their being faced with red signals at the next traffic lights, whereas by conforming with the limit they could maintain an even and acceptably fast speed without having to stop at the lights. Their installation in Slough, and subsequently in West London, was followed by a substantial reduction in the serious casualty rate(71). But their use is limited to stretches of road where a series of signals can be linked in this way, and the timing of the phases cannot then respond to traffic volumes on adjacent roads.

Speeds can also be controlled by the use of speed humps. Since the early 1970s research has been conducted by the TRRL to determine a safe profile for speed humps; to establish the extent to which vehicle speed and thereby road accidents can be reduced; and to ascertain the attitudes of drivers and residents along the routes on which the humps are installed.

It has been shown that humps are very effective: typically, mean speeds have been nearly halved and the 15 percentage of drivers previously exceeding the limit has been cut by a third; the roads have become safer; adjacent roads carrying diverted traffic have been found to be no less safe; and the humps have been judged to be acceptable to residents and drivers alike(72). As a result, the Highways (Road Hump) Regulations were introduced in 1983 enabling local authorities to instal humps on a permanent basis on roads other than special trunk or principal roads. Their costs are low: solid moulded rubber humps which can be laid in minutes by unskilled operatives only cost £60 a metre(73). But to use them to control speeds on all the roads in an area, such as a housing estate, would be more expensive than that figure suggests, since it would be necessary to construct them at intervals of 100 metres or perhaps less, and illuminated advisory signs, which are relatively expensive, would have to be installed at each entry point.

Existing roads can be altered much more radically, by changes in their widths, alignments and surfaces, in order to induce low speeds, especially on residential roads. There has been little experiment along these lines in Britain, but successful continental experience is described in Chapter VIII. In new developments, the opportunities to design from the outset in a way which will limit vehicle speeds, and flows as well, are much greater; this subject too is discussed in Chapter VIII.

There is clearly considerable scope both to develop existing methods of enforcement and to apply them more widely. In particular, the potential to use road engineering to enforce very low speeds in roads whose traffic function is confined to access, but which have very important non-traffic functions as well, has yet to be properly exploited. Nevertheless, attempts to limit drivers' speeds by changing their environment are unlikely to succeed unless they take into account the most important feature of that environment: the vehicle itself.

Enforcement through vehicles

At the most basic level of ensuring conformity with the law relating to the maximum legal speed at which vehicles can be driven, it seems to us that there is strong justification for requiring manufacturers to fit tamper-proof controls to prevent vehicles being driven at speeds over 70 mph, or perhaps 75 mph to allow some small tolerance. Indeed, we view the absence of legislation on this as little short of incitement to drivers to break the law, particularly as it would be both cheap and technically easy to cut engine power at maximum speed: the components required are the same as those used in existing speed control devices, and the likely sensation for drivers would be no different from that experienced when driving a lower performance vehicle(74).

Such controls would ensure compliance with the national speed limit, but the problem of enforcing any lower limit, such as the 30 mph urban limit, would remain. A simple way to encourage conformity with lower limits would be to equip vehicles with a manually operated switch on the dashboard, which drivers would set at the limit for the area through which they were travelling. This switch would activate an internal warning device to alert the driver, and an external one, perhaps on the roof of the vehicle, to alert other people, particularly the police, if the limit were being exceeded.

Thus in an area where the statutory limit was 30 mph, the driver would push the appropriate colour coded switch. This would put on, say, a yellow light on the vehicle's roof and dashboard. Should the driver inadvertently accelerate beyond 30 mph, a buzzer would sound in the vehicle to warn him that the limit was being exceeded; at the same time the external yellow light would start to flash. This seems to be a straightforward method which as technology advances should become increasingly reliable and cheap.

A more radical approach would be to have not merely speed indicators but speed governors which would make it impossible for the vehicle to exceed the limit. Assuming that the governors were built into the vehicle, they could be switched on by the driver in much the same way as the indicators described above. One problem with governors that does not arise with indicators is the possible need for some override device to deal with those emergency situations when to accelerate, even above the speed limit, is the appropriate evasive action. Whether this is really an important problem is a question to which we return below.

A more sophisticated means of activating either speed indicators or speed governors would be by some external device, such as a cable buried under the roads at points of entry into built-up areas. The cable would send out signals to sensors in vehicle engines. These would activate governors to set maximum speeds at which vehicles could then travel until the next signal was received. The cables might serve other purposes too, such as recording information for charging under a system of road pricing.

In the past few years, several member countries of the OECD have experimented with automatic control devices. A recent report concluded that, although the results varied, the prospects were generally promising(75). In 1976, the former Director of the Office for Traffic Safety Measures of the Prime Minister's Secretariat in Japan recommended that motor vehicles should be equipped with a governor that imposed a maximum speed on the vehicle itself of 60-70 kph on main roads and 100-110 kph on motorways. Although this has not happened, since 1974 Japanese cars are required by law to be equipped with an internal alarm to alert drivers when the maximum speed limit is being exceeded(76). (In addition, the cars they manufacture for their home market are less powerful than those for export, albeit because of the more stringent environmental standards on exhaust emissions with which they have to comply). The French government has already ruled that all heavy lorries be fitted with a mechanical device restricting their speeds to a maximum of 56 mph(77); and some buses in the US have governors limiting top speed to 57 mph(78). In the UK, speed governors are being sold principally to ensure that lorry drivers minimise wear and tear on engine transmission, brakes and tyres and that they do not consume diesel fuel at an excessive rate(79).

If it were made mandatory to equip all road vehicles with some such devices, compliance with the existing speed limits would be vastly improved. In addition, they would enable lower limits to be set to match particular local needs without running the risk that through low levels of compliance the law would be brought into disrepute. This flexibility would help to overcome one of the objections to speed limits, namely that they are a crude device which cannot conceivably be appropriate for all circumstances.

The force of this point is shown by the high accident rates during the hours of darkness, on wet roads, and on heavily trafficked routes. For example, casualty rates per kilometre travelled by car users, motor cycle riders and cyclists are between a quarter and a third higher in the three months from October to December than in the three months from April to June. With these improved means of enforcement it would be possible to legislate that during the hours of darkness or when road surfaces are wet, the mandatory limit is one 'notch' lower than that set for daylight hours on dry roads.

It seems unlikely that, even with speed governors, controls on the vehicles would entirely replace road engineering as a means of speed enforcement. The very low speeds desirable in housing estates and on many residential streets and country lanes will perhaps always be best enforced by humps or other features of the roads themselves. But one of the possible dangers of humps, that they can be dangerous when vehicles approach them at too high a speed, would be reduced if on-vehicle controls were in use in the surrounding area.

Statistics show that young and inexperienced drivers are particularly accident-prone. There is something to be said for the introduction of a probationary period, lasting for perhaps a year after the driving test has been passed, during which time drivers' speeds would be restricted. On-vehicle controls would help to make such a rule enforceable. They would also reduce one disincentive noted above to the development and use of light low-performance vehicles, that the occupants of such vehicles are especially vulnerable in a collision with a larger vehicle. The difference in mass would remain but would become less important if the speed at impact was reduced; also, collisions would become less likely.

Self-identification through indicators, or better still self-enforcement through governors, would help the police with a task which they now dislike. Because enforcement is so difficult and many drivers do not regard speeding as a crime but only as a technical infringement, the police find that to attempt to enforce speed limits damages their relationship with a significant sector of the public upon whose cooperation and goodwill they wish to rely in fighting crime generally. This concern was borne out in a recent survey in which it was found that three times as many motorists as other members of the general public considered their relationship with the police to be bad or very bad(80). Self-enforcement would enable the police to deploy their limited resources in those areas - such as mugging and burglary - about which they believe the public to be more concerned. It would be likely, too, to lead to a considerable reduction in the burden on the judicial system: as noted earlier, each year over 300,000 people are prosecuted in Magistrates Courts for speeding(81).

We have not found any recent British studies on the cost of governors: research on them at the TRRL(82) was curtailed in the 1970s on the grounds that, in the absence of political interest, there was no prospect of implementation. In 1969, the National Highways Safety Board in the United States commissioned the

Battelle Institute to examine the cost and feasibility of speed limiting devices on cars. The Institute's report stated that the devices can provide a satisfactory peformance with an acceptable degree of accuracy of +3 mph. At the time, it was calculated that the unit cost would be $19, with a further $11 to make it relatively tamper-proof. (The alternative could of course be a heavy fine for interfering with the mechanism, as is the case with speedometers in this country.) The cost of retrofitting existing vehicles was calculated to be between two and five times these costs(83). The use of electronic ignition systems is now becoming widespread. It is estimated that a control which would limit the rate of firing when the car was in top gear to some preset maximum would be simpler and less expensive than the cheaper models of electronic wristwatches or pocket calculators(84).

The 1968 the consultation document 'How Fast?' devoted one paragraph to governors and rejected them for two reasons(85). One was that a governor which restricted engine speed would operate not only when the vehicle was in top gear, and was therefore travelling at the set limit, but throughout the range of gears when such a restriction was unnecessary and undesirable. This objection does not apply to more modern governors which, as seen above, need come into operation only when the vehicle is in top gear and, according to our expert American source, 'do not need to affect any aspect of performance at speeds lower than those for which they are set'(86). The other objection was that a governor 'removes the driver's reserve of speed, which might be essential in an emergency or when overtaking'. Although this objection is the one most frequently raised both by transport professionals and by laymen, it seems to us implausible. Whether a governor is fitted or not, there must be some limit to any vehicle's reserve of speed. Each driver takes this reserve into account when deciding how to drive and when to overtake. If the performance were controlled by a governor, the margins of safety would alter and the driver of a high-performance vehicle would no longer perform certain manoeuvres which he now regards as safe. In addition, those occasions, already rare, when the right response to dangerous behaviour on the part of another driver is to accelerate would become less frequent if the vehicles of other drivers were also governed. In any case, according to the American source quoted above, modern governors 'can be readily designed to temporarily allow speeds above their normal limits'(87).

An American study based on insurance data of the accident histories of cars manufactured in 1973 compared the records of models within the same model series but with different engine sizes. It was found that there is in general a 'direct relationship between engine size and collision claim frequencies, average loss payment per claim and average loss payment for insured vehicle year.' Such relationships still held when the driver's age was taken into account(88).

Fears that limiting engine performance would increase the risks of driving seem therefore to be unfounded; nor could any such objections be raised about internal and external speed indicators.

Research and development

It is very surprising that there should still be substantial differences of opinion about the causal connections between speed and accidents. We recommend that an independent statistical study should be made of the existing evidence from all countries - as was called for in an OECD report in 1972(89). In this country, there should also be careful experiments to show the effect on the number and severity of accidents both of the strict enforcement of existing speed limits and of setting and enforcing lower limits. Such experiments should cover the whole range of situations from motorways to residential streets.

On the basis of available evidence, it would seem that a solution to the problem of enforcement would open up opportunities for introducing highly effective lower limits. Tentative calculations suggest that this would be advantageous on all types of road, especially in urban areas, and indeed practice abroad indicates that this is becoming widely recognised: limits of 15-30 kph in residential areas - much lower than the 50 kph thought to be the lowest limit possible in 1977(90) - of 40-50 kph on other urban roads, and of 80-90 kph on motorways have been adopted in Denmark, Sweden, Australia and Japan in order to lower the level of road accidents.

The effect of lower speeds on travel times also needs to be studied, since it is much less simple than it may appear, especially in towns, where speeding along particular stretches of road can often result in no corresponding saving of journey time but only in a longer delay at the next junction or traffic light. When speed does bring an advantage to a particular driver, it is sometimes only at the expense of others, with no net gain to the community. It may be that properly enforced lower limits would initially involve commercial operators in some financial loss, for instance, owing to long distance lorry drivers having to make overnight stops that could otherwise have been avoided. However, it is possible that the longer term effect would be that operational planning changes would be set in train leading to no increase in costs, or even lower costs.

Given that the relationships between fuel consumption and speed and manner of driving are fairly well known - driving at lower speeds is less fuel intensive, particularly for vehicles with low maximum speeds and acceleration(91) - these studies would provide most of the data needed for simplified cost-benefit studies of what the optimal speed limits should be, assuming that compliance could be assured, for roads of different types. Such studies would take account of only four elements of cost and benefit: travel time, accidents and casualties (but not anxiety and stress), fuel consumption and other vehicle operating costs, and the cost of enforcement. They would also rest on the simplifying assumption that the pattern of journeys remained unchanged, although in reality if average speeds were lower some journeys would transfer to other modes, others would be replaced by shorter journeys, and others would be foregone. Because of these simplifications, the optimal speeds that would be calculated by such studies would he higher than the true optima. Nevertheless to establish an upper bound would be very useful. But even the simple studies should be based on higher values for casualties and more complete accident statistics than those now in use.

This discussion also reinforces the point made in Chapter II that the information in the accident records should be amplified so as to include details of vehicle models, and that engine size should be among the features recorded.

Public attitudes to speed limits and their enforcement require further study. General studies should be concentrated on the connection between attitudes and beliefs: is any hostility towards lower limits and stricter enforcement explained by, or at least associated with, a belief that they would not save accidents? It would be very useful to tell the people interviewed in such surveys, or a sub-sample of them, the results of the statistical investigations and experiments just mentioned in order to see whether the findings were believed and, if they were, how this knowledge affected attitudes. That does not mean, however, that work on the attitude studies should be delayed until these other results are available; much can be done meanwhile. Other studies accompanying particular experiments with speed restraint are required to show how drivers' attitudes and their actual compliance are affected by the way the limits are presented, especially by the extent to which limits are 'built in' to the driver's environment. Surveys could also be used to establish what factors contribute to the attractiveness of driving fast, and how the perceived risks of doing so are balanced against these attractions.

Development work on speed indicators and governors should be resumed in order to establish technical points of engineering, reliability and costs. For governors, there should also be trials with relatively small samples of drivers to ascertain any problems in use, followed by trials with larger samples to ascertain their effect on fuel consumption and accidents (including, for reasons of sample size, damage-only accidents).

Throughout this programme of research, the maximum co-operation of other countries in the EEC, ECE and OECD should be sought with a view to setting international standards, especially for speed indicators and governors.

Implications for the road safety effort

The treatment of speed is a worrying lacuna in the British road safety effort. The only recent advance of any significance has been the development of speed-control humps. This development itself took a very long time: the 1974 Road Traffic Act authorised an experimental programme of humps on public roads and it was not until 1983 that regulations were issued permitting their install-ation on a regular basis. Of course it is necessary for policy to be based on sound research, but the benefits foregone because humps could not be used during this nine-year period must have been considerable.

The lack of interest in speed control is partly accounted for by a belief that the relationship between speeds and accidents is not very close. But if, as we have argued, this belief rests on weak grounds, the question then arises why more searching studies and experiments were not undertaken, especially in the light of exper-ience in many countries of the effect on accidents of the speed limits imposed in response to the 1973 energy crisis. In 1977, the American Secretary of Transportation in a Report to the President described the 55 mph limit as 'perhaps the most important safety measure in modern times'(92).

It seems to us that the fact that speed control has not been pursued more vigorously shows both that road safety does not have the standing it deserves within the Department of Transport and that outside pressure has been lacking. It is a safe prediction that if the Department proposed any reduction in speed limits it would arouse much protest; there would be support too, but much less vocal and organised.

A further lesson is that any national pressure group for road safety must have sufficient resources and expertise to commission and oversee or to conduct the technical research that it judges to be necessary; or failing that must at least have enough expertise to influence the Department's own research programme by making positive, detailed, technical suggestions.

References

(1) D. Gordon and T. Mast, 'Drivers' judgements in overtaking and passing', Human Factors, 1970, Vol.12, No.3, pages 341-346.

(2) K. Rumar and V. Berggrund, Overtaking performance under controlled conditions, Report 148, Department of Psychology, University of Uppsala, Sweden, 1973.

(3) R.F. Newby, 'Effectiveness of speed limits on rural roads and motorways', Traffic Engineering and Control, December 1970.

(4) Ibid.

(5) S.J. Ashton, 'Pedestrian injuries: the influence of vehicle design' in H.C. Foot (ed) et al., Road Safety Research and Practice, Praeger Publishers Ltd, 1981, pages 59-66.

(6) Samuel Daniel et al., Considerations in the Development of a Pedestrian Safety Standard, NHTSA, US Department of Transport, 1978/9.

(7) Accident Investigation and Prevention Manual, Department of Transport, 1974.

(8) Circular Roads 1/80, Local Speed Limits, Department of Transport 1980, paras. 11 and 27.

(9) Memoranda submitted by the Automobile Association and the Royal Automobile Club to the House of Commons Transport Committee Inquiry, Road Safety, Minutes of Evidence, 19 April and 3 May 1983, HMSO, 1983.

(10) House of Commons Transport Committee, Road Safety: Inquiry not completed, and Minutes of Evidence, dated 19 April, 3 May and 10 May, HMSO, 1983.

(11) Association of Chief Police Officers' evidence to the House of Commons Transport Committee, 22 February, 1984.

(12) G.C. Staughton and Valerie J. Storie, An in-depth investigation survey: basic results, Transport and Road Research Laboratory Working Paper WP/A1/9, January 1978. This unpublished document is available on direct personal request from the TRRL.

(13) Georgina M. Burney, Estimation of distances while driving, TRRL Supplementary Report 262, 1977.

(14) Barbara E. Sabey and H. Taylor, The known risks we run: the highway, TRRL Supplementary Report 567, 1980.

(15) Barbara E. Sabey, Potential for Accident and Injury Reduction in Road Accidents, Paper presented to the Traffic Safety Research Seminar, New Zealand, 1976, page 10.

(16) Ibid., page 11.

(17) Consultation Paper on National Speed Limits, Department of Transport, November 1976.

(18) Special tabulation obtained from survey findings by Social Community and Planning Research on the subject of Road Traffic and the Environment.

(19) Mayer Hillman, Irwin Henderson and Anne Whalley, Transport Realities and Planning Policy, Political and Economic Planning, 1976.

(20) R. Sumner et al., Speed Control Humps in Cuddesdon Way, Cowley, Oxford, TRRL Supplementary Report 350, 1978.

(21) B. Mostyn and D. Sheppard, A national survey of drivers' attitudes and knowledge about speed limits TRRL Supplementary Report 548, 1980.

(22) Automobile Association, The British Motorist, 1982 (based on a survey of 14 thousand motorists in Britain).

(23) B. Mostyn, op.cit..

(24) See also R. Hogg, A study of male motorists' attitudes to speed restrictions and their enforcement, TRRL Supplementary Report 276, 1977.

(25) Department of Scientific and Industrial Research, Road Research 1958, HMSO, 1959.

(26) Advertisement, 21 October 1983.

(27) Report in the Times, 15 October 1982.

(28) Report in the Guardian, 19 October 1982.

(29) Report in the Times, 14 February 1984.

(30) Report in the Guardian, 27 October 1982.

(31) Report in the Observer, 16 October 1983.

(32) Report in the Times, 14 Janaury 1984.

(33) Report in the Guardian, 23 Janaury 1984.

(34) Report in the Times, 12 February 1984.

(35) Report in the Observer, 15 May 1983.

(36) Report in the Observer, 27 June 1981.

(37) Report in the Observer, 12 December 1982.

(38) Letter from Peter Thomson, Director General of the Advertising Standards Authority, to Don Mathew, Transport Campaigner, Friends of the Earth, 4 January 1984.

(39) Annual volume of Transport Statistics Great Britain, HMSO.

(40) Calculated from figures supplied by Autocar.

(41) Calculated from figures published in the Sunday Times, Road and Car Supplement, Autumn 1983.

(42) G. Grime and T.P. Hutchinson, Some implications of vehicle weight for the risk of injury to drivers, Transport Studies Group, University College London, 1979.

(43) Leonard Evans and Dennis Blumenfeld, 'Car occupant life expectancy: car mass and seat belt effects', Risk Analysis, Vol. 2, No.4, 1982.

(44) B. Mostyn and D. Sheppard, op.cit.

(45) R.A. Cameron, Drivers' knowledge of speed limits: a study based on police records, TRRL Supplementary Report 382, 1978.

(46) K.S. Rutley, 'Control of drivers' speed by means other than enforcement' in Ergonomics, 1975, Vol.18, No.1.

(47) B.L. Hills, 'Vision, visibility and perception in driving', Perception, Vol.9, 1980, p.184.

(48) C.F. Harvey, D. Jenkins and R. Sumner, Driver error, TRRL Supplementary Report 149UC, 1975.

(49) T.C. Willett, Drivers after sentence, Tavistock Publications, 1973.

(50) K.S. Rutley, op.cit..

(51) D.G. Jenkins, 'Cross national attitudes and opinions survey: Report of UK findings', International Drivers' Behaviour Research, SR 403, TRRL, 1978.

(52) Sunday Times Road and Car Supplement, Autumn 1983.

(53) Ibid.

(54) R. Hogg, op.cit.

(55) Calculated from figures in Transport Statistics Great Britain, 1971-81, op.cit.

(56) Department of Transport, National Speed Survey 1983, Statistical Bulletin STC4 (84) 2, February 1984.

(57) Magistrates Association, Suggestions for Traffic Offence Penalties, 1983.

(58) Home Office, Offences relating to motor vehicles, England and Wales 1981, Supplementary Tables.

(59) Circular Roads 1/80, op.cit., para.10a.

(60) Quoted in Memorandum submitted by the London Boroughs Association to the House of Commons Transport Committee, Road Safety: Inquiry not Completed, HMSO, 1983, page 105.

(61) TRRL Digest, A New Motorway Signal, LR 1075, 1983.

(62) Sussex Police and Police Scientific Development Branch of the Home Office, A Report on the operational evaluation of a portable traffic data collection system, June 1981, Appendix 2.

(63) J.M. Munden, An experiment in enforcing the 30 mph speed limit, RRL Laboratory Report 24, 1966.

(64) M. Syvanen, Effect of police supervision on the perception of traffic signs and driving habits, TALJA (The central organisation for traffic safety in Finland), 1967; and Sussex Police and Police Scientific Development Branch of the Home Office, A report on the operational evaluation of a portable traffic data collection system, June 1981.

(65) Quoted in Memorandum submitted by the Transport and Road Research Laboratory to the House of Commons Transport

Committee Inquiry on <u>Road Safety</u>, Minutes of Evidence, 3 May 1983, page 108.

(66) Quoted in <u>Speed limits and enforcement</u>, SWOV (Institute for Road Safety Research in the Netherlands), 1973, page 15.

(67) D.C. Andreassend, 'An examination of Melbourne Metropolitan Speeds 1962-69', <u>Proceedings of the Australian Road Research Board</u>, Vol.5, No.3, 1970.

(68) See, for instance, <u>Research on Traffic Law Enforcement</u>, OECD, 1980; and E. Hauer et al., 'Speed enforcement and speed choice', <u>Accident Analysis and Prevention</u>, Vol.14, No.4, page 267-78, 1982.

(69) Article in the <u>American City</u>, June 1972.

(70) K.S. Rutley, <u>op.cit.</u>

(71) Ministry of Transport and Civil Aviation, <u>Road Safety, the Slough Experiment 1955-57</u>, HMSO, 1957; and A.D. Crook, 'Effect on accidents of area traffic control in West London', <u>Traffic Engineering and Control</u>, May 1970, pages 30-31.

(72) See numerous TRRL Reports published in the last ten years, including LR 597, 878 and 1017 and SR 292, 350, 423 and 456.

(73) 'Portaramp' manufactured by the Moseley Rubber Company.

(74) W. Haddon, President of the Insurance Institute for Highway Safety, Washington DC, USA, private communication, 20 September 1983.

(75) OECD, Road Transport Research, <u>Traffic Safety of Children</u>, OECD, 1983, page 68.

(76) Reference to governors in Katsumi Takeoka, 'Recent Trends in Traffic Accidents: Japan's amazing progress in lowering traffic deaths and injuries, <u>The Wheel Extended</u>, Vol. 6, No.3, Winter 1976, p.30; and reference to the internal alarm obtained from private communication with J. Hanyu, Japanese Information Office, Embassy of Japan.

(77) Article in <u>Transport Retort</u>, Transport 2000, February 1983.

(78) W. Haddon and S. Baker, 'Injury Control', in <u>Preventive and Community Medicine</u>, ed. D. Clark and B. MacMahon, Little, Brown and Company, 1981, pages 109-140.

(79) Lucas Kienzle Instruments Ltd.

(80) The Automobile Association, <u>Survey on the Motorist and the Police</u>, 1983.

(81) <u>Transport Statistics Great Britain, 1972-82</u>, Table 2.45.

(82) R.C. Moore, 'A system for transmitting speed commands to motor vehicles', Technical Note TN 706, TRRL, 1972.

(83) National Highway Safety Bureau, <u>Enforcement</u>, NHSB Report PB 186, 1969.

(84) W. Haddon, <u>op.cit.</u>

(85) Ministry of Transport, <u>How Fast? A paper for discussion</u>,

HMSO, 1968, para.59.
(86) W. Haddon, op.cit.
(87) Ibid.
(88) W. Haddon, Auto insurance losses collision coverages, Research Report A-6, Highway Loss Data Institute, 1976.
(89) OECD, Speed limits outside built up areas, OECD, 1972.
(90) H. Taylor, 'The Pedestrian's Environment', in OECD, Special Research Group on Pedestrian Safety, 1977, page 56.
(91) Mayer Hillman and Anne Whalley, Energy and Personal Travel: obstacles to conservation, Policy Studies Institute, 1983, Chapter III.
(92) Brock Adams, Report to the President on Compliance with the 55 mph Speed Limit, Department of Transportation, Washington DC, 1977, page 3.

Table III.1   Changes in road accidents following imposed or lowered speed limits

Ref.	Date	Location	Imposed or lowered limit	Type of accident or casualty	Per cent change
1	1935	London, UK	30 mph	fatalities	-23
				serious injuries	-14
2	1935	Great Britain (built-up areas)	30 mph	fatalities	-15
				injuries	-3
3	1955	Sweden (built-up areas)	50 kph	fatal & serious injuries	-9
				all injuries	-8
4	1956	N. Ireland (built-up areas)	30 mph	fatal & serious injuries	-31
				all injuries	-25
5	1956	Slough, UK	linked signals	fatal & serious injuries	-55
6	1957	Belgium	70 & 80 kph	fatal & serious injuries	-17
7	1957	West Germany (built-up areas)	50 kph	fatalities	-30
				all injuries	-18
8	1957	Netherlands (built-up areas)	n/a	fatal & serious injuries	-10
				slight injuries	-6
9	1958	London, UK (formerly unre-structured roads)	40 mph	fatal & serious injuries	-28
				all injuries	-19
10	1958	West Germany (motorways)	100 kph	fatalities	-18
				all injuries	-41
11	1959	Switzerland (built-up areas)	60 kph	fatalities	-21
				injuries	-6
12	1959	Jersey, UK (built-up areas)	40 mph	fatal & serious injuries	-39
				slight injuries	-8
13	1961	Sweden	90 kph	fatalities	-40
				serious injuries	-27
14	1961 -64	Great Britain (summer weekends)	50 mph	injuries	-24
15	1962	Finland (3 counties)	90 kph	fatalities	-42
				other injuries	-16
16	1964 -65	UK (six roads)	30 mph	fatal & serious injuries	-23

Ref.	Date	Location	Imposed or lowered limit	Type of accident or casualty	Per cent change
17	1965	UK (motorways)	70 mph	expected fatalities	−39
				expected serious injuries	−11
	1965	UK (dual carriageways)	70 mph	serious injuries	−21
18	1965 -67	Switzerland (built-up areas)	90 & 100 kph	injury rate per km	−42 to −90
19	1966	Finland	110 kph	serious injuries	−21
20	1967	Eire (road to Dublin)	50 & 60 mph	injuries	−56
21	1967	USSR (two roads)	70 & 80 kph	fatalities	−30 to −50
				injuries	−40 to −46
22	1969	France (five roads)	mainly 80 kph	fatalities	−36
				serious injuries	−40
23	1971	Sweden (rural roads)	70 & 90 kph	injuries	−18
24	1971 -76	UK (12 sites)	40 mph	injury accidents	−44
25	1973	New Zealand (rural roads)	50 mph (in lieu of 55 and 60 mph)	fatalities	−37
				serious injuries	−24
				minor injuries	−22
26	1973 -74	UK (motorways)	50 mph (in lieu of 70 mph)	accident rate	−33
27	1974	USA (rural highways) interstate	55 mph	fatality rate	−50
				injury rate	−28
		other 4-lane		fatality rate	−70
				injury rate	−34
		2-lane		fatality rate	−68
				injury rate	−32
28	1974	Denmark Odense	60 & 110 kph	fall especially young pedestrians & cyclists	n.a.
29	1974	France (roads & motorways)	90 & 120 kph	fatalities	−22
30	1979	Sweden (rural roads)	130-110 kph	injuries	−30
			110-90 kph	injuries	−25
			90-70 kph	injuries	−22

References to Table III.1

1 J.M. Munden, An experiment in enforcing the 30 mph speed limit, RRL Laboratory Report 24, Road Research Laboratory, 1966.
2 R.J. Smeed, 'The influence of speed and speed regulations on traffic flow and accidents', Roads and Road Construction, January 1961.
3 Ibid.
4 T.M. Coburn and N.C. Duncan, 'The effect on speed and accidents of a 30 mph speed limit in built up areas in Northern Ireland', International Road Safety and Traffic Review, Vol.VII, No.3, 1959.
5 Ministry of Transport and Civil Aviation, Road Safety, the Slough Experiment 1955-57, HMSO, 1957.
6 National Swedish Council on Road Safety Research, Bulletin, Effects of speed limits outside built-up areas, 1971.
7 R.J. Smeed, op.cit.
8 Ibid.
9 R.F. Newby, 'Effect on Accident Frequency in the London Area', Traffic Engineering and Control, March 1962.
10 Speed limits on rural roads, Road Research Laboratory Leaflet LF 223, 1971.
11 R.J. Smeed, op.cit.
12 Ibid.
13 National Swedish Council, op.cit.
14 B. Sabey, 'Experience of Speed Limits in Great Britain', Paper to International Symposium on Traffic Speed and Casualties, Denmark, 1975.
15 P.P. Scott, 'Speed limits and road accidents', Paper to Traffex '77 Traffic Engineering and Road Safety Conference, Stoneleigh, Warwickshire, 1977.
16 J.M. Munden, op.cit.
17 Ministry of Transport, Report on the 70 mph Speed Limit Trial, RRL Special Report No.6, HMSO, 1967.
18 National Swedish Council, op.cit.
19 Speed limits on rural roads, op.cit.
20 National Swedish Council, op.cit.
21 Ibid.
22 Ibid.
23 G. Nilsson, The effect of speed limits on traffic accidents in Sweden, National Road and Traffic Research Institute, Sweden 1982.
24 A.M. Arman, The Value of Realism in Setting Speed Limits, Paper to PTRC Summer Annual Meeting 1982, University of Warwick.
25 W.J. Frith and J.B. Toomath, 'The New Zealand Open Road Speed Limit', Accident Analysis and Prevention, Vol.14, No.3, 1982.
26 Road Accidents Great Britain 1974, page viii.
27 Tim Borg, Evaluation of the 55 mph speed limit, School of Civil Engineering, Purdue University, 1975.
28 A. Nielsen, 'Experiences from actual traffic speed limitations' in Traffic Speed and Casualties, Odense University Press, 1975.
29 Christian Gerondeau, 'The impact of fuel-saving measures on road safety in France and Western Europe', Robot, June/July 1974.
30 G. Nilsson, op.cit.

Table III.2 Fatalities as a proportion of all casualties among different road users on roads subject to different speed limits

roads subject to limit of:	pedestrians	fatalities as percentage of all casualties					
		pedal cyclists	motor cyclists	car occupants	bus riders	light lorries	heavy lorries
30 or 40 mph	2.5	0.7	1.2	0.8	0.3	0.7	0.9
50,60 or 70 mph	11.9	3.4	3.3	2.8	0.2	2.1	2.9

Source: Calculated from figures in Road Accidents Great Britain 1982, Table 23.

Table III.3   Changes in road accidents following the raising of speed limits

Ref.	Date	Location	Raised limit	Type of accident or casualty	Per cent change
1	1956-58	London, UK (outer area)	30 to 40mph	fatal & serious injuries injuries	+7 *
2	1964-65	Kent, UK (20 sites)	30 to 40mph	fatal & serious injuries slight injuries	-33 -12
3	early 1970s	London, UK	30 to 40mph 40 to 50mph	expected accidents	-15
4	1973-74	Midlands, UK (9 sites)	30 to 40mph	accidents	*
5	1977	UK (49 dual and single carriageway sites)	60-70 mph 50-60 mph	accidents	*
6	un-dated	UK (6 sites in 5 counties)	30-40 mph	accident rate	-44 +9 -55 +30 -69 +12

* Change not significant

References
1 Barbara Sabey, 'Experience of Speed Limits in Great Britain', Paper to International Symposium on Traffic Speed and Casualties, Denmark, 1975.
2 A.M. Arman, The Value of Realism in Setting Speed Limits, Paper to PTRC Annual Summer Meeting, University of Warwick, 1982.
3 Department of Transport, Circular Roads 1/80, 'Local Speed Limits', 1980.
4 A.M. Arman, op.cit., and further survey findings supplied by the same author.
5 Department of Transport, op.cit.
6 Ibid.

IV SMALL-SCALE ROAD ENGINEERING SCHEMES

Scope and value

Major road schemes are primarily intended to increase road capacity and hence to save travel time, although, at least on the Department of Transport's usual assumption that their effect is only to divert traffic from existing less safe routes and not to generate new traffic, they also save some accidents. But there is also a class of small-scale and relatively low-cost road engineering schemes which are designed only with accident reductions in mind. A great variety of measures may be involved: for example, the redesign or relocation of road signs to make them more visible; converting straight-across junctions into staggered ones so as to compel drivers to slow down; the provision or improvement of pedestrian islands and other crossing facilities; the provision of median strips or road markings to bring about traffic channelisation; the use of skid-resistant surface dressings at junctions; alterations in the road camber; improving visibility by minor changes in the layout of the carriageway and by selective restrictions on on-street parking; edge-lining to improve visibility at night; and so on.

The development of such techniques was pioneered by the County Surveyor of Oxfordshire in the 1930s and some local authorities were applying them in the 1950s. In the 1960s the Ministry of Transport set up a number of Road Safety Units to cover different areas of the country. These units achieved a considerable degree of success[1,2], although their work was sometimes impeded by the fact that whereas they came under the Ministry, the power to take action often lay with local authorities whose responsibilities for road safety were at that time permissive only. But when local government was re-organised in 1974, a statutory duty was laid on those local authorities which were also highway authorities to promote road safety in their areas[3]. They are now responsible for investigating accidents and designing and implementing appropriate remedial measures both on their own roads and also, in virtue of agreements made with the Department of Transport, on motorways and trunk roads in their areas(4).

The TRRL has estimated that some 20 per cent of road accidents could be saved by accident-specific road engineering measures, although this estimate allows for action which goes rather beyond the kind of measures listed above to include the re-routeing of traffic by traffic management schemes(5).

It has been known for many years that small-scale safety schemes yield very good value for money. The Ministry's Road Safety Units in the 1960s produced many examples of schemes which paid for themselves several times over in a year(6). In 1978-79, the work of the GLC's blackspot team showed a first-year rate of return in excess of 300 per cent; this figure allows for staff and computing costs as well as the costs of the physical works themselves(7). A recent report on ten years' work on low-cost remedial measures in Hertfordshire shows that the programme as a whole achieved a first-year rate of return of 139 per cent(8). This calculation allows only for the cost of the physical works, and not for design or staff time, which are relatively much more important for small schemes such as these than for major works. But if such costs are allowed for on the assumption that they would add 75 per cent to the cost of the physical works, the first-year rate of return is still 79 per cent.

The first-year rate of return criterion, although commonly used and officially recommended to assess these small-scale schemes, does not allow a direct comparison to be made with major road investment, which is assessed by a discounted cash flow method assuming a seven per cent discount rate and a 30-year planning horizon. For small-scale schemes, a 30-year planning horizon is regarded as unrealistic. Many of the schemes, for example resurfacing with skid-resistant dressings, would have to be completely renewed in a much shorter time, even though some, such as the staggering of road junctions, effectively last for ever. On the benefit side, changing traffic patterns and other developments make it unsafe to assume that accident savings at any particular site will continue to accrue for many years into the future. Thus, a planning life of five years only is commonly assumed in the appraisal of these safety-inspired schemes, although that is recognised to be a conservative assumption. The ratio of discounted benefits to costs, assuming a seven per cent discount rate and a five-year planning horizon, which is equivalent to a first-year rate of return of 79 per cent is 3.4. Major road works are accepted so long as there is any excess of discounted benefit over cost. Thus, small-scale safety schemes are a much better investment than the larger schemes primarily intended to save travel time. The substantial under-reporting of accidents in the police statistics, and the low values that are officially given to accident costs, mean that the advantage of the small schemes is even greater than it appears. It is unlikely that many other investments, either in the transport sector or elsewhere in the economy, can show a similar rate of return.

This being so, conventional economic logic suggests that more resources should be devoted to small-scale remedial measures until the point comes when the rate of return from them falls to that which can be obtained elsewhere in the transport sector. This logic has not been followed, however.

Precise information on counties' activity in this field is hard to come by (a fact which itself says something about the low importance attached to it), although more should be known very shortly when a survey recently completed by the Institution of Highways and Transportation (formerly the Institution of Highway Engineers) has been analysed. It is widely believed that not all local authorities keep proper records, by location, of the accidents which occur on their roads, which is a pre-requisite to any systematic attempt to tackle the problem(9). The expenditure figures for local authorities given in Transport Statistics Great Britain suggest that the total amount that local authorities spend on road safety, including education as well as small-scale engineering schemes, is considerably less than one per cent of their transport expenditure(10). This may be misleading, since in some counties at least, some money which is in fact spent on small-scale safety schemes may be entered under other headings. Unfortunately, the forms that local authorities have to return to the Department of Transport each year for the purposes of Transport Supplementary Grant no longer recognise spending on road safety as a separate item, so they cannot be used as a check. But in any case, it is clear that the amount spent on these remedial measures is small, even in the most progressive counties, nor is there any evidence of an upwards trend.

Reasons for not investing more in small-scale remedial measures

What is the explanation for the failure to pursue such a profitable line of investment? Discussions with people closely involved in local authority transport planning have brought to light a number of possible reasons.

As a preliminary, it should be mentioned that criticisms have been made, on statistical grounds, of the estimates of accident savings that these small schemes have achieved. The first criticism concerns the identification of black spots - points on the road network where an unusually high number of accidents occur and which are therefore selected for remedial treatment. It is claimed that a clustering of accidents at a given spot in a particular year will sometimes occur purely by chance. The reduction in subsequent years, which is attributed to the remedial action, would usually have occurred in any case(11,12). Secondly, it is suggested that the effect of remedial work is sometimes not to save accidents altogether but only to change the location on the network where they occur(12). Fortunately, it is not necessary in the present context to examine the force of these points, nor the extent to which they are already allowed for in current methods of calculating accident savings. Whether or not the estimates of accidents saved should in reality be reduced, it is not because of these statistical doubts that decision makers have held back from investment; nor, indeed, has anyone suggested that current methods are so greatly in error as to invalidate the basic claim that this is a highly profitable form of investment.

Low prestige

One problem appears to be that experience in this field, where the results in physical terms are often inconspicuous, does not always carry the same prestige in the civil engineering profession as experience in large-scale construction. As one person put it to us, a photograph of a bridge with his name on it is a better recommendation for an engineer seeking a new job than a successful record in accident prevention. Not all employers would agree with that, but the same point was made to us spontaneously often enough to suggest that there is something in it. Politicians, too, may prefer to be associated with some conspicuous achievement, such as a by-pass, than with a programme of work which commonly has no visible result on the ground.

This low prestige would also help to make sense of another explanation that has been suggested to us, which is that although the benefits from road safety schemes are very large, they do not accrue to the authority that spends the money. Although this is an important point, which we have borne in mind in our later suggestions for institutional change, the same could be said of most other transport investment. The benefits of major road-building schemes, or of public transport investment or subsidies, accrue mainly to travellers; highway authorities are, indeed, likely to incur an extra cost commitment from major road schemes in the form of an increased maintenance requirement. However, the prestige of the larger schemes is such that the extra incentive of a return to the authority which has to spend the money is not required.

Insufficient pressure from above

One reason why economic criteria have not been used to determine how much money to spend on small-scale safety schemes is that the Department of Transport has never recommended that they should be. The Department has indeed given advice on how to calculate first-year rates of return, but only so as to enable such schemes to be ranked against each other, so that the most promising ones are tackled first, not as a way of helping to decide how much to invest in this kind of work as a whole. In fact, so far from suggesting that money should be invested in safety schemes until the point comes when the rate of return from them is no higher than can be obtained elsewhere, the Department has explicitly set much higher targets for such schemes than would be demanded from other investment. Thus, a Departmental circular issued in 1975 to draw the attention of local authorities to their new responsibilities in road safety recommended that for small safety schemes a first-year rate of return of at least 50 per cent should be sought. Nor was it then suggested that the size of the annual budget for such schemes should be determined by reference to this target. It seems to have been accepted that the budget would be determined independently and would be much lower than such a target would suggest. The circular took the example of a county where 500 accidents a year, costing the community (in 1975 prices) £1 million, could be saved by means of small schemes. On the basis of a first-year rate of return of 50 per cent, it would be worth spending £2 million to achieve such a saving. It was then assumed that the annual budget for small road improvements might be some £50,000, from which the conclusion was drawn that a 40-year programme would be required(13); the very large benefits that would be foregone during the 40-year period were not seen as a reason for increasing the annual budget. Elsewhere, the circular used extremely diffident language in commending road safety in general and small road improvements in particular to local authorities. Road safety is very important - but times are hard and local authorities cannot be expected to devote too many resources to it. Small road improvements produce great savings at little cost - so local authorities might consider making use of any spare staff capacity they may have available to look into them.

'5. The guidance given by Circular 171/74 on the need to restrict local authorities' expenditure and manpower requirements in 1975/76 makes it clear that this is not an opportune time for the assumption of new functions and the Department recognises therefore that local authorities may be constrained in the resources they can at present commit to

119

work on the promotion of road safety. But road accidents cause 7,500 deaths and 350,000 injuries a year, at a cost to the community of £700 million, and without assiduous action both locally and nationally this waste of life and resources is likely to increase. The authorities are therefore urged to take the largely hidden cost of road casualties into account in weighing the conflicting claims of different services.'

'7. Annex 2 outlines an empirical approach to the promotion of road safety programmes explaining current thinking on some of the many factors contributing to road safety. One of the most important of these is the small road improvement scheme. The Department wishes to stress the value it places on such schemes, based on detailed accident study. They produce great savings at little cost and justify high priority in local authorities' road safety programmes. Road works for which there are emotional local pressures often fail to save as many accidents and to produce as good economic returns as schemes less in the public eye. But to identify the most profitable locations for road improvements means careful and detailed accident analysis, a study of individual problems and the evaluation of options. If authorities temporarily have spare staff capacity available in consequence of the reduction of capital expenditure on highways they may consider whether such staff could usefully undertake investigation and planning work or individual problems as an investment for the future. Indeed the carefully selected remedial work itself might well be undertaken at very small expense to other highways work, for it is not universally appreciated what a minute proportion of total highways expenditure such works take. Advice on the likely savings in life and resources to be achieved from these schemes and methods of determining investment levels are given in Annex 3, which deals with the preparation of road safety policies and programmes.'

Advice issued by the Institution of Highway Engineers in 1980 does indeed point out that the decision of how much to spend on small remedial schemes should take into account that they are generally the most cost-beneficial form of road expenditure(14). Nevertheless, the Institution still recommends that for each single site treated a first-year rate of return of at least 50 per cent should be sought. For similar action involving more than one site, lower targets are recommended, although still far exceeding what is demanded from major road works(15).

A problem for a local authority that did wish to use economic principles to allocate transport expenditure between road safety schemes and other uses is that ways of calculating rates of return have not been developed, or are only now being developed, for some of the important alternative items of local transport expenditure, such as road maintenance and public transport subsidies. Since there is no inherent reason why economic criteria should not be applied in these fields also, the failure to develop them itself requires some explanation. But even where methods of calculation have not been developed, local authorities could be encouraged to allocate budgets in the spirit of economic rationality, i.e. to ask themselves whether it is likely that the rates of return from alternative expenditure are as high. And for one particular choice, between large capacity-oriented schemes and small safety-inspired schemes, the allocation can indeed be made on the basis of a calculation, or at least with the aid of a calculation.

One reason for the reluctance of decision makers to adopt this approach appears to be that the larger schemes are thought to be superior to smaller ones because the gains they bring are permanent. But this advantage should be taken into account by choosing different investment horizons, and is generously allowed for by assuming a horizon of thirty years for large schemes and five for small. Sometimes a major scheme can bring environmental improvements not allowed for in the calculated rates of return, which take account only of time and accident savings, whereas a small scheme is unlikely to have any such side-effects. But the way to take any extra benefits into account is to give some extra weight or priority to the particular large schemes which produce them - it is not as if the environmental effect of a major road scheme was always positive - rather than to impose a penalty, in the form of very much higher benefit targets, on the whole set of smaller schemes.

In spite of this discrepancy in the rates of return required, the Department of Transport has on various occasions, particularly in connection with the annual TPPs (Transport Policies and Programmes) and TSG (Transport Supplementary Grant) submissions, drawn the attention of local authorities to the great potential and value for money of small-scale safety schemes. In the circular describing the arrangements for TSG submissions for 1976/77, local authorities were advised that their submissions should describe their policies for accident study and their programme of proposed remedies(16) and it was also said that 'Where as a result of the detailed accident study, a programme of small road works is proposed, the provision made in the estimates should be separately stated ...'(17). In the corresponding circular

121

for 1977/78, it was stated that the allocation of the TSG programme would take account of proposals for accident remedial work based on a systematic programme(18). Although the point that TSG allocation would take particular account of road safety proposals has not been repeated, the circular for 1978/79 again drew attention to the merits of small-scale schemes and asked that the TPPs should contain a section on policies and measures designed to promote road safety, with information about accident analysis and remedial work(19). These points were repeated in the circular for 1979/80 which also asked for a statement of the expenditure incurred on small road schemes in the year 1977/78(20). The circular for the following year stressed the need for accident investigation teams and for a separate budget for small schemes specifically designed to reduce accidents. It asked local authorities to set out their approach to accident analysis and remedial work in the knowledge that the cost ot the community of road accidents was then in the neighbourhood of £1,300 million a year(21).

These TPP circulars, however, represent the peak of the Department of Transport's efforts to encourage local authorities to invest in small-scale road safety schemes. The last four circulars have not mentioned road safety, although an important reason for that is that the circulars have been drastically shortened as a matter of policy, and, as was mentioned above, road safety is no longer a heading on the finance forms which have to accompany a TPP submission. Nor is there any evidence that even at their peak these exhortations had any significant effect, a fact which is partly explained by the inherent weaknesses of the TPP/TSG system which are discussed below.

It is characteristic of accident remedial work that the ratio of staff costs, in data analysis, site investigation and design, to the costs of the physical works is relatively high. If there is a particular pressure to keep down local authority staff numbers, over and above the general pressure to keep down total costs, the effect is to squeeze activitites such as road safety with a high staff content. In effect there is such a pressure, albeit of an informal kind, in the form of government exhortations and the 'manpower watch' statistics. This appears to be illogical and distorting. What matters to the ratepayer is the total amount of money spent by the local authority and the value obtained from it; the division of expenditure between the authority's own staff, contractors and materials has no significance in itself. Nor is accident investigation and remedial action a suitable field for privatisation. Outside consultants might have some part to play in setting up a unit in the first place, or in advising on such matters as the appropriate computer systems, and it can also be useful from time to time for an outside expert to look with a fresh eye at the problems of any particular local authority. But the need for continuity, local knowledge and coordination with other aspects of local road and transport planning requires the bulk of the work to be handled within the local authority itself.

Local public opinion

The inadequacy of pressure from central government is not suffic- ient to explain the small amount of resources that local authorities put into road safety and into small-scale remedial works in particular. Local authorities have a great deal of autonomy in deciding their expenditure and priorities. Much more would be put into road safety if the local electorate insisted on it. The fact that it does not demands some explanation. Concern over the local environment, and in particular over the intrusion of traffic, has been growing and becoming much better organised over the years. It was seen in Chapter II that danger on the roads is the aspect of traffic intrusion which causes most resentment. Why then has this resentment not been translated into effective political action?

The problem is not a lack of concern. It is partly that the concern is not organised, although the groups and associations which work at the level of the street or neighbourhood, as opposed to the civic societies which operate at the level of the town or, in larger cities, the district, often have road safety as a main raison d'etre. Either through such groups, or direct from individual citizens or through the local press, local authority members and officials are likely to be under considerable pressure to take action or road safety.

From the point of view of the professionals in road safety, this pressure is not of the right form and may even be counter- productive, in the sense that if they are obliged to give way to it the result may be that resources are diverted from more promising action which has not aroused public opinion. Sometimes people are concerned about locations which they believe to be dangerous but which have no history of accidents. When an accident occurs, especially if it is a particularly sad one, perhaps involving a child, there will be pressure to do something about that particular site; even though it is not a blackspot, there is no reason to believe that accidents will recur there, and the accident may have been of a type which does not lend itself to an engineering remedy. Often there is a demand not merely to take some action at a site which has aroused concern but to take a particular action suggested by the local people, although the diagnosis of the trained professional may suggest another remedy.

We do not believe that the local citizens are necessarily always in the wrong when their demands conflict with the judgment of professionals. In the first place, their concerns may be different. The professionals' aim, and their measure of success, is simply to reduce the number of accidents. But citizens may also wish to be free from anxiety and from the need to take the evasive action, such as forbidding their children to play in the streets, which dangerous conditions make necessary. They may be quite justified, therefore, to ask for attention to be paid to sites where treatment would bring peace of mind and greater freedom of action rather than a reduction in accidents. Although some of the sites where action is demanded because an accident has occurred may deserve less priority than those already listed by the local road safety unit, they may nevertheless be sites which would show a high enough rate of return to be on the list if the budget more closely matched the needs. Nor are local citizens necessarily wrong in their views as to what action is required. Two constant concerns of local groups are that speed limits should be enforced, or lower limits set, and that more pedestrian crossings should be provided. The demand for lower speed limits inevitably gives rise to a conflict when the official line is that 'unrealistic' speed limits should be raised, but Chapter III gives reasons for thinking that it is the official line that is mistaken. Pedestrian policy lies outside the scope of this report, but there are ample grounds for saying that the importance of walking has been neglected and that the criteria for determining the provision of crossings are too restrictive(22).

Despite these points, it is quite fair to say that the pressure from the local electorate is not of the kind required. What is needed is not intermittent agitation about individual locations that cause anxiety, but a steady rational pressure for a continuing campaign, based on systematic investigation and a much larger budget, to improve conditions generally.

One of the reasons why such pressure has not developed, particularly from the larger and better organised local environmental societies which might have been expected to generate it, may well be the fact that their particular suggestions, for example on speed limits or pedestrian crossings, so often seem to meet with opposition from the county engineers. The ordinary concerned citizen may be made to feel that this is a difficult technical subject where he will be treated as an intruder and will be rebuffed. There also appears to be a widespread, if tacit, feeling that accidents are a concomitant of our modern society and motorised transport system which have to be accepted as inevitable, like the weather. The fact that the British accident record is good by international standards may contribute to the feeling that there is not a great deal more to be done about it. Moreover, the accident problem, however important, may appear less urgent than the other problems which face local people and societies. If action is not taken to save a building threatened by demolition, or to keep open a railway line or whatever, the opportunity may be lost for ever, whereas the accident problem remains and action to deal with it can always be postponed.

Implications for the road safety effort
A reporting and accounting system
More effective pressure both from the central government and from the local electorate is required to ensure that local authorities devote to road safety schemes their due share of the transport budget. One common requirement to bring about both pressures is information. There should be an annual report on the work of each council's programme of accident investigation and remedial work. The report should be on the lines of a company report, setting out what costs have been incurred by the accident unit and what benefits have been achieved and are expected from its work. Every authority's report should be in the same format and use the same conventions, so that comparisons can be drawn with other authorities. This would help the local electors to bring rational and constructive pressure to bear on their council by enabling them to ask questions of the form 'Why are we spending less on this activity than county X or obtaining less for our money than county Y?' Central government can ask similar questions.

In order to ensure comparability, various points would have to be specified by the Department of Transport. The first concerns the data that should be collected and the statistical analysis performed in order to calculate what accident savings have in fact been achieved (in other words, to estimate the number of accidents that would have occurred in the absence of remedial work). Appropriate money values for accident savings would also be supplied by Ministers, as discussed in Chapter I. Although it would not be possible now, because the basic research has not been done, the Department should in future also offer guidance on the evaluation of benefits other than accident savings, such as relief from anxiety. On the cost side, the Department should lay down the conventions to be used on such matters as the allocation of overheads.

Controls and incentives
It was stated above that even when the Department of Transport has strongly urged local authorities to undertake road safety schemes, and has said that the attention paid to them would

influence the allocation of TSG, it is not clear that there has been any effect.

There is little doubt that the TSG system could be strengthened and that more use could be made of it to promote road safety. One puzzling feature at present is that no reasons are stated for giving or withholding grants; no doubt the reasons become known to those immediately concerned through informal channels, but that does not help to produce a well-informed local public opinion. Nor is there any obligation on a local authority to spend the money it receives in the way set out in its bid. It would seem possible to remove these defects and further to strengthen the system by making it a condition of receiving any TSG money at all that the plans under each major heading, of which road safety should be one, were satisfactory.

Nevertheless, we do not think that the TPP/TSG system is the most satisfactory mechanism for controls and incentives in road safety. For one thing, there is some doubt about whether the system should continue at all, on the grounds that it is anomalous to have a system of supplementary grants, additional to the ordinary Rate Support Grant, in just one field of local authority activity. Secondly, the Road Safety Division of the Department of Transport is not directly involved in the process of approving TPPs and allocating TSG, a responsibility which falls to the Roads and Local Transport Division. This probably helps to explain why road safety is not one of the expenditure headings on the forms; in any case, it would seem desirable that the links between the Road Safety Division, or any equivalent central government body, should be as direct as possible. In addition, although this chapter has concentrated on one particular way, albeit an especially promising one, in which local authorities could improve road safety in their areas, there are a whole host of other ways, some of which fall outside the scope of a TPP. Some examples are land use and locational policy, which has a very powerful influence on the length and mode of journeys and hence on the likely number of accidents; pedestrianisation; the detailed layout of new residential areas. In our view, the incentives offered by central government to local authorities should be related to results achieved, but should not be formulated in such a way as to favour any particular means of achieving them. Therefore, any system of incentives should operate independently of the TPP system.

Suggestions for incentives, which in effect amount to a system of payment by results, are put forward in Chapter IX. It is perhaps worth mentioning here that as well as creating a more direct and satisfactory relationship between the Road Safety Division and local authorities, they should also help to strengthen the pressure of local electors on their councils, since a financial interest, as ratepayers, would be added to their ordinary concern as citizens for safe and agreeable surroundings.

The size of a local authority's transport budget

Among the reasons suggested to us in discussion for the low level of effort put by local authorities into small-scale road safety schemes is that they do not have enough money to spend on transport generally. The tighter the budget, the more important it is that it should be allocated in a way that will achieve the highest return, which almost certainly means that more should be allocated to road safety. We do not therefore accept that tight transport budgets justify a low level of expenditure on road safety, and we are also suspicious of the claim that transport deserves a higher share of public expenditure generally. However, it would be possible to increase local authorities' transport budgets without increasing total public expenditure on transport by a transfer from central to local government.

At present, central government's expenditure on motorways and trunk roads is about one-third of local government's expenditure on transport purposes and its expenditure on new roads exceeds that of local government(24). The justification claimed for having two road-building authorities is that the central government's programme serves different purposes, of a national and strategic kind, from those served by the local authorities' programmes. In fact, however, the great majority of the benefits arising from most trunk road schemes are accounted for by short local journeys. The effect of the present arrangement is that public expenditure on transport in any area is split between two budgets: one under the control of the local authority which can be spent on any transport item as needs indicate, and the other which, regardless of the merits of competing claims, can be spent only on trunk roads. Such a division must lead to distortions in investment and to an allocation of resources which is less than optimal. It would be rational, therefore, to transfer the bulk of the Department of Transport's present responsibilities for road building, and the funds involved, to local authorities. The funds would no longer be earmarked a priori for major road building and maintenance, but would be an addition to the local authority's transport budget, or perhaps even to its general budget, to be spent in whatever way gives the highest rate of return. Presumably the better schemes now in the national road programme would survive, but one would expect some diversion of funds to other purposes, among which small schemes to improve road safety would rank high. We return to this reorganisation of responsibilities in Chapter IX.

127

Summary
In order for local authorities to invest in small-scale road safety
schemes on a scale commensurate with the rates of return, changes
are required in their relationships both with the Department of
Transport and with their own electorates. Each local authority
should publish an annual report on its accident investigation and
remedial work in a form which would allow the scale and effectiveness of the work of different authorities to be compared. The
Department of Transport should set up a system of incentives for
road safety which would be independent of the TSG system and
would apply to all accident savings however achieved. The division
of responsibility for roads between the Department of Transport
and local authorities reduces the amount of money that might be
made available for accident investigation and prevention and leads
to other distortions in the allocation of resources. It should be
brought to an end by a transfer of as many roads as possible from
the Department to local authorities.

References
(1)   J.T. Duff, 'The effect of small road improvements on
       accidents'. Traffic Engineering and Control, October 1971.
(2)   K.L., 'Road Safety Units', Traffic Engineering and Control,
       February 1969.
(3)   Road Traffic Act 1974, Section 8.
(4)   Communication from the Department of Transport, March
       1983.
(5)   Barbara E. Sabey, Road Safety and Value for Money, TRRL
       Supplementary Report 581, 1980, Table 7
(6)   As ref. 1.
(7)   J.R. Landles, Accident Remedial Measures, the Work of the
       GLC Blackspot Team, PTRC Education and Research
       Services Ltd., summer 1980.
(8)   Black Sites Before and After Study Up Dated to January
       1982, Hertfordshire County Council Highways Department,
       H.C.C. T/292/1, 1982.
(9)   The following extract comes from the Automobile Associat-
       ion's evidence on road safety to the House of Commons
       Transport Committee (Minutes of Evidence, Tuesday, 19 April
       1983, HMSO, 1983, page 62).
       'A first requirement in identifying sites for treatment is
       the collection of accident data, so that accident clusters
       can be thoroughly studied. Not all local authorities
       compile such records, and many only do so on a basis which
       means that accident clusters are identified on a three year

basis - from serious injury accidents only. Minor reported accidents are excluded, for administrative savings. If they were included, sites for treatment could be identified within a twelve month period'.

(10) Transport Statistics Great Britain 1971-1981, HMSO, 1982, Table 1.18.

(11) E. Hauer 'Selection for treatment as a source of bias in before-and-after studies', Traffic Engineering and Control, August/September, 1980.

(12) C.C. Wright, The Interpretation of Road Accident Data for Engineering Remedial Work, Department of Civil Engineering, Middlesex Polytechnic, 1983.

(13) Circular Roads 12/75, Department of the Environment, 1975, Annex 3.

(14) Highway Safety, Accident Reduction and Prevention in Highway Engineering, Guidelines. The Institution of Highway Engineers, May 1980, section 4.

(15) Ibid., para. 6.1.

(16) Transport Supplementary Grant Submissions for 1976/77, Department of the Environment Circular 43/75, para 35.

(17) Ibid., Annex G, para. 3.

(18) Transport Supplementary Grant Submissions for 1977/78, DoE Circular 125/75, para. 39.

(19) Transport Supplementary Grant Submissions for 1978/79, DoE Circular 1/77, para. 31.

(20) Transport Supplementary Grant Submissions for 1979/80, D.Tp. Circular 3/78, para. 30.

(21) Transport Policies and Programmes Submissions for the 1980/81 TSG Settlement; D.Tp. Circular 4.79, para. 29.

(22) Mayer Hillman and Anne Whalley, Walking Is Transport, Policy Studies Institute, September 1979, especially pages 6 to 8.

(23) As ref. 10.

V CYCLING

Accidents, travel and risk

Statistics on cycling have to be treated with especial caution. It was seen in Chapter I that although all cycling deaths are reported, only a minority of severe casualities and a smaller minority, of the order of 20 to 30 per cent, of slight casualties to cyclists appear in the police records and hence in the annual statistics. Doubts have also been raised whether the Department of Transport's roadside counts, which are the basis of the figures on trends in travel, properly represent the minor roads on which much cycling takes place(1).

Nevertheless, it is probably legitimate to draw some conclusions from the long-term trends shown in Table V.1. The table shows that cycle mileage declined very rapidly from the early 1950s to a low point in 1974, since when there has been a certain revival. Casualties also fell substantially, though not at the same rate as travel, until 1974 and have also since increased.

It does not necessarily follow from the fact that casualties have fallen less rapidly than travel that cycling has become more hazardous. Table V.2 shows that casualty rates are especially high among young cyclists. If it is chiefly the older, safer riders who have given up cycling, that would produce an upward trend in the overall casualty rate even though the rates for each separate age group had not changed at all.   However, an analysis by the Department of Transport comparing casualties in 1958 and 1981 suggested that although there had been a change in the age distribution of cyclists towards the lower ages, that was not sufficient to account for the rise in the overall casualty rate. It was estimated that between those two years the casualty rate for a cyclist of a given age had increased by 25 per cent(2).

Table V.3 shows that cyclists themselves constitute the great majority, over 90 per cent, of the people killed or injured in accidents in which a bicycle is involved. It was seen in Table II.3 that for a given distance travelled cyclists are less likely than cars to hit and injure pedestrians and very much less likely to do so than motorcyclists. The difference is especially marked for collisions which result in the death of the pedestrian.

Children and young people figure prominently among cycle casualties. In 1981, 11 per cent of cyclists killed or seriously injured were under ten, 38 per cent were under fourteen and 60 per cent were under twenty(33). It is possible, however, that injuries to young cyclists, or at least to children, are reported more fully than injuries to adults.

Suppressed demand

These casualty figures would in themselves justify a major campaign to make cycling safer, especially as they are rising and are likely to rise still further, unless remedial action is taken, as cycling itself continues to revive. The large number of child casualties is a particular cause of concern. But another major reason for action is that the present dangerous conditions deter large numbers of would-be cyclists and thereby create massive distortions in travel patterns. In Chapter I evidence was presented of the scale of this distorting effect, which suggested that in reasonably flat towns over 40 per cent of journeys to work would be made by bicycle if conditions were relatively safe. It was mentioned that the present experience in the Netherlands, where the bicycle is the main mechanical means of transport for short journeys, appeared to support this finding.

The Netherlands is not the only example. In West Germany, it has been officially claimed 'based on actual scientific results of behavioural research on mode choice' that 25 per cent to 35 per cent of all car journeys in towns, up to a length of 15 kilometres, could be replaced by bicycle trips'(4). The experience of several German towns where particular efforts have been made to provide cycling facilities also demonstrates the relationship between cycling conditions and cycle use. In Bocholt, a flat town of 66,000 population where 53 kilometres of cycle paths have been built, 40 per cent of journeys to school and almost the same proportion of journeys to work are made by bicycle, which is also a major means of transport for shopping(5). In Bremen, a city of over half a million population and more than 400 kilometres of cycle track, it is claimed that the number of trips made by bicycle is more than twice what would be expected in a less well endowed city of the same size: 55 per cent of journeys for educational purposes and 19 per cent of all journeys (both figures exclude journeys on foot) are made by bicycle(6). The fact that well over 20 per cent of all road users in Erlangen travel by bicycle is attributed to the town's geography and to the exceptional facilities, including a cycle path network of 150 kilometres(7).

It should not be thought that such results represent the most that could be achieved by planning for cyclists. It was pointed out in Chapter I that conditions could have been improved in even the best of the British towns classified in the Waldman study as safe. Cycling in the Netherlands is substantially safer than in Britain but, as will be seen below, the accident rate is still high. Provision for cyclists in Bocholt, though better than in comparable towns or cities, is nevertheless still described as 'inadequate'(8). Apart from danger, there are other deterrents to cycling, for example vehicle fumes and the lack of parking facilities, which can be alleviated by policy.

The demand that would be released if cycling could be made really safe - safer than the competing modes of mechanical transport - and otherwise attractive could therefore be greater than is suggested by the use made of the bicycle today even in the relatively good areas. Accidents would be reduced in more than one way. The accident rate would fall among people who cycle now; there would be fewer accidents among those who transferred to the bicycle from other and (in the conditions assumed) more dangerous modes; the reduction in motor traffic arising from the transfer and from the decrease in 'escort' travel should make conditions safer both for the remaining motorised travellers and for pedestrians.

Improved facilities for cyclists should also reduce the stress of travel both among cyclists and among the other road users who now have to share the roads with them. People who took up cycling should gain in health; user costs of travel would fall, as would the costs of road provision and maintenance; noise and air pollution would be reduced; energy would be saved. There seems to be only one possible disadvantage: that cycling would take some passengers from public transport and would thereby reinforce the vicious spiral of declining custom, rising fares and reduced services. Although there might be some such effect, some transfer of public transport trips to cycling could also work to public transport's advantage if some uneconomic peak trips were to transfer. Journeys to work and school seem to be the most promising candidates, so this might well happen. Also, advantage could be taken of the reduced pressure on road capacity which should follow from any switch from cars and motorcycles to bicycles to create bus priority schemes; even without such schemes, a reduction in cycle traffic on bus routes should allow buses to travel faster.

Official policy on cycling safety
The machine and rider's equipment
There have always been regulations for bicycles, as for other vehicles, covering their design, equipment and maintenance. These regulations have been tightened up over the years, with particular regard to brakes and conspicuity. Regulations laid before Parliament in 1983, which will come into force in late 1984, require various reflectors to be fitted, some of which, such as spoke reflectors and pedal reflectors, have not been compulsory up until now, and also require that the brakes should be of a type which work reasonably well in wet weather[9]. More action along these lines would appear to be possible and desirable. On conspicuity, a simple and (everyday experience suggests) effective measure would be to insist that cyclists wear reflective sashes or some similar clothing, and there are also other ways in which the bicycle itself could be made more conspicuous: for example, by having tyres with reflective sides. Even when the new regulations are in force, the braking requirements are considerably less stringent for wet than for dry conditions - a stopping distance of 7.5 metres from a speed of 16 km/h as opposed to a stopping distance of 5 metres from a speed of 24 km/h[10]. A TRRL study published in 1979 showed that reflective discs projecting sideways from the bicycle, as commonly used in Finland, or flags, as commonly used in Sweden, encouraged motorists to leave a reasonable margin when overtaking[11]; more might be done to promote the use of such equipment.

Training
Great importance has always been attached to training child cyclists. The National Cycling Proficiency Scheme was launched by RoSPA in 1959 and is still run under RoSPA's auspices, although the responsibility for training both children and instructors now lies with county councils. It is claimed that 300,000 children are trained annually through this scheme and that almost half the children in the nine/ten age group take part[12,13]. The TRRL has played a major part in developing Cycleway, a new version of the NCPS which is now being gradually introduced into schools; both the NCPS and Cycleway have the strong support of the Department of Transport; the Department of Education and Science is also promoting Cycleway in circulars to local education authorities[14].

In spite of this official involvement and approval, it is not clear exactly what claims are made or would be justified for training child cyclists. Any idea that training is likely to be more efficacious than traffic segregation as a means of reducing accidents was rejected by the Department of Transport in its evidence to the Transport Committee of the House of Commons in

133

1983, but in spite of recent changes, discussed below, towards a more favourable official attitude to cycling provision, total segregation is not regarded as practicable(15). For reasons given below, we think that the resources devoted to making provision for cyclists are still far too modest. But given the existing conditions, what can be said about the efficacy of training in reducing casualties to child cyclists and how should training affect the line that the authorities or parents take about children's use of bicycles?

The NCPS scheme is designed to improve the performance of child cyclists both generally and in relation to particular manoeuvres, such as right turns, which are especially hazardous. There is evidence that children's performance on such manoeuvres does indeed improve as a result of training, and that some at least of the beneficial effect is lasting(16,17). Nevertheless, a substantial number of errors are still committed. One trial conducted by the TRRL with 15 children showed that immediately after training, the majority still behaved incorrectly in several manoeuvres, including turns at traffic lights(18). In addition, much of the effect of training wears off over time(19,20). Cycleway, which was designed after these experiments and partly in consequence of them, is intended to improve the former methods in a number of ways, and in particular to improve children's retention of what they learn, but it is too early to evaluate it.

Although it is clearly sensible for training to concentrate on the more hazardous manoeuvres, it does not follow automatically that an improvement in the ability to perform them will lead to a commensurate, or perhaps to any, reduction in the number or severity of casualties. We know of four studies that have attempted to relate the training of child cyclists to their involvement in accidents. Two of these concluded that although training probably had had some beneficial effect in reducing accidents per child, it was small and confined to certain categories of children(21,22). However, given that children who have passed the test appear to cycle more as a result(23,24), these findings may underestimate the success of training in reducing rates per distance travelled. The other studies come to more optimistic conclusions, but the statistical inferences are doubtful(25,26).

None of these studies is very recent, and they cannot, therefore, be taken as showing the potential of the improved new methods that are now being introduced. Nevertheless, it seems to us, in the light of the casualty rates by age shown in Table V.2, that children under ten should be discouraged from cycling on public roads except when fully segregated facilities have been provided. Indeed, Swedish studies have suggested that children cannot ride a bicycle competently until the age of 13(27).

The parents of older children face an agonising choice. If they allow their children to cycle, they expose them to high risks. If they forbid it, they are denying them a very important part of childhood. Parents who make the first choice should probably also get their children trained and should also make their permission to cycle contingent upon their children's passing the test, since the accident rate among those who fail it is high(28). But official support for training should not lead parents to suppose that it reduces the risk more than slightly. The main emphasis in official policy should not be put on training but on changing the conditions which create these unacceptable choices in the first place.

The provision of facilities for cyclists

Until recently, the provision of facilities for cyclists was not officially regarded as an issue in transport planning. In one or two new or expanded towns, notably Stevenage, and in a handful of older towns, cycling was taken seriously, but this was because of the personal enthusiasm of the engineers concerned, not because of direction from above. The land-use transportation studies which were the favoured instrument of urban planning in the 1960s and 1970s took no account of either walking or cycling. The circulars issued to local authorities in the early years of the TPP/TSG system, following local authority reorganisation, although containing very detailed advice on local transport planning say nothing about cycling. Literally the only mention of cycling is that one of the TSG finance forms, to do with expenditure on road maintenance, has the item 'footways, cycle tracks, kerbs, fencing and barriers' under the heading 'other highway works'(29). At a meeting on bicycles held by the Transportation Engineering Group of the Institution of Civil Engineers in 1975, it was stated that(3):

> 'The Department of the Environment (at that time there was no separate Department of Transport) was aware of the interest in cycling and recognised responsibilities for providing advice but could not at present spare resources to take positive action: it merely monitored initiatives from local councils ...'.

The beginnings of a change came with the consultation document 'Transport Policy' issued in 1976 and the White Paper of the same name issued in the following year, both of which discussed cycling very briefly. The consultation document noted the bicycle's advantages of being cheap, energy-saving and free from pollution and noise. It warned that to provide for the use of bicycles for the journey to work in crowded city centres would involve 'extensive and sometimes costly segregation measures'. It was said that in the right conditions (not necessarily in city centres or in towns) 'local authorities will be justified in examining the economic case for diverting some of their available resources to improving facilities for cyclists'. The White Paper, a very long document, had only the following to say about cycling.

'The increasing cost of travel has led more people to think of cycling as a cheap and convenient way of getting about, and more would no doubt cycle if conditions were made safer and more pleasant. Completely segregated cycle routes would be impracticable or far too expensive in most cities, but local authorities should consider ways of helping cyclists when preparing traffic management schemes. Some local authorities have marked out lightly-used streets as cycle routes and more of this could be done when the roads are suitable. More cycle stands in town centres and at or near public transport terminals would also help.

Altogether, there is scope for many more practical initiatives, and for local authorities generally to take account of both pedestrian and cycle schemes which have been shown to be successful. Local authorities will be asked to identify their proposals for such schemes in their annual transport policies and programmes. The Department of Transport will strengthen its Traffic Advisory Unit, whose work covers provision for pedestrians and cyclists as well as traffic management. The Department, with its Regional Offices, will improve its advice to local authorities on useful measures and make generally available examples of successful schemes. The Department will shortly publish advice about planning to help pedestrians. It will also contribute to the cost of selected experimental schemes for cyclists, and help to devise and monitor them.'

The Department has since taken all the actions mentioned in the second paragraph of this extract. A consultation paper specifically on cycling was issued in May 1981 and was followed in January 1982 by a statement on cycling policy by the Secretary of State for Transport, who welcomed the revived interest in cycling and expressed the hope 'that the growing recognition of cyclists' needs will lead to more widespread action to improve facilities which in turn will encourage more people to cycle'(33).

But although cycling is now recognised, no policy document has yet raised the crucial question of how many people might cycle in the right conditions and what resources should therefore be devoted to improving the conditions. The statistical analysis of cycling to work, mentioned above and in Chapter I, suggested that cycling could be very important, but no policy document has mentioned this study, which indeed seems to be very little known within the Department(34). Nevertheless, the Department's advice on cycling is clearly based on the presupposition that it does not merit many resources. It has been seen that the 1977 White Paper stated that the provision of segregated facilities in cities would usually be impracticable or far too costly, although no evidence was produced in support of that assertion. Although local authorities are now asked to consider cycling in their TPPs, this still seems to be only in the context of traffic management (35,36) and the possible use of disused railway lines(37). According to the Secretary of State's Statement on Cycling Policy, the Department's financial help for innovatory cycle schemes is intended to 'assess the effectiveness of new arrangements and to demonstrate what can be done for cyclists at relatively modest cost', although the need for one or two larger projects 'to monitor the effect on cycling demand of developing a continuous urban route or network' is also acknowledged(38).

The renewed official interest in cycling does not amount to much in physical or financial terms. As far as was known to the Department of Transport, cycling facilities had been provided in only 27 of the 47 English counties by November 1982(39). The amount of money spent by local authorities on cycling facilities is not known, but a survey by Friends of the Earth suggests that most of the schemes are modest: less than a third of the local authorities (county and regional councils and district councils) which had provided any facilities for cyclists by 1982, or were planning to do so, had built or were planning segregated routes (40). By March 1984, the Department of Transport had helped to support 17 schemes in 12 counties at a total cost to the Department of £240,000 and five more schemes have been agreed(41). Most has been done in London, where thanks to an energetic campaign by a well organised pressure group (the London Cycling Campaign) and a sympathetic administration, the GLC agreed in 1981 to devote one per cent of its annual capital budget for transport, amounting to some £1.7 million a year, on facilities for cycling.

The dangers of a half-hearted policy
The government's policy towards cycling appears to be therefore that cycling is desirable, that local authorities should encourage it

137

by providing facilities, but that not much money should be spent on it. In terms of road safety, the obvious risk in such a policy is that the hoped-for increase in cycling will put up the total number of road accidents. The reason is that, quite apart from the possibility of new travel, cycling is much more hazardous under present conditions than the modes of transport with which it competes, always excepting two-wheeled motor vehicles. The following figures relate to 1978/79 and show the number of fatal and serious casualties per hundred million kilometres travelled by each mode of transport(42).

Bus or coach passenger	2
Car passenger	9
Car driver	9
Pedestrian	85
Cyclist	120
Motorcyclist	270

These aggregate results reflect the facts that casualty rates are higher among the young and that cyclists tend to be younger than other travellers. But Table V.4 shows that casualty rates are very substantially higher for cyclists than for car drivers of the same ages and are higher for cyclists than for pedestrians at all ages below 60. Although this table does not show children, the very detailed breakdown of pedestrian casualty rates by age in <u>Road Accidents Great Britain 1980</u> confirms that for children cycling is much more dangerous than walking.

These figures do not take into account the fact that when a cyclist is involved in an accident it is fairly rare, as compared with accidents involving motorised means of transport, for the other party to be injured. National figures might in any case not be very helpful in predicting the change in the number of casualties that might follow from a switch to cycling from other modes in any particular place. Nevertheless, the differences in casualty rates are large enough to show that, unless cycling becomes very much safer, one should expect an increase in cycling to result in an increase in the total number of casualties.

Even if all a local authority's efforts to encourage cycling took the form of action which made cycling safer, it is still possible that the net effect would be to increase the total number of road casualties. Casualties among the hard core who cycle even in present conditions would go down, but unless cycling casualty rates were cut drastically, the extra casualties among travellers transferring from other modes, together with the casualties associated with generated cycle travel, might offset that reduction.

Cycling should, therefore, be encouraged only if the investment in providing facilities is sufficient to ensure that the decline in casualty rates keeps pace with the increase in cycle travel.

If that condition were met, as it is not now in Britain, then at least total road casualties would not rise as a result of an increase in cycling. But to justify a policy of encouraging people to cycle who now do not, it could be argued that a further much more stringent condition should be met: that casualty rates for cyclists should fall to approximately those of travellers by competitive means. In our view, that condition would be unreasonably strong, since the implication is that if it cannot be met, nothing should be done to improve conditions for those people who are prepared to cycle at present. Also, even if people who took up cycling were more at risk as travellers than if they had continued to use their former means of transport, the exercise should benefit their health in other ways, not least in a reduced risk of heart disease.

Danger is not the only deterrent to cycling. Others include difficulties of parking and problems of carrying a bicycle on public transport. Action to remove such deterrents in present conditions would have an adverse effect of road safety. Such action should, therefore, be undertaken only in the context of a wider policy to make cycling very much safer. This point is not recognised, or at least not emphasised, in official documents. Thus, both the 1977 White Paper quoted above and the Secretary of State's recent Statement(43) refer to the desirability of providing for cycle parking without warning that such action would be misguided on its own.

Doubts about the wisdom of encouraging cycling are not new. In the 1970s, and perhaps still now, many local authorities took the view that cycling was so much more dangerous for the traveller than other means of transport that anything done to encourage cycling would effectively encourage more accidents: it was better to let the number of cyclists continue to decline(44). In 1975, the GLC road safety officer expressed the opinion that two-wheeled transport had no place in London(45). In 1978, an OECD report on the safety of two-wheelers concluded that 'at present such a policy (to promote the use of bicycles and mopeds) is likely to worsen the accident situation unless it is accompanied by drastic counter-measures in the field of traffic engineering and town planning'(46). In 1968, Ernest Marples said 'there is a great future for the bicycle if you make conditions right. If you make them wrong, there isn't any future'(47). In spite of these warnings that cycle policy must be bold or nothing, at present in Britain it is likely to fall squarely between two stools.

Policy in other countries

We have not attempted a comprehensive review of foreign practice, but clearly cycling is treated as a major means of transport in a number of countries.

Cycling has always been a major form of transport in the Netherlands, but its use declined in the 1960s and early 1970s. In the mid-1970s, a major change in national transport policy took place. This resulted from a realisation that had been growing over the preceding years that the growth in the numbers of cars could no longer be seen 'in a purely favourable light' and that 'a steering policy was needed for traffic and transport instead of an adaptive policy'(48). A main aim of policy was to 'encourage the use of the bicycle and the moped as much as possible'. In towns it was recognised that 'people will be attracted towards the idea of using bicycles and mopeds if safe routes, separate from other traffic, are provided ...'. Hence the following principles were stated(49):

'All the major destinations in the town, e.g. schools, must be easily accessible by bicycle along the separate cycle routes. They are also an attractive way of getting to the recreation areas outside the towns. Where a cycle route crosses a major road, bicycles and mopeds should have equal priority. At less important intersections the cycles should always have priority. Where necessary and circumstances permit, a system of charges to discourage the use of cars in urban traffic or in peak periods will be introduced in the large urban centres. This can also be applied to parking. Car-pooling must be encouraged and working hours staggered where this is possible and would prove advantageous.

Outside the city centres, the older districts in particular must be made attractive by being redesigned. This can be achieved by separating residential areas from traffic areas; through traffic will be barred from these residential areas. Cars that must enter them will then have to give priority to cyclists and pedestrians. Residential areas are primarily places for people to live and shop in and safety is the most important factor.'

Importance was also attached to providing for cyclists outside towns: the policy is now gradually to create a nationwide network of cycle routes linking the various urban networks(50).

The central government is now spending over £11 million a year in subsidies for building bicycle paths and routes(51). It has also financed major demonstration projects in the Hague, a city of

750,000 people where £2.6 million was spent on a cycleway 6.5 kilometres in length, and in Tilburg, a town of 150,000 people, where £3.6 million was spent on reconstructing a street to provide a cycleway of 4.5 kilometres(49). The town of Delft, with a population of 90,000, is spending £5 million (1976 prices) on a comprehensive cycle network which includes new underpasses and new bridges over canals(53).

In Japan, where bicycle utilisation has experienced 'tremendous jumps'(54), national action 'for the improvement of the bicycle traffic environment and the promotion of publicity concerning proper bicycle riding' was agreed in 1973. In that year there existed 5,000 kilometres of bicycle paths, including some paths shared with pedestrians; by 1981 the number had risen to 32,000(55). The 1981 national traffic safety budget included a sum of over £300 million to provide, or subsidise the provision of, safe facilities for pedestrians and cyclists(56). Other measures to encourage cycling or to make it safer include the provision of parking lots(57) and a system to regulate bicycle maintenance. By the end of 1981, there were over 37,000 retail outlets in which officially approved bicycle safety maintenance was carried out(58).

Some of the German experience with cycling schemes has already been noted. Sweden and Denmark have both since the early 1970s been building segregated paths for pedestrians and cyclists; the Swedish parliament asked in 1973 for an investigation into how conditions for cyclists could be improved, which led to the production of a design guide and generally stimulated bicycle planning(59). In France, a policy to rehabilitate two-wheeled travel as a mode of transport was adopted in 1974. The effort put behind it seems to be rather less than in the more northern countries; nevertheless, at least 180 new cycle track schemes were provided between 1974 and 1978(60).

Foreign experience shows that it is possible for cycle casualty rates to be lower than in Britain and for the rates to fall faster than the use of bicycles increases. In the Netherlands in 1979-81, the rates per hundred million kilometres travelled, for cyclists over the age of fourteen, were 4.1 for fatal casualties and 39.3 for fatal and serious casualties together(61). The corresponding figures for Britain in 1979 were 6.3 and 90.6(62). In Sweden, the equivalent rate for fatal casualties, for cyclists of all ages, was 4.1 in 1982. Table V.5 shows that the fatal casualty rate in Sweden is less than half what it was ten years ago; thus deaths have fallen substantially although the use of bicycles, in vehicle kilometres, has increased by two-thirds over the low point of 1972. In Japan also, the number of cyclists killed has fallen over a period in which cycling considerably increased(63). According to an OECD report, similar results have been achieved in individual Swedish and Japanese towns which have adopted traffic measures in favour of cycling(64). However, there is no evidence of cycle casualty rates as low as those of the safer modes of transport, such as car or bus passenger, with which cycling competes.

Reasons for the neglect of cycling in Britain

The official revival of interest in cycling has been later and far weaker in Britain than in some other countries, including some of our continental neighbours with very similar problems and circumstances. Probably the most important reason for this is that the idea that the main task of transport planning was to provide for the increasing use of cars took a firmer grip in Britain in the 1960s, and since then has been harder to shake off, than in most other countries. This also largely accounts for the greater reluctance to support public transport in Britain, discussed in the next chapter, and perhaps also in part for Britain's relatively poor record in pedestrian safety, as described in Chapter VIII. But other reasons, more specific to cycling, have contributed.

It seems that the very merits of the bicycle, that it is inconspicuous, cheap to use and relatively easy to provide for, have been treated as reasons for not taking it very seriously. Because cycling facilities are cheap, therefore little should be spent on them. Perhaps this attitude reflects the same penchant for large and conspicuous projects which also partly accounts for the relative neglect of small-scale safety schemes. In the report of the meeting on cycling held at the Institution of Civil Engineers in 1975, it is noted that 'although good cycles had been made since the First World War, this discussion was the first meeting of the Institution to concern itself totally with the bicycle'(65). (In fact, the introduction of the safety bicycle had a profound impact long before the First World War: Flora Thompson's book Lark Rise to Candleford describes how dramatically it affected life in a small English country town in the 1890s.)

A great merit of formal methods of investment appraisal is that such prejudices do not enter into them. As the last chapter shows, there is no guarantee that if the appraisals are undertaken the action they suggest will be followed, but at least the evaluation itself is objective. But cost-benefit methods to evaluate investment in cycling facilities have not been developed, although it was one of the recommendations of the study of cycling to work that they should be(66). This omission is the more surprising, since the Department has suggested at least twice, once in the 1976 Green Paper quoted above, and again in the document Ways of Helping Cyclists in Built-up Areas(67), that local authorities should undertake a formal assessment of cycling facilities. Presumably it was thought that such assessments were very simple, so that no advice on methods was needed. In reality, the difficulties both in prediction and in evaluation are considerable, as the professional economists in the Department of Transport would certainly appreciate. If cycling had been regarded as an important mode of transport, their skills would have been used to develop the necessary criteria.

Cycling policy again raises the question of what the relationship between central government and local authorities is and ought to be. Sometimes Ministers and the Department take the line that it is entirely up to local authorities to decide their own priorities. Local autonomy appears to have been particularly stressed with respect to cycling. For example, the Under-Secretary of State said in the House of Commons in 1981 'I have no power to require counties to include particular items in their TPPs but local authorities are well aware of the importance of taking account of the needs of cyclists in their local transport planning'(68). In fact, the Department has, if not powers, at least very strong means of persuasion through the TSG system, and on other aspects of policy a more centralised line has often been taken. For example, the circular on TSG submissions for 1978/79 says(69):

'In order to assess a county's progress in the light of national objectives, the Department require a statement of the Council's policy on the role of public transport and the objectives of that policy for both urban and rural area ...'

The equivalent circular for the year 1983-84 says(70):

'As in recent years, the aim has been to keep the procedures as simple as possible, to minimise the work and costs of producing TPPs; but the Secretary of State would like to have rather more information about some aspects of the programmes which will enable him to make a judgement about the most effective distribution of the resources available, and to support counties which respond to certain policy initiatives.'

Thus it would be possible for the government to have a national policy on cycling and to promote it through the TPP/TSG system. But if that is thought inappropriate, on the grounds that local autonomy should be respected, it is at least the Department's responsibility to develop methods of economic appraisal of cycling schemes for local authorities to use. In addition to the theoretical work, this must involve several major demonstration projects to ascertain the casualty rates that can be achieved in very favourable conditions and also the effect on the use of other modes of making cycling safe and agreeable throughout a town.

In those countries where cycling is taken seriously, its environmental and ecological advantages are an important part of the reason. In Germany, for example, it is the Federal Ministry of the Interior, in virtue of its responsibilities for the protection of the environment, that has organised an interdepartmental committee to develop a programme to encourage cycling(71). The relative neglect of cycling in Britain partly reflects the small attention paid to environmental considerations here in the formulation of transport policy.

The neglect of cycling also reflects the weakness of the pressure groups. The Cyclists' Touring Club, founded in 1878, must be one of the oldest road user associations in the world. There is also a manufacturers' association, the British Cycling Bureau; and various environmental groups, especially Friends of the Earth, as well as a small band of enthusiastic professional transport planners, have been active in promoting cycling. But this amounts to little as compared with the pressure brought to bear by other road interests. No doubt because of the difficulties that have been experienced in having cycling recognised at all, the cycling lobby has been so moderate in its demands that it is in danger of encouraging just that policy of modest help to the cyclist which has been criticised in this chapter as likely to lead to the worst of both worlds. The guidelines on cycling provision published recently by the Institution of Highways and Transportation seem to treat the differences between Britain and those countries where cycling has been pursued more vigorously as facts of life that have to be accepted, rather than as a reason for a fundamental re-appraisal of the British approach.

> 'The Guidelines are aimed purely at the application of relevant techniques in the United Kingdom. For this reason considerable account has been taken of UK Government publications and experience already obtained. Some information has been imported from the continent of Europe and elsewhere but it has been necessary to do this with caution since the levels of cycling and spending on it in some other countries are markedly different from those in the UK'(72).

A constant theme in the documents of the cycling lobby is that cycling is not as dangerous as the statistics make it appear(73,74,75). A wish to reassure prospective cyclists is very understandable; bicycle manufacturers, in particular, would not wish to draw attention to the dangers of using their products, even when those dangers do not arise from any defect in the products themselves. But the arguments are not convincing(76), nor is it really good tactics to play down the present risks, since to do so only weakens the case for major investment to make cycling safer.

Implications for the road safety effort

Road safety is usually thought of in terms of making a given amount and pattern of travel safer. In that context, the steps taken in 1983 to improve the braking and conspicuity of bicycles represent an advance, although they may not go far enough. The surprise is that it has taken so long to introduce these regulations, since no new technology and very little expense are involved and accidents to cyclists have been a matter of concern for decades, perhaps since the advent of motor traffic. This suggests that the traditional lines of attack on the problem of road accidents could be pursued more vigorously.

More important, however, is the failure to treat cycling as a major mode of travel now grossly underutilised because of the risks. Techniques to evaluate cycling schemes, and hence to answer the question how much should be spent on investment for cycling, have not been developed, nor have experiments been undertaken to obtain the data necessary to apply such techniques. It has nevertheless been assumed, despite the evidence to the contrary in this country and some very promising foreign experience, that cycling deserves only minor attention and resources and can be dealt with at the level of traffic management.

This attitude may partly reflect the insufficient attention given to safety in transport policy, and the failure to realise that the costs of danger on the roads included the distortion of travel patterns as well as the occurrence of accidents, but more is involved. It seems to represent a continuation of outdated ideas that the main aim of transport policy should be to accommodate the growth of motor traffic. In Chapter VI, it is suggested that the structure of responsibilities for transport, with the Department of Transport having a direct interest in trunk road provision but not for public transport, helps to explain the relative neglect of public transport in Britain as compared with other countries. Possibly this organisational point also has a bearing on the neglect of cycling; possibly the relatively weak pressure that the cycling lobby can bring to bear explains it. In any case, it is clear that changes in the attitudes and probably the structure of the Department of Transport will be required in order to ensure that provision for cycling, in common with other aspects of transport policy other than trunk roads, is given due attention. These points are taken up in Chapter IX.

References
(1)   See for example Mike Hudson, The Bicycle Planning Book, Open Books/Friends of the Earth, 1978, Chapter 2.
(2)   Road Accidents Great Britain 1981, para. 11.1.
(3)   Ibid., Table 6.
(4)   Fahrrad und Umwelt, ISSN 0343-1312, Der Bundesminister des Innern, 1983, English summary.
(5)   Wilhelm Kolks, 'Bocholt a town for cyclists', Proceedings of the First International Bicycle Congress VELO/CITY, 10-12 April 1980, Bremen West German Federal Minister of Transport, 1981.
(6)   Ivar Miloschewski, 'The bicycle in Bremen', as ref. 5.
(7)   Dietmar Habermeier, 'Erlangen: Priority to the bicycle', as ref. 5.
(8)   Wilhelm Kolks, op.cit.
(9)   Pedal Bicycles (Safety) Regulations 1983 referred to in Department of Transport Press Notice No. 222, 8 July, 1983.
(10) Cycles Part 1.   Specifications for safety requirements for bicycles, British Standards Institution, BS6102: Part 1: 1981.
(11) G.R. Watts, Bicycle safety devices - effects on vehicle passing distances, TRRL Supplementary Report 512, 1979. A more recent report by the same author on a study among school children in Manchester (TRRL Supplementary Report 801, 1983) supports the finding that overtaking vehicles allow more room to bicycles fitted with 'spacers'. But it shows that spacers can cause problems in some circumstances, especially when cyclists are riding abreast, and it is suggested that their use should be discouraged near school entrances at busy times. According to this report, other work has shown that fluorescent yellow jackets are as effective as spacers in reducing the incidence of close passes and would also increase overall conspicuity, but it is pointed out that their cost and appearance may deter young people from using them.
(12) Department of Transport's minutes of evidence to the House of Commons Transport Committee Inquiry on Road Safety, 22 March 1983, HMSO, 1983, pages 21 and 22.
(13) Royal Society for the Prevention of Accidents minutes of evidence to the House of Commons Transport Committee Inquiry on Road Safety, 19 April 1983, HMSO, 1983, page 80.
(14) As ref. 12.

(15) The relevant paragraph from ref. 12. reads as follows:
'The need for pedal cycle training is, of course, important and the Department will continue to promote its benefits. However, the scope for reducing accidents through rider training alone is inevitably limited. Far greater casualty savings could be achieved in urban areas through the segregation of pedal cycle and other traffic. Though total segregation is impracticable in both planning and resource terms, it is particularly important to provide cycle facilities which enable cyclists to avoid heavily trafficked and potentially dangerous roads. The Secretary of State's Cycling Policy Statement, published in January 1982, provides the national policy framework for the provision of such improved facilities for cyclists. The Department has already agreed to fund 20 innovatory cycle schemes put forward by local authorities and is ready to consider support for others'

(16) Marie Bennett, Barbara A. Sanders, C.S. Downing, Evaluation of a cycling proficiency training course using two behaviour recording methods, TRRL Laboratory Report 890, 1979, page 14 and elsewhere.
(17) Pat Wells, C.S. Downing, Marie Bennett, Comparison of on-road and off-road cycle training for children, TRRL Laboratory Report 902, 1979, page 12 and elsewhere.
(18) Ibid., page 2.
(19) As ref. 16.
(20) As ref. 17.
(21) A. Risk and S. Raymond, Child Cyclists, Salford University, 1979.
(22) Barbara Preston, 'Child Cyclist Accidents and Cycling Proficiency Training'. Accident Analysis and Prevention, Volume 12, 1980, page 40 and elsewhere.
(23) Ibid., page 35.
(24) J.O. Darlington, Children and Cycling, The Effects of the National Proficiency Scheme in the County of Hereford and Worcester, December 1976, pages 11 and 12.
(25) The Hereford and Worcester study (ref. 24) involved distributing 2,000 questionnaires to parents of children who had passed the test and 2,000 to parents of children who had not been trained; 487 questionnaires were returned from the first group and 572 from the second. Four children from the first group and 14 from the second had been injured in a cycling accident in the year preceding the survey.

As a measure of the success of training, the first group should also have covered children who received training but failed the test, since there is evidence (ref. 28) that the accident rate among those who fail the test is high. The parents of the children who passed the test were asked only about the accidents which had occurred since that time: it would seem from the table in the report which compares the age of the children at the time of the survey with their age when they took the test that a significant number of the replies would not have been based on a full year's riding. Children who take the test are not a random selection of child cyclists: there may be factors other than the quality of training, such as parental concern, which explain both why some children receive training and why they are involved in fewer accidents. The low response rate creates large opportunities for bias.

(26) J.M. Sully, 'Child Cycling', Town and Country Planning, 1976, Vol. 44, pages 332-3. This article relates to school children in parts of Yorkshire. It is claimed that although about a quarter of the children over nine in Leeds, York and Huddersfield had taken the NCPS test, this group were involved in none of the accidents that occurred to child cyclists in those towns over a three-year period. However, the article gives no details of sources, definitions or statistical methods.

(27) P.W. Arnberg, E. Ohlsson, A. Westerberg, C.A. Ostrom, The ability of pre-school and school children to manoeuvre their bicycles, National Road and Traffic Research Institute, Linkoping 1974, mentioned in J.G. Avery and P.J. Avery, 'Scandinavian and Dutch lessons in childhood road traffic accident prevention', British Medical Journal Vol. 285, 1982.

(28) Barbara Preston, op.cit., page 35.

(29) Transport Supplementary Grant Submissions for 1977/78, D.Tp. Circular 125/75, Annex H.

(30) P. Trevelyan (speaker) and M. Heraty (reporter), 'Bicycles', Proceedings of the Institution of Civil Engineers, Part 1, 1975, pages 485-487.

(31) Transport Policy, A Consultation Document, HMSO, 1976, para. 11.3.

(32) Transport Policy, HMSO, June 1977, paras. 228 and 229,

(33) Cycling Policy, Statement by the Secretary of State for Transport, January 1982, para. 2.

(34) Various conversations with senior civil servants of the Department of Transport.

(35) Transport Supplementary Grant Submissions for 1979/80 D.Tp. Circular 3/78, para. 24.

(36) Transport Policies and Programme Submissions for the 1980/81 TSG Settlement, D.Tp. Circular 4/79, para. 21.

(37) Transport Policies and Programme Submissions for 1983/84, D.Tp. Circular 3/82, para. 12.

(38) Cycling Policy, op.cit., para. 7.

(39) House of Commons, Hansard, 16 November, 1982, column 125. But we understand from the Department of Transport (private communication of February 1984) that the last round of TPP submissions shows that 'almost all counties are providing, or considering the provision of, facilities to cyclists.

(40) Caren Levy, On Our Bikes, a survey of local authority cycle planning in Britain, Friends of the Earth, 1982, page 16.

(41) Private communication from the Department of Transport, March 1984.

(42) Road Accidents Great Britain 1980, Tables D,E,F. Road Accidents Great Britain 1981, page viii. For pedestrians, casualty figures are taken from Road Accidents Great Britain 1979, Table 4, and an estimate of distance walked has been made from Table 3.3 of National Travel Survey 1978/9 Report.

(43) Cycling Policy, op.cit., para. 6. See also Ways of helping cyclists in built-up areas, Local Transport Note 1/78, Department of Transport 1978, paras. 4.19 to 4.21.

(44) Mike Hudson, op.cit., page 31.

(45) Reported in ref. 30.

(46) Safety of Two-Wheelers, OECD, Paris, 1978, page 106.

(47) Mike Hudson, op.cit., page 9.

(48) Transport policy and the development of the transportation network in the Netherlands, Ministerie van Verkeer en Waterstaat, 1977 or 1978, page 3.

(49) Ibid., page 5.

(50) New Multi-Year Plan for Passenger Transport, Information sheet No. 20E, Ministerie van Verkeer en Waterstaat, April 1980, page 6.

(51) Ibid., page 8.

(52) H.J. Van Vulpen, Evaluation and Conclusions of the Cycleway Pilot Projects in the Netherlands, undated but not before 1980.

(53) The Delft Bikeway System, Public Works Department, Delft, 1975.

(54) Japanese Government White Paper on Transportation Safety, May 1982, page 9.

(55) Ibid., page 35.

(56) Ibid., page 81.

(57) Ibid., page 106.
(58) Ibid., page 150.
(59) Mike Hudson, op.cit., page 45.
(60) Amenagements existants en France destines aux deux-roues legers, Centre d'Etudes des Transports Urbains, May 1979.
(61) Figures provided by SWOV (the Dutch Institute for Road Safety Research).
(62) Derived from Road Accidents Great Britain 1980, Table D and Road Accidents Great Britain 1979, Tables 4 and 30.
(63) Japanese Government White Paper on Transportation Safety, op.cit., page 17.
(64) Michael Taylor, 'Pedestrians and Cyclists', Urban Transport and the Environment, OECD, Paris, 1979, Vol. 1, page 22.
(65) As ref. 30.
(66) J.A. Waldman, Cycling in Towns: A Quantitative Investigation, LTR1, Working Paper 3, Department of Transport, December 1977, page 13.
(67) Ways of helping cyclists in built-up areas, Local Transport Note 1/78, Department of Transport 1978, page 15.
(68) House of Commons, Hansard, 19 March 1981, Columns 173-4.
(69) Transport Supplementary Grant Submissions for 1978/79, D.Tp Circular 1/77, para. 18.
(70) Transport Policies and Programme Submissions for 1983-84, D.Tp Circular 3,82, para. 1.
(71) See ref. 4.
(72) Guidelines for Providing for the Cyclist. The Institution of Highways and Transportation, July 1983.
(73) Cycling: The Healthy Alternative, a digest of ten reports to the British Cycling Bureau, British Cycling Bureau, June 1978, page 17.
(74) Mike Hudson, op.cit., pages 27 to 31.
(75) Mike Hudson, Caren Levy, John Nicholson, Richard Macrory, Peter Snelson, Bicycle Planning, Policy and Practice, Architectural Press, 1982, page 35.
(76) The main reason given for doubting the impression given by the statistics is that if casualties are related to trips made or to time spent travelling, the casualty rates for cycling, do not appear so unfavourable, vis-a-vis those for other modes, as when casualties are related to distance. It is true that some types of journey, shopping journeys for example, would tend to become shorter if bicycles were used rather than cars, but that is not a sufficient reason to change the basis on which casualty rates are calculated. Although there are occasions when time-related rates would be more appropriate than distance-related rates - for example if one were calcu-

lating the relative risks of spending a day's holiday in driving or in cycling through the countryside - they are very few. The very large degree of under-reporting of cycling casualties in the statistics is likely to compensate for any other biases.

Table V.1   Bicycle casualties and travel 1952-1982

		Casualties				Travel	
Year	Fatal	Seri-ous	Slight	All sever-ities	Index 1960= kms	Billion kms	Index 1960= 100
1952	743	10,526	35,975	47,244	99	23.0	190
1960	679	9,752	37,302	47,733	100	12.1	100
1962	583	8,461	31,624	40,668	85	9.3	77
1964	583	8,048	28,993	37,624	79	8.0	66
1966	514	6,705	22,930	30,149	63	6.3	52
1968	391	5,881	19,958	26,230	55	5.0	41
1970	373	5,253	17,480	23,106	48	4.3	36
1972	367	5,034	16,581	21,982	46	4.2	35
1974	281	4,163	14,441	18,885	40	3.8	31
1976	300	4,631	18,296	23,227	49	4.4	36
1978	316	4,432	17,453	22,201	47	4.3	36
1980	302	5,234	19,252	24,788	52	4.6	38
1981	310	5,194	19,802	25,306	53	4.8	39
1982	294	5,673	22,170	28,137	59	5.5	45

Sources: Annual editions of Road Accidents Great Britain, Transport Statistics Great Britain, and Highway Statistics

Table V.2   Casualty rates for cyclists per 100 million vehicle kilometres travelled, 1979

| Age of cyclist | Severity of casualty | | All casualties |
	Fatal	Fatal and serious	
0-9	13	500	2,300
10-14	11	190	890
15-19	4	110	540
20-29	5	96	490
30-39	2	58	310
40-49	4	63	270
50-59	7	67	240
60 and over	21	140	390
All ages	7	120	540

Note: The National Travel Survey, which is the source of the travel information on which these rates are based, does not cover that part of children's cycling which consists of riding around or playing, which may be quite a substantial amount of their travel as compared with purposeful trips. Hence, the casualty rates shown for the younger age groups must be somewhat overstated.

Source: Road Accidents Great Britain 1980, Table D

Table V.3 Casualties in 1981 in accidents involving bicycles, analysed by severity and by class of road user

Class of road user	Fatal		Serious		Slight		All casualties	
	No.	%	No.	%	No.	%	No.	%
Cyclist	310	94	5194	91	19,802	91	25,306	91
Pedestrian hit by bicycle	7	2	217	4	524	2	748	3
Other pedestrian	2	1	16	*	63	*	81	*
Rider or passenger of 2-wheeled motor vehicle	6	2	188	3	753	3	947	3
All others	5	2	94	2	613	3	712	3
All road users	330	100	5709	100	21,755	100	27,794	100

* less than 0.5 per cent

Source: Department of Transport, special tabulations of the 1981 road accident statistics

154

Table V.4   Fatal and serious casualties for cyclists, car drivers and pedestrians per 100 million kilometres travelled, 1979

Age	Pedestrians	Cyclists	Car drivers	
			Men	Women
20-24	64	{	18	16
25-29	42	{ 96	10	11
30-39	43	58	6	8
40-49	48	63	5	7
50-59	60	67	5	9
60-70	75	(	(	(
70-80	147	(140	(10	(18
80 and over	360	(	(	(

Note: The rate for pedestrians in the 20 to 24 age group is estimated from the rates shown in the source for each of the five ages 20, 21, 22, 23, 24.

Source: Road Accidents Great Britain 1980, pages xiv, xv, xvi.

Table V.5   Trends in cycling in Sweden, 1970-1982

Year	Cycle travel, 100m. kms	Cycle fatalities	
		number	per 100m. kms
1970	15	141	9.4
1971	14	118	8.4
1972	13	138	10.6
1973	12	144	12.0
1974	14	139	9.9
1975	13	147	11.3
1976	14	127	9.1
1977	14	121	8.6
1978	15	114	7.6
1979	16	94	5.9
1980	18	112	6.2
1981	19	76	4.0
1982	20	82	4.1

Sources: Travel statistics, Swedish Transport Commission. Accident statistics, National Swedish Road and Traffic Research Institute.

VI TRANSPORT POLICY AND THE VOLUME AND PATTERN OF ROAD TRAFFIC

The road safety task is usually thought of as how to reduce the number and severity of accidents associated with a certain volume and pattern of traffic. It is accepted that the routes that drivers choose can be influenced in the interests of road safety, either by means of traffic management(1) or by building new roads, but otherwise the traffic situation is implicitly regarded as given. Thus the introduction to the 1967 White Paper Road Safety - A Fresh Approach, which is in general a very forceful document, after painting an alarming picture of what accidents could be expected if the prevailing trends continued, made the following statement(2).

> 'That is the outlook if we do nothing about it. But we know too, that accident rates can be lowered and that the consequences of accidents can be made less severe. We must keep the totals down and work ceaselessly in the face of a rapid and continuing growth in the use of vehicles.'

Logically, however, it is clear that, desirable as it is to reduce the accident and casualty rates associated with each mode of travel, the number of accidents would also fall if journeys were shortened or if there were some change from the less safe to safer means of travel. These ways of tackling the accident problem are especially attractive since, provided suitable means were employed, they should bring benefits of other kinds as well, in environment, conservation and transport efficiency.

It is not possible to treat this subject fully in this report, since the whole of transport policy is at issue. Nevertheless, the road safety effort must be directed in a way which takes account

156

not only of measures which reduce accident rates but of those which reduce traffic volumes, either in total or of the more dangerous modes. This chapter therefore looks briefly at some aspects of policy concerning buses, railways and subsidised car use. The next chapter considers the way in which land-use and locational planning can reduce the need for travel and encourage the use of safer modes.

Buses

It was seen in Chapter V, page 138, that the fatal and serious casualty rate for bus and coach passengers is less than a quarter of those for car passengers and drivers and a minute fraction of those for pedestrians, cyclists and motorcyclists. Aggregate rates, which gloss over important differences in operating conditions and user characteristics, can be very misleading; nevertheless, with differences as large as these it is safe to conclude that buses and coaches are the safest form of road travel. It does not follow that a switch to buses from other modes, or at least from cars, would always bring down accident numbers, since a bus journey more often involves a walk at one or both ends than a car journey, and walking is relatively dangerous. Nevertheless, there must be many occasions when that would not be a significant consideration; also, some means of encouraging bus travel, for example by excluding cars and motorcycles from a town centre, would simultaneously make walking safer as well.

The decline in bus travel is one of the major trends in personal travel over the last thirty years. In 1982, travel by bus and coach, in passenger kilometres, was half what it had been in 1952(3). But this statistic, since it includes contract and private hire coaches, which have been a growing market, masks the extent of the decline of local stage services. The number of journeys made by stage services fell by 30 per cent in the decade 1972 to 1982(4). The mechanism of this decline is also familiar. Increased wealth leads to increasing car ownership and to a switch from bus to car; the resulting loss of revenue leads to a reduction of services and/or to an increase in fares, both of which lead to a further decline in custom. The congestion caused by increasing car use adds a further twist to this vicious spiral of decline, both by increasing the operator's costs, forcing him once more either to withdraw services or to put up fares; and by making the services slower and less reliable, and therefore less attractive to passengers.

There is nothing inevitable about this process. A comparative study by the TRRL of urban public transport in 15

157

OECD countries between 1965 and 1977 showed that the fall in the number of journeys had been greatest in the UK; in five countries (France, the Netherlands, Canada, Finland, Sweden) there had been substantial increases in the use of urban public transport and in four others use had remained stable(5). The particularly sharp decline in Britain may be partly explained by the fact that Britain started from an exceptionally high base, in the form of unusually well developed and used local public transport services, but that could not account for the difference between a falling and a rising market.

One way to intervene in the vicious spiral of decline is to subsidise. In all but one (Finland) of the five countries where the use of urban public transport has been growing, subsidies are much higher than in Britain(6). Within Britain, one county, South Yorkshire, has adopted a policy of substantial subsidies. In 1975-76 bus fares were frozen at the existing level; as a result of inflation, they had fallen by 55 per cent in real terms by 1981-82. The number of bus passengers rose by three per cent in South Yorkshire over this six-year period, whereas elsewhere in the country it fell by 23 per cent(7). The effect on accidents has not been estimated, but was presumably beneficial: it was seen in Chapter II that motorcycle use apparently declined in South Yorkshire among the particularly vulnerable 16-24 age group, whose use of the bus increased(8).

In London, fares were reduced by 32 per cent in October 1981, in accordance with the election manifesto of the Labour Party, which gained control of the GLC in the spring of that year, and were raised again in March 1982 following a judgement in the House of Lords that the amount of subsidy involved was illegal. The low fares had a significant effect on travel patterns in London and a study was undertaken at University College, London, to estimate the effect on accidents of reverting to higher fares. It was estimated that in the following year casualties were between seven and eleven per cent higher than they would have been if the low fares had continued. The best estimate was nearer the higher than the lower figure and amounted in absolute terms to some 6,000 casualties, of which over 600 were fatal or serious, with a cost to the community in the order of £20 million(9). These figures are based on the ordinary accident records, without any adjustments for under-reporting, and on the Department of Transport's money values for casualties of each degree which, for the reasons given in Chapter I, err substantially on the low side.

Although subsidies to local public transport are lower in Britain than in many other countries, they have grown in recent years. The 1968 Transport Act empowered central government, but not local authorities, to make grants for the purchase of new buses and also brought in a rebate on fuel duty. It enabled either central government or local authorities to make grants of a capital nature 'for the provision, improvement or development of facilities for public passenger transport in Great Britain', and also empowered local authorities to subsidise rural bus services which were not commercially viable. The 1972 Local Government Act, which came into force in 1974, enabled county and district councils to subsidise current as well as capital expenditure, in towns as well as the country, and profitable as well as unprofitable services(10). Subsidies on current account are now a significant element in local authorities' spending, amounting in 1982/83 to some 22 per cent of their transport expenditure(11).

The original justification of the new bus grant was to encourage operators to equip themselves with one-man buses, which were seen as part of the solution to the economics of bus operation(12). Other subsidies have never been given a very clear rationale, but in general terms their purpose was seen as social: to provide a minimum transport service to people who would otherwise suffer deprivation. The attitude of local authorities to subsidies has varied; that of central government has been reluctant, particularly towards subsidies on current account which have been seen as wasteful and a discouragement to efficiency in management. The South Yorkshire County Council's policy of freezing fares led to the witholding by the Secretary of State (then Mr. Rodgers) of some Transport Supplementary Grant and, as has been seen, the GLC's policy of cheap fares was found to be illegal.

Subsidies can in fact have an economic as well as a social justification. The use of public transport imposes less costs, per passenger kilometre, on the community, than does the use of cars and motorcycles. This is true not only of accidents and congestion, but also, at least when bus design is suitable, of noise and fumes. Thus if subsidies to buses succeed in diverting travel from these modes they bring an economic benefit. Although this point follows from orthodox economic theory, and has been pointed out by the environmental movement at least since 1974(13), it has not until now been acknowledged by the Department of Transport, which presumably partly accounts for the grudging official attitude. Only very recently have official attempts been made to calculate the benefit from subsidies. Although the benefits to road users that have been considered so far consist only of time savings (it is planned to extend the analysis to include accidents, but not, apparently, environmental effects), it has been shown that subsidies can bring substantial benefits when used to keep down fares, as well as when used for the purpose, which has always been recognised as respectable, of maintaining a more extensive service than can be supported from fare revenue alone. The only use that is officially envisaged for the model which has been developed to make these calculations is to determine how best to spend a given amount of subsidy, not to help to decide what the amount should be(14). In fact, however, although the model cannot help in deciding how much to spend on transport vis-a-vis other services, it would be quite appropriate to use it to help allocate a transport budget between subsidies and other items of maintenance or investment.

Another way to encourage bus travel is to improve operating conditions. Two broad ways of doing so are possible, which are not mutually exclusive. One is by bus priority measures, which protect buses from general congestion and from impediments such as parked cars. The other is by traffic restraint to enable buses, in common with the rest of the remaining traffic, to move freely.

The merits of bus priorities have been recognised since the late 1960s, when the Ministry of Transport was trying to persuade local authorities, at that time mostly reluctant, to introduce them. The argument used was a simple one: in terms of passengers carried, buses utilise road space better than cars. Since that time the principle has become generally accepted and more sophisticated methods of appraising bus priority schemes, by means of cost-benefit analysis, have been developed by the TRRL(15). These methods are suitable only for assessing the effects of individual bus priority schemes taken separately, and perhaps even then do not do justice to the benefits of increased reliability both to passengers, especially on journeys where the precise time of arrival is important, and to operators. In addition, there appears to be a presupposition that bus priority schemes necessarily slow down other vehicles, whereas it has been shown in London that the disentangling of different types of vehicle can sometimes help them all(16).

The benefits that would arise from a comprehensive system of priority routes in a town are greater than the sum of the benefits from individual priority schemes considered separately. Among other things, it is now established that there is a link between the availability and quality of public transport and the level of car ownership(17, 18). The people who would be saved the expense and trouble of acquiring and running a car which they would rather be without would not be the only beneficiaries. Everyone else would gain from the reduction in congestion, pollution and accidents; public transport generally, long-distance as well as local, would have a larger customer base. (These considerations should also be taken into account in assessing the benefits of subsidies.) But although the environmental movement has advocated comprehensive bus priority networks since at least 1971(19), bus priority schemes are still limited and fragmentary.

Parking control is a commonly practised and a potentially flexible method of traffic restraint. When parking meters were first introduced into Britain, in London in 1958, they were seen as a means of coping with very local problems of congestion and safety. The importance of parking control as an instrument of transport policy generally was gradually realised. A limitation of parking control, which could be crucial in some places, especially in large cities, is that it does not affect through traffic, which may indeed increase to take advantage of the road space vacated by the stopping traffic on which parking controls do impinge(20). There are many towns where that would not be a significant problem but where parking controls cannot be effectively applied because most drivers make use of private off-street parking spaces over which the local authority has no control In the mid-1970s, the Department of Transport worked on legislation to allow such spaces to be brought under control(21, 22) but the plans were dropped, apparently because of insufficient interest from local authorities(23).

Another method of selective restraint is to limit the right to take a motor vehicle, or a motor vehicle of a given type, into a certain area. In some Italian cities the right to take a car into the centre is limited to residents, or sometimes to residents and certain categories of worker, and this right may itself be conditional upon the possession of an off-street parking place(24). Schemes for restraining entry by car into central London, either by price or by other means, have often been considered, but have been turned down because it was thought that they would be either inequitable or very cumbersome to administer(25).

At least since the 1950s(26), some transport economists have advocated road-use pricing as a means of control. Drivers would pay by the mile for the use of their vehicles; the charge would vary according to the area of use, with the highest charges in city centres, and by time of day. This idea was not originally advocated as a means of bringing about improvements in safety or the environment, nor even particularly in order to favour high-capacity vehicles such as buses over cars, although that point was recognised, but as a way of discouraging the marginal car user and giving priority to people whose need to use a car was more urgent. Objections have been raised partly on grounds of equity, partly on grounds of the cost and perhaps the feasibility of devising a cheap, reliable and cheat-proof system of metering.

Another, though less selective and less powerful, way of limiting vehicle mileage would be by changing the balance of taxation away from Vehicle Excise Duty towards fuel taxes. Plans to do so were well advanced in the late 1970s, but were rejected at a political level on the grounds of alleged hardship to people living in the country dependent on cars. This was, however, a rather implausible objection, since the financial position of people living in the country who drove less than some 10,000 miles a year would have improved as a result of the change(27). Another objection traditionally given to such a change in taxation is that British car manufacturers would lose sales to their foreign competition whose cars use less petrol. But with the new models such as the BL Metro this should no longer apply(28).

Managing the roads in favour of buses has many advantages over subsidising public transport. Better operating conditions would improve bus speeds and reliability and would allow the same service to be supplied with fewer vehicles. This increase in productivity could be used, like subsidies, either to increase the service or to hold down fares. But speed and reliability are also qualities of a bus service which travellers value highly in their own right. It is unlikely that any policy of subsidisation, even free fares, would divert enough travel from cars to create the same operating conditions that a policy of managing the roads in favour of buses would provide. Thus although subsidies are not a substitute for management, management can be a substitute for them. Also management involves much less public expenditure.

Especially in view of this last advantage, one would have expected a great deal of official attention to have been given to selective traffic managment and restraint in the last few years, but in fact interest has declined in Britain since the late 1970s. The explanation of this may be partly that restraint is equated with a restriction on freedom, although the naive view that freedom consists of an absence of rules, whereas in reality it depends on an appropriate framework of rules, has been criticised by environmentalists for many years(29, 30). Possibly the concept of public transport has also suffered from the reaction against public and toward private enterprise. However, as is discussed below, there is considerable room to increase the commercial element of public transport operations. In terms of making efficient use of road space and limiting accidents and other external costs, the case for preferential treatment for buses has nothing to do with public or private ownership, but only with the distinction between shared and individual means of transport.

162

It is less easy to compare British and foreign practice on traffic restraint than on subsidies. But the general impression is that the case for restraint as a positive instrument of urban policy was accepted earlier and more readily in many other developed countries than in Britain. An OECD conference in May 1975 on 'Better Towns with Less Traffic' perhaps marks the moment when restraint was established as an official doctrine. Since that time policy in other countries appear to have developed steadily in this respect, whereas in Britain it has lapsed.

It has been seen that one reason for a distrust of subsidies, especially revenue subsidies, has been the fear that they deprive management of the incentive to be efficient and lead to a poorly run operation. Inefficiency is a real problem, but its cause is not subsidy but monopoly. If there were a system of competition such that inefficient operators lost business, that would be a sufficient spur, even though only part of an undertaking's revenue came from fares and the rest from subsidy. One such system would be for operators to run services under contract to local authorities for a specified period. Contract management can apply to different sectors of large towns or to the entire bus system of smaller ones. In the USA, where the first such system started in 1962, there were by 1979 five companies supplying local public transport services on a contract basis, which between them ran 72 services(31). In France, the law making contract management possible was enacted in about 1970 and private companies started to operate four or five years later; by the end of the 1970s contract management was accepted in France as a well tried method of running local public transport services(32). In Oslo, 19 companies supply services under contract to the public transport authority(33). Although similar services have not developed in Britain, the Transport Act 1983 authorises Public Transport Executives in metropolitan counties to seek outsiders tenders for carrying out any of their activities and obliges them to seek such tenders if directed to do so by their Public Transport Authority.

Railways

Differences in definition complicate comparisons between road and rail safety. Global comparisons are in any case unhelpful, since rail cannot always replace road and tends to be a substitute for relatively safe road travel, e.g. motorway travel. Nevertheless it is clear that rail is safer by an order of magnitude than all forms of road transport other than bus or coach, and is probably safer even than motorway coaches which are the safest form of road passenger transport(34). Although the noise of railway operations

163

can be disturbing, rail causes fewer other external costs than road. To what extent are these advantages now taken into account in transport policy?

The best way to take them into account would be by regulating or taxing road transport in a way which would either reduce the external costs it causes, per vehicle mile driven, or would discourage its use in circumstances where the total costs involved, internal and external, exceeded the benefits. To set and enforce lower speed limits would discourage some road use and in doing so would bring about some transfer of traffic from road to rail, although the justification of lower speed limits does not depend on such a transfer. A switch in vehicle taxation from an annual tax to a mileage-related tax would have similar effects and, again, any transfer to rail could be regarded as a useful side-effect of a measure which could be justified independently. However, as has been seen, both these ideas have so far been rejected. Railways would also benefit from the abolition of subsidies to cars discussed below and from the more purposive land-use planning discussed in Chapter VII. These too are reforms which should be put in hand even if railways did not exist.

Unless and until road transport is taxed and regulated in a way which takes due account of external costs, there are strong economic grounds to subsidise railways, similar to those for subsidising buses, except that freight is also involved. The economic case for subsidising rail freight is, indeed, especially strong because of the external costs caused by lorries, not least in terms of safety. Table VI.1 shows the casualties arising from accidents involving heavy goods vehicles in 1982. Only 5.4 per cent of all casualties, but 14.7 per cent of fatalities, occurred in such accidents, which indicates that an accident is far more likely to prove fatal when a lorry is involved. The table also shows that it is the other party who is most often injured in an accident involving a lorry. This is true for all degrees of casualty, but most of all for fatalities; 92.3 per cent of people killed in fatal accidents involving lorries were other road users.

Although lorries cause great offence in other ways, especially by their noise, social surveys have established that the most resented nuisance is that caused to other road users. Thus in a large survey of the adult population of Great Britain carried out in 1979/80, 12 per cent claimed to be bothered 'very much or quite a lot' by nuisance from lorries when indoors at home, but 38 per cent were bothered to the same degree as car occupants or motor-cyclists(35). The base of the percentage includes people who did not live in car-owning households and were not motorcyclists.

Another question in the same survey showed that the nuisance caused by lorries to people out walking in their area is much more resented than the nuisance caused to them when at home and that the nuisance caused to people as car occupants or motorcyclists is more resented than that caused to them as pedestrians(36). Nuisance to pedestrians must include noise as well as danger, but the survey suggests that danger is very important; lorries were seen by slightly more people than cars as a source of pedestrian danger, notwithstanding the far greater number of cars on the road(37). The detailed list of problems caused to car drivers and motorcyclists shows that most are associated with danger; Table VII.2 illustrates this point. The survey did not inquire into cyclists' views on lorries, but it is a fair inference that if pedestrians, motorcyclists and car drivers find them a source of fear, then cyclists do as well.

The fear of lorries presumably gives rise to some distortion or suppression of travel and of other street activity, such as children's play, as described in Chapter I. But the fact that lorries worry car drivers and motorcyclists as well as pedestrians and cyclists suggests that they may distort travel behaviour in another way as well, by affecting drivers' choice of route. If some people deliberately avoid routes which are heavily used by lorries, such as motorways, this is likely to have an adverse effect on accidents because alternative routes will usually have a higher accident rate. In this way it is possible for lorry traffic to give rise to accidents other than those in which a lorry is involved.

Subsidies to rail freight would be well spent if they helped to avoid accidents, intimidation and other nuisance caused by lorries. Nevertheless, the official view, since it fails to recognise the economic but only the social case for transport subsidies, has been opposed to subsidies for freight(38). Fortunately, this hostile policy has been tempered by grants for private sidings where an environmental advantage is likely to arise.

The criteria used for investment appraisal systematically favour road against rail. Rail investment is usually assessed by the purely commercial criterion of the profitability of the railways, although wider criteria have been used on occasions(39). Road investment is assessed by means of a cost benefit formula. Commercial criteria take account of benefits to users only insofar as they are recaptured through the operator's charging system, but cost-benefit criteria take account of all benefits to users. The two criteria would coincide, in their treatment of users, only if the railways could charge each individual traveller the full amount which the improvement in question was worth to him, which is, of course, impossible. In addition, the road criteria take account of the relief which new roads bring to existing roads in reduced congestion, accidents and maintenance requirements, whereas the relief which rail improvements may bring to the road system is not allowed for. The road criteria do not, however, allow (although comprehensive cost-benefit criteria would) for any adverse effects which road building may have in drawing custom from other safer and otherwise socially more desirable modes or on the profitability of those operators. It may be rare for particular road improvements to have a significant impact on the use of rail, but clearly the road programme as a whole has a substantial effect.

These differences between road and rail investment criteria were discussed at length in <u>Changing Directions</u>, published in 1974, and again by the Leitch Committee in 1977. Both reports showed that the choice of criteria made a substantial difference to the calculation of benefit, and both recommended that cost-benefit methods should be used to appraise rail as well as road investment(40,41). In the meantime, the 1977 White Paper had also stressed the importance of using similar criteria to assess different kinds of transport investment(42). Nevertheless, these recommendations have not so far been taken up. Railway electrification was considered only on the basis of commercial criteria, and the Serpell Report, which was intended to be a long-term look at the future of the railways, also adopted a purely commercial point of view(43).

In December 1982, the Department of Transport announced that at the request and on behalf of the Standing Advisory Committee on Trunk Road Assessment (the successor to the Leitch Committee), a study, based on an actual case, was being commissioned on the feasibility of applying a cost-benefit appraisal to a rail improvement(44). We understand that the study is now complete although not published.

The treatment of the railways in Britain is markedly less favourable than in most comparable countries. A study of eleven European countries showed that only in Sweden did the railways receive less subsidy than in Britain(45). The use of cost-benefit criteria, or similarly generous methods, to appraise railway investment is widespread. Competition to the railways, both in the passenger and the freight markets, tends to be more tightly controlled: the number of licences issued may be limited and there may also be controls over fares, routes and timetables(46). Even apart from the unique system of company car tax concessions in Britain, which is discussed in the next section, taxes on the ownership and use of a car are lower in Britain than in any of the eleven countries covered except Sweden, and in some countries motorway tolls constitute further use-related charges(47).

Car subsidies

If car subsidies encourage the more widespread ownership and use of cars than would otherwise exist, they affect travel patterns generally and accidents in particular. There may be instances where subsidies have the effect that journeys which would otherwise have been made on two wheels are made by car, in which case the effect on accidents is favourable. But to the extent that car subsidies encourage the use of cars rather than public transport, or lead to more travel generally, the effect is adverse.

The subject of car taxation and subsidisation is complex and bedevilled by problems of definitions and data. It is possible to treat it only very briefly here.

In the sense that the use of a car imposes external costs, which are not covered by taxation, the rest of the community is subsidising car users. But the subsidies of a more familiar financial kind which motorists receive are also large. It is doubtful how far the various grants that the Government has made to ailing car manufacturers should be included: it could be argued that in their absence the ownership and use of cars would have been much the same but foreign manufacturers would have held a larger share of the market. But many car owners enjoy a much more direct financial benefit through the subsidisation of company cars.

The present position is that many companies provide cars to their employees purely as a benefit in kind, even when the car is not needed for business purposes. Employees earning less than £8,500 a year do not have to pay tax on this benefit; those earning more do have to pay tax, but the benefit is assessed for tax purposes at much less than its true worth. In 1979, the benefit as assessed for tax purposes was calculated to lie between 32 percent and 36 per cent of the true benefit, as estimated from AA figures(48). The taxable benefits have been raised since then, as part of a deliberate programme of fiscal reform, at a rate higher than general price increases; nevertheless, they are acknowledged by the Chancellor of the Exchequer to be substantially less than the true benefit. The present scale is shown in Table VI.3; further increases have been announced. The amounts shown in the table are adjusted downwards if the user of the car drives less than 2,500 miles and upwards if he drives over 18,000 miles on business in a year. From the point of view of transport policy and the distortion of travel patterns, these conditions are unfortunate, since they may encourage people to drive more just in order to cross the relevant threshold.

In addition to providing a car and paying for its upkeep, employers may also pay for the petrol and oil used in company cars on non-business travel. Until 1983, this benefit was not subject to any tax. It now is, but the amounts of taxable benefit are less than what the benefit is worth except for people whose annual mileage is substantially lower than the average. The annual taxable benefits for fuel depend only on the cubic capacity of the engine: 1300 cc or less, £325; 1301-1800 cc, £425; over 1800 cc, £650(49).

In 1979 the Inland Revenue estimated that there were some 1.5 to 2 million company cars, out of a total at that time of 14.5 million cars. The National Travel Surveys of 1975/76(50) and 1978/79(51) showed that some 30 per cent of cars in private households were subsidised in some way by the employer, although less than half of them had been bought by the employer. Many of these cars would have been owned anyway, or perhaps a different model would have been owned, but it has been estimated that if it were not for company cars the number of households owning more than one car would be reduced by at least 14 per cent(52). Company cars tend to be more used than others. In 1975/76, 20 per cent of the mileage performed by household cars was accounted for by cars wholly or partly bought by the employer of one of the household's members(53). Subsidised cars are used much more than non-subsidised cars not only on business but also for commuting(53,54).

These are not the only ways in which the present rules on company cars maintain artificially high levels of car ownership and use. Their indirect effect through the second-hand market may be even more important. According to the Inland Revenue, 70 per cent of the new cars registered in 1978 (1.1 million out of 1.6 million) were provided for the business sector(55). Other surveys suggest that this percentage may now be a little higher(56). Company cars are sold after a shorter period than new privately purchased cars. The number of cars, particularly of relatively new cars, on the second-hand market would be smaller, and prices correspondingly higher, if company cars were not provided as a benefit in kind.

The institution of company cars, if not unique to Britain, appears to be much more highly developed here than in other countries(56,57). In 1974, the report Changing Directions drew attention to the distorting effect on travel and recommended that the rules be overhauled in such a way that the benefit would be taxed at its true worth(58). The House of Commons Select Committee on Energy Conservation recommended in 1975 that the rules be tightened and better enforced(59); in addition to the effect of the present rules on car ownership and mileage, company cars tend to have larger engines and therefore a higher rate of fuel consumption than others(60). Even before issuing its consultative paper in 1979, the Inland Revenue had been pressing for changes on grounds both of fiscal equity and of energy conservation(61). Recently, academics(62) and interest groups(63) have become concerned because of the transport implications. It appears, however, that the Department of Transport does not see company cars as an issue in transport planning. They were not mentioned in the 1976 consultation document Transport Policy, nor in the 1977 White Paper of the same name, nor in more recent statements of transport policy.

Research on company cars now in progress at the TRRL(64) may perhaps lead to some revision of the National Road Traffic forecasts, on which the assessment of the road programme depends, but at present these forecasts implicitly assume no change in the rules on company cars, even though it is the Government's stated policy to reform them and changes are in fact being made.

People without company cars who use their own cars on their employer's business are usually reimbursed at rates which reflect the average rather than the marginal costs of motoring. This means that they have an incentive to use a car on business rather than public transport, for which the reimbursement would simply be the exact costs involved. Although unusually high mileage allowances are subject to tax(65), such an incentive is inherent in the standard rates which do not attract taxation. Relatively little attention has been paid to this point, although in a study for the Dutch Ministry of the Environment published in 1980 it was suggested that rates should be related to the marginal, or distance-related costs, with perhaps a small extra payment to compensate the driver for using his own equipment on company business(66). This report also mentions that some government departments in the Netherlands reimburse car users only to the extent of what the cost would have been if the journey had been made by public transport. A problem about making such a rule universal is that cost is not the only consideration: public transport may not always be convenient for business travel. Nevertheless, there must be many occasions when this rule could be applied.

Many employers provide their staff with free parking spaces at their place of work. This benefit is not normally taxable, although it can be valuable to the employee and may also affect how people travel to work and perhaps even where they live, with consequences for congestion, accidents and other social costs. Since the studies on the control of private non-residential parking in the 1970s that were mentioned above this topic has not attracted any attention. The rules on the provision of car parking in new housing development, discussed in Chapter VIII can also be thought of as a subsidy to car ownership.

Implications for the road safety effort

This chapter has been concerned with road safety not as a separate and specific problem but as an element in transport planning generally.

Over the last 25 years, it has gradually become clear that the vast growth of motorised travel, and especially travel by car, requires not merely new policies but a whole new approach. Roads can no longer be thought of as a facility which anyone can use indiscriminately, subject only to minimal conditions of eligibility, fitness to drive and driving behaviour, and which should be expanded indefinitely, regardless of expense, to keep pace with the growth of traffic. Public transport, whether by bus or rail, can no longer be treated as a quite separate field of activity, governed by different and much more stringent commercial criteria. In addition to considerations of safety and the environment, efficiency both in the use and the provision of transport facilities demands a more discriminate and integrated approach.

The magnitude of the changes in legal powers and the structure of responsibilities that were necessary in order to make a uniform approach possible should not be underestimated, nor should the progress that has been made. Twenty years ago it was not even possible, except in very special circumstances, to reserve any roads for particular types of vehicle, to subsidise a bus system or to control lorry routes. Nevertheless, progress has been agonisingly slow and has slowed down further in recent years. The 1977 White Paper recognised the need for an integrated approach to transport planning and for common investment criteria, and stated that '... we should aim to decrease our absolute dependence on transport and the length and number of some of our journeys; and to plan more consciously for those who walk as well as those who use mechanised transport'(67). But this has not been followed up, and in some respects understanding of the problems, and of their interconnections, seems to have slipped. The British experience also appears to be in contrast with that of many other countries, including some of our near neighbours in Europe, where innovation to redress the more perverse tendencies inherent in an unco-ordinated transport system has continued.

Some of the reasons for this are embedded deeply in the British governmental system. For example, the unusual, if not unique, degree of central control over local authorities may have inhibited bold experiments of traffic restraint as found in a highly decentralised country such as Italy. The constant re-shuffling of Ministers - there have been eight Ministers or Secretaries of State for Transport since 1970, and junior ministers have changed equally rapidly - militates against continuity and means that Ministers cannot possibly give the reflection to the problems that they deserve.

Institutional weaknesses of a kind more specific to transport, and one hopes, easier to correct than these, also help to account for the continuing imbalance in transport policy. Over the years the bus industry has done little to press the tremendously strong social and economic arguments for subsidising buses and giving them priority in traffic; the burden of making out the case has been left to environmental groups and independent researchers. This is partly because of the difficulty that has been experienced in forming a body that could speak for the industry as a whole. That difficulty has now been resolved with the foundation of the Bus and Coach Council in 1982, replacing the former Confederation of British Road Passenger Transport; the launching of an energetic campaign in the same year centred on the publication The Future of the Bus gives hope that the case for the bus will be more fully presented in future. The railways have not had the same difficulty in finding a common voice, but until recently relationships with the Department of Transport, both at political and working level, were marked by mutual reserve and suspicion; one of Sir Peter Parker's achievements as chairman was to improve this relationship. Public transport passengers have been poorly represented, and indeed the whole machinery of representation has been systematically weak. The weaknesses are so clear, and have been pointed out so many times over the years, for example by the Consumer Council in 1968(68), the Independent Commission on Transport in 1974(69) and the National Consumer Council in 1976(70), as well as by the Central Transport Consultative Committee itself(71), without any fundamental reforms being undertaken, that it must be concluded that the Department of Transport prefers to deal with weak consumer bodies. Environmental organisations and bodies representing pedestrians and cyclists have for the most part backed their strong case with good arguments, but have not succeeded in making much impression. One reason is that the Department of Transport's consultation procedure appears not to be completely genuine, in the sense that action does not follow from good arguments presented in response to requests for views, and promised reforms in the procedure have not materialised(72).

An important reason why pressure from outside for change has been so ineffectual, and why it is necessary in the first place, has been an imbalance in the Department of Transport's responsibilities. It has a direct responsibility and interest in the trunk road programme, but only an indirect responsibility for other equally significant, and sometimes competing, features of transport policy. The responsibility for formulating common criteria for road and rail investment clearly rests with the Department of Transport; it is difficult to believe that it would not have been discharged long since if the Department stood in the same relation both to roads and to railways. Local authorities have had powers to subsidise buses since 1974. If they had been left free to exercise these powers, without central intervention, that might explain the absence until very recently of any attempt by the Department to formulate economic criteria for evaluating bus subsidies. Even then, however, it would have been appropriate for the Department to have studied the question of subsidies, so that it could issue advice on them just as it now advises on points of road design, signs, criteria for pedestrian crossings etc. But since in fact the Department immediately stepped in to stipulate the total amount of subsidy to buses, for the country as a whole, that would be acceptable, there was a clear need for it to develop rational criteria(73). The Department did indeed work very hard to replace Vehicle Excise Duty by fuel duty, for reasons which included the reduction of road vehicle mileage and some improvement in the competitive position of public transport, but has taken no part in the campaign to end concessions to company cars, the perverse effect of which is probably much greater.

In Chapter III, it was argued that the Department's responsibilities for trunk roads distorted local transport planning. An equally powerful reason for transferring them is that they have also stunted the development of national transport policy, to the detriment of safety as of other things.

References
(1)   See Urban Safety Project, TRRL Leaflet, LF 938, December 1982, for a description of a major new demonstration project, involving five towns, on the re-routeing of traffic to save accidents.
(2)   Road Safety - A Fresh Approach. Cmnd. 3339, HMSO, 1967, para. 5.

(3)   Transport Statistics Great Britain, 1972-1982, Table 1.1.
(4)   Ibid., Table 2.10.
(5)   P. H. Bly, F.V. Webster and Susan Pounds, Subsidisation of urban public transport, TRRL Supplementary Report 541, 1980, page 19 and Figure 5.
(6)   Ibid., page 17.
(7)   Subsidised Public Transport and the Demand for Travel, The South Yorkshire Example, Summary, Transport Studies Unit, Oxford University, February 1983, page 2.
(8)   Ibid., page 8.
(9)   Report by the Controller of Transportation and Development to the Transport Committee of the GLC, Item T.937, 12 October 1983.
(10) Changing Directions, the Independent Commission on Transport, Coronet Books, 1974, paras. 6.36 to 6.45.
(11) Transport Statistics Great Britain 1971-81, Table 1.18.
(12) Changing Directions, op.cit., para. 6.43.
(13) Ibid., paras. 6.31, 6.41.
(14) Department of Transport's Minutes of Evidence to the House of Commons Transport Committee on Bus Subsidy Policy, 20 April 1983, page 73, paras. 18 to 20.
(15) Bus Priority Systems, NATO Committee on the Challenges of Modern Society, CCMS Report No. 45, TRRL 1976, especially section 16.
(16) Review of Bus Lanes, Report by the Director of Planning and Transportation to the Transport Committee of the GLC, TP950, 15 October, 1974.
(17) For a study covering the New York region, see Boris S. Pushkarev and Jeffrey M. Zupan, Public Transportation and Land Use Policy, Indiana University Press, 1977.
(18) J. J. Bates and M. Roberts, The Interrelationship of Car Ownership and Public Transport, paper given to the PTRC Summer Annual Meeting, 1979.
(19) Transport Strategy in London, London Amenity and Transport Association and London Motorway Action Group, 1971, paras. 8.3.10, 8.4.18 and 8.4.19.
(20) A. D. May, 'Supplementary Licensing: an Evaluation', Greater London Intelligence Quarterly, No. 30, GLC, March 1975.
(21) Consultation document, The Control of Private Non-Residential Parking, Department of Transport, 1976.
(22) Consultation document, Additional Powers for Local Authorities to Control Off-Street Parking, Department of Transport, 1977.

(23) M. E. Beesley, Influence of Measures Designed to Restrict the Use of Certain Transport Modes, Paper for the European Conference of Ministers of Transport, September 1978.

(24) S. P. C. Plowden, 'Transport Efficiency and the Urban Environment', Transport Reviews, Vol. 3, No. 4, 1983, page 386.

(25) D. Bayliss, D. Blide, T. May, T. Miyazaki, 'London', Managing Transport, OECD, 1979.

(26) M. E. Beesley and G. J. Roth, 'Restraint of Traffic in Congested Areas', Town Planning Review, Vol. XXXIII No. 3, October 1962. This article contains references to a number of earlier studies.

(27) The Future of Vehicle Excise Duty, Department of Transport, HMSO, November 1978.

(28) Sir Geoffrey Howe's budget statement as reported in The Times, 11 April, 1981.

(29) Stephen Plowden, Towns Against Traffic, Andre Deutsch, 1972, Chapter 2.

(30) Changing Directions, op.cit., paras. 6.19 to 6.21.

(31) T. Crosby, 'Contract management - the way to go?'. Mass Transit, August 1979.

(32) S.P.C. Plowden, op.cit., page 394.

(33) Ibid., page 393.

(34) Road Accidents Great Britain 1982, Section 10.

(35) C.J. Baughan, B. Hedges, J. Field, A national survey of lorry nuisance, TRRL Supplementary Report 774, 1983, Tables 5 and 6.

(36) Ibid., Table 8.

(37) Ibid., Table 7.

(38) White Paper Transport Policy, HMSO 1977, see especially paras. 52 and 56.

(39) Sir George Leitch (Chairman), Report of the Advisory Committee on Trunk Road Assessment, HMSO, 1977, paras. 25.16 to 25.19.

(40) Changing Directions, op.cit., especially paras. 7.23, 7.64.

(41) Report of the Advisory Committee on Trunk Road Assessment, op.cit., paras. 25.20 to 25.26, 27.11, 27.12.

(42) Transport Policy, op.cit., para. 66.

(43) Sir David Serpell, KCB, CMG, OBE, et al. Railway Finances, Department of Transport, HMSO, 1983. See especially para. 5 of the Introduction '... our review has been concerned with the railway's finances, not transport policy'.

(44) SACTRA study of methods of road and rail investment appraisal, D.Tp, Press Notice No. 450, 20 December 1982.

(45) A Comparative Study of European Rail Performance, Institute for Transport Studies at Leeds University and British Railways Board, December 1979, Table 5.6.

(46) Ibid., Appendix 4.

(47) Ibid., Table 4.5.

(48) The Taxation of Cars and Petrol as Benefits in Kind, Inland Revenue, August 1979.

(49) Communication with the Inland Revenue.

(50) Stephen Plowden, Taming Traffic, Andre Deutsch, 1980, page 73.

(51) Mayer Hillman and Anne Whalley, Energy and personal travel, obstacles to conservation, PSI, 1983, page 191.

(52) Ibid., page 197 quoting a memorandum by J. J. Bates on the Inland Revenue's 1979 consultative paper.

(53) Stephen Plowden, op.cit., page 74.

(54) Mayer Hillman and Anne Whalley, op.cit., page 199.

(55) As ref. 48.

(56) Mayer Hillman and Anne Whalley, op.cit., page 188.

(57) The Taxation of Cars and Petrol as Benefits in Kind, op.cit.

(58) Changing Directions, op.cit., para. 6.47.

(59) Mayer Hillman and Anne Whalley, op.cit., page 185.

(60) Ibid., page 195.

(61) As ref. 48.

(62) For example, M. Dix and R. Pollard, 'Company financed motoring and its effects on household car use', Traffic Engineering and Control, November 1980 and Stephen Potter 'State subsidies and the corporate motorist', Modern Railways, November 1983.

(63) At the time of writing, both the British Railways Board and the London Amenity and Transport Association have commissioned studies on company cars.

(64) Mentioned in John Tanner, 'Traffic Forecasting', Transport Statistics Conference, The Chartered Institute of Transport and the Standing Committee of Statistics Users, November 1983.

(65) As ref. 49.

(66) S.P.C. Plowden, op.cit., page 372.

(67) Transport Policy, op.cit., para. 35.

(68) Consumer Consultative Machinery in the Nationalised Industries, The Consumer Council, HMSO 1968, especially page 50.

(69) Changing Directions, op.cit., paras. 6.9 to 6.12 and page 264.

(70) Consumers and the Nationalised Industries, Report by the National Consumer Council to the Secretary of State for

Prices and Consumer Protection, National Consumer Council Report No.1, HMSO, July 1976.

(71) Central Transport Consultative Committee Annual Report for 1972, HMSO 1973.

(72) In 1978, the London Amenity and Transport Association sought a meeting with the Parliamentary Under-Secretary of State for Transport, then Mr. John Horam, about the treatment of replies to consultation. LATA was concerned that suggestions it had made in its own replies had not been taken up, but neither had there been any answer from the Department giving reasons for not doing so. LATA requested that in future either suggestions should be adopted or reasons for refusal should be stated. This request was accepted by Mr. Horam but the Department's practice has not changed accordingly.

(73) Rate Fund Expenditure and Rate Calls in 1975-76, Department of the Environment Circular 171/74. Paragraph 25 states that 'the Government's aim is that bus operations in general should move much closer towards a position of commercial viability'. It was accepted that since bus operating costs had risen substantially, fares would have to rise by at least as much. By introducing a constraint on the total amount which local authorities collectively could spend on bus support, the circular also dealt a blow to the principle of integrated transport planning and budget allocation at the local level, since there is no way, unless the national total is divided between local authorities at the outset, whereby a particular local authority can tell whether its own subsidy plans would lead to an over-spend nationally.

Table VI.1   Casualties in accidents involving heavy goods
              vehicles in 1982

	Severity of casualty			
	Fatal	Serious	Slight	All casualties
1. Casualties in all road accidents	5,934	79,739	248,623	334,296
2. Casualties in accidents involving a heavy goods vehicle	875	4,816	12,426	18,117
3. (2) as per cent of (1)	14.7	6.0	5.0	5.4
4. Casualties to people other than their occupants in accidents involving a heavy goods vehicle	808	4137	10,160	15,105
5. (4) as per cent of (2)	92.3	85.9	81.8	83.4

Note: The definition 'heavy goods vehicle' in the accident
         statistics is a goods vehicle of over $1\frac{1}{2}$ tons unladen
         weight.
Source: Road Accidents Great Britain 1982, Tables 5 and 24.

Table VI.2   Problems caused by lorries to car drivers and motorcyclists

Unit: per cent of car drivers and motorcyclists

	Ever bothered by this problem	Found this to be the worst problem of lorries
Spray from lorry tyres in wet weather	82	31
Lorries driving too fast	75	18
A strong wind or draught as you pass a lorry or it passes you	75	9
Smoke or fumes from lorries	64	9
Lorries blocking roads when turning or when they are parked	63	6
Not being able to overtake a lorry	57	9
Noise from lorries	29	1
Other problems	30	9
No problems	3	N.A.

Source: C.J. Baughan, B. Hedges, J. Field, A national survey of lorry nuisance, TRRL Supplementary Report 774, 1983, Table 11.

Table VI.3   The benefit attributed to the holder of a company car as assessed for income tax purposes in the tax year 1983/84

Original market value of the car and engine size	Taxable benefit (£)
£14,000 or less	
Engine size: 1300 cc or less	325
1301 to 1800 cc	425
Over 1800 cc	650
£14,000 to £21,000	950
Over £21,000	1500

Source: Inland Revenue

VII   LAND-USE AND LOCATIONAL PLANNING

The connection between land use and transport is one of the most familiar ideas in transport planning.   Nevertheless, transport planners tend to think of the land-use pattern as something that they have to know about in order to predict travel patterns, rather than as something they can use and change in order to help solve transport problems, including road safety. One reason is that land use is identified with the basic layout of a town, which in existing settlements is thought to change only very slowly unless a very drastic and expensive intervention is contemplated. This attitude is illustrated by the following two quotations, the first from a report published by the County Surveyors' Society in 1978, dealing with transport generally, and the second from a report by the TRRL published in 1974, concerned with urban freight.

> 'Although land use can be planned to minimise some journeys, the real possibilities for changing travel patterns by this means are limited in the next twenty years, particularly in conurbations'(1).

> 'A third possible solution would lie in the redesign of urban areas in such a way that the operation of goods vehicles did not create environmental costs or congestion. This solution was favoured in the Buchanan Report for urban traffic in general.   However, comprehensive rebuilding of urban areas to segregate traffic from other land use functions can only be considered as a long-term solution, since there are prohibitive costs involved. Hence, less grandiose improvements to the urban road system must be considered'(2).

The pace of change
In fact, even the pattern of settlement can change quite fast. Between 1971 and 1981, the population of the principal metropolitan cities in England and Wales fell by 12 per cent and that of inner London by 18 per cent. Over the same period, the population of rural areas as a whole rose by 10 per cent, and that of the rural areas at the fringes of large cities by 16 per cent(3). Nor should the land-use pattern be thought of only in terms of broad settlement patterns. The number, size and location of facilities have an important influence on lengths of journey and means of transport. Table VII.1 shows the decline in the number of shops, especially food shops, in Great Britain between 1961 and 1971. Although exactly comparable figures are not available for more recent years, the decline continued even faster in the 1970s: by 1980 the number of retail outlets in the United Kingdom had fallen by more than 30 per cent as compared with 1971(4). It is not surprising that in the six years between 1972/73 and 1978/79, the average length of shopping journey increased from 3.9 to 4.5 kilometres and the proportion of shopping journeys made by car from 27 per cent to 32 per cent(5). The same tendency for the size of establishments to increase while their number decreases has affected other facilities such as schools, hospitals and doctors' practices(6), and has presumably had a similar effect in increasing journey lengths.

Within any town structure, as defined by size, density and the number and location of dwellings and facilities, the pattern of journeys is also affected by the locational decisions of the individual citizens. Any individual person may take such a decision only rarely, but there is a steady stream of them being taken the whole time. Thus, some 10 per cent of adults change house each year and about the same number change jobs(7); the number changing jobs was higher but has declined with rising unemployment. Clearly, the decisions taken at such moments affect subsequent journey lengths and means of travel.

Objectives and means of influence
A primary aim of planning should be to facilitate and encourage short journeys. To the traveller himself, a short journey is as valuable as a long one provided that it satisfies his journey purpose equally well; indeed, if it saves him time, trouble or expense, a short journey is preferable. To avoid accidents and other external costs of transport, the shorter the journey the better. This would clearly be true even if the length of the journey did not affect the choice of mode, but in addition, the shorter the journey the more

180

likely it is to be made by non-motorised means, which are the least polluting and in the right conditions - though as has been seen not always at present - should also be the safest. This is shown in Table VII.2, which also suggests that the competitive position of the bus vis-a-vis the car declines for journeys of over three miles in length.

Tables VII.3 and VII.4 show the relationships between residential density and lengths of journey and modes of transport. At higher densities, journeys are shorter and are more often made on foot or by public transport rather than by car. The reason why journeys are shorter is clearly that there are more opportunities per square mile to satisfy journey purposes in high-density areas. The shortness of the journey in turn affects the choice of mode, but that is not the only influence at work. Table VII.5 shows that people living at high densities are less likely to own cars than people in the same income groups elsewhere. Partly this is because there is less need to own a car, since travel needs are more easily satisfied on foot or by public transport; in addition, the expense and difficulty of keeping and using a car is greater than elsewhere. For similar reasons, car owners living in areas of high density are less likely than those elsewhere to use their cars for everyday travel within a town. To maintain high densities is therefore a powerful way of encouraging journeys to be short rather than long and to be made on foot or, when a motorised mode is chosen, by public transport, rather than by car. All this should work towards reducing accidents, provided that other policies are employed to ensure that walking and, when applicable, cycling are safe.

Even in ideal conditions, a traveller will sometimes have a very strong reason to make a long journey rather than a short one. For most people in a position to choose, the choice is then likely to be between a car and public transport. To minimise accidents and other social costs, the more often public transport is chosen the better. The choice will be influenced not only by transport planning in the narrow sense - the quality and price of public transport, the methods of traffic restraint in use - but also by locational planning and in particular by the proximity of origins and destinations to the public transport networks.

The greatest opportunities for controlling the pattern of land use clearly arise in connection with new or expanded towns. But the more gradual change in the pattern of settlement, of the kind that has been described, can also be strongly influenced through development control. The environmental aspects of transport policy are also important in influencing the demand for developing in one place rather than another. In the General Household Survey, people are asked whether they are thinking of moving house and if so for what reason. At any given moment, one in six households is contemplating a move and the most important reason, other than that the accommodation is of the wrong size to meet the household's needs, is the physical environment and, in particular, the nuisance of traffic(8).

The number and location of facilities can also be influenced by policy. Planning permission for large facilities which attract many personal journeys can be restricted to sites well served by public transport; as a further measure, control can be exercised over the number, availability and pricing of car parking spaces. Property taxation can in principle be used to favour small establishments or establishments in desirable locations, such as corner shops, although changes in the law might be required to make the rates an effective instrument for this purpose. Many important facilities are provided by the public sector: for example, sports centres, hospitals, schools, post offices, and local authority offices. A deliberate policy could be adopted of providing 'small and many' rather than 'large and few'.

Current practice

Policy has in practice sometimes taken account of these principles. For example, proposals for very large out-of-town shopping centres have in general been turned down because of their unfortunate effects on traffic generation and, in the longer term, on the availability of shops within towns for people who cannot shop by car. At least as often, however, opposite principles have been followed. Most New Towns have been built at low densities in a form difficult to serve by public transport, although Runcorn, which was planned round a reserved bus way, is an exception. The preference for such a layout springs partly from the garden city ideal and the related idea that high density is incompatible with a good environment. This is ironic indeed, in view of the British record in the eighteenth and nineteenth centuries of building attractive towns to high densities and with some private gardens, as in Bath, Edinburgh, Brighton and many parts of London. It is a pity to abandon such forms when the problems of air pollution and sanitation that used to be associated with them have been solved. Another reason for favouring low densities in New Towns has been the idea prevalent in the 1960s that the aim of transport policy should be to provide for 'full motorisation'. For example, the Buchanan Report suggested that a good measure of the accessibility of an area would be the proportion of journeys to it that could be made by car(9).

The trends of inner city decline and population growth in the rural fringe have not been checked by public policy which in some respects has actively encouraged them. A recent example is the draft circular on land for housing and green belts issued by the Department of the Environment in the summer of 1983(10) but since withdrawn because of the protests it aroused, which appeared to favour housing growth at the edge of cities, in apparent contradiction to the policy of inner city revival. Moreover, the form which this growth would have taken would have necessitated long journeys and the use of cars or motorcycles. A consortium of builders was planning to develop some fifteen new settlements within 50 miles of London, each occupying about 700 acres and accommodating 14-20,000 people in some 7,000 homes(11). Employment opportunities within each settlement would have been limited, so that commuting would have been necessary, and this scattered pattern of development is not easy to serve by train or even by bus.

Continental practice seems more often to favour high densities and public transport. For example, in the Netherlands, the satellite town of Bijlermeer was planned in such a way that 80 per cent of the target population of 110,000 would live within 500 metres of a station on one of the two metro lines joining the town to Amsterdam(12). The expansion of Stockholm and of Copenhagen has also taken place along railway lines(13). In Belgium, the centre of the new university town of Louvain-la-Neuve, with a target population of 50,000, is built over the railway station, and the town itself is planned for the pedestrian(14).

Implications for the road safety effort

The two main trends in land use at the moment are a decline in the number, accompanied by an increase in the size, of facilities of various kinds, and a dispersal in the pattern of settlement. As a consequence, journeys become longer and harder to serve on foot, by cycle or by public transport. This has unfortunate consequences for road safety and for transport generally and would also appear to lead to a continuing loss of countryside and a perpetuation of inner city decline. Clearly, therefore, a major study and policy initiative is required into ways of checking and reversing these undesirable trends.

The implications for road safety are only one element of this wide problem but this chapter reinforces the lesson of the last one that road safety should not be seen only in terms of how to reduce the accident rates of particular modes: it also involves questions of land use, journey lengths and modal choice. In our view, this wider approach to the subject is unlikely to be adopted unless road safety is given much more prestige and standing within the organisation of central government.

This chapter also reinforces the point made in Chapter IV that a new system of incentives to local authorities to reduce road accidents should take account of all reductions, however achieved, rather than being tied narrowly to the work of the local authority road safety units, highly important though their work is.

References

(1) Transportation - The next twenty-five years, An appraisal of the prospects and possibilities for development of the country's transportation system up to the end of the century, the County Surveyors' Society, September 1978, para. 4.2.

(2) P. J. Mackie and G. B. Urquhart, Through and access commercial vehicle traffic in towns, TRRL Supplementary Report 117 UC, page 2.

(3) Data from the Census of Population quoted in Mayer Hillman and Anne Whalley, Energy and personal travel: obstacles to conservation, PSI, 1983, page 129.

(4) Annual Abstract of Statistics, 1981 and 1983 editions.

(5) Data from National Travel Surveys quoted in Mayer Hillman and Anne Whalley, op.cit, page 141.

(6) Stephen Plowden, Taming Traffic, Andre Deutsch 1980, Appendix A.

(7) General Household Survey 1981, HMSO, 1983, page 88.

(8) General Household Survey 1980, HMSO 1982, page 43.

(9) Colin Buchanan et al., Traffic in Towns, Appendix 2, para.16 and Appendix 3.

(10) Land for Housing and Green Belts, DoE, Draft Circular X/83.

(11) Transport Retort, Vol.7, No.7, Transport 2000, 1983.

(12) S.P.C. Plowden, 'Transport Efficiency and the Urban Environment', Transport Reviews, Vol. 3, No. 4, 1983, page 379.

(13) J.M. Thomson, Methods of Traffic Limitation in Urban Areas, OECD, 1972, pages 76-77.

(14) Various editions of Bulletin d'information de l'universite catholique de Louvain.

Table VII.1   Retail outlets in Great Britain in 1961 and 1971

Type of Outlet	1961	1971	Change per cent
Grocers and provision dealers	151,154	108,282	-28
Other food retailers	127,304	100,806	-21
Confectioners, tobacconists, newagents	70,662	52,751	-25
Clothing and footwear shops	96,612	93,644	-3
Household goods shops	63,476	72,877	+15
Other non-food retailers	64,349	71,646	+11
General stores	3,750	4,775	+27
All outlets	577,307	504,781	-13

Source: Census of Distribution

Table VII.2   Mode of travel analysed by length of journey

| | Length of journey (miles) | | | | | |
Mode of travel	Under 1	1 < 3	2 < 3	3 < 5	5 < 10	10 or more
	Percentage of journeys within each distance band					
Rail	-	*	1	2	4	8
Bus	1	15	27	30	20	10
Car	6	39	55	61	74	80
Two-wheeled motor vehicle	*	1	2	2	2	1
Bicycle	2	5	3	2	1	*
Walk	91	40	12	3	-	-

*   less than 0.5 per cent

Note: For the purpose of this table, a walk made to or from a public transport stop would count as a separate journey. This helps to account for the large number of journeys of under one mile made on foot.

Source: National Travel Survey, 1978-79 Report, Table 3.3.

Table VII.3   Mean journey lengths for selected journey purposes analysed by residential density
Units: kilometres

Journey purpose	Residential density in persons per hectare									
	Less than 1.25	1.25 to 2.5	2.5 to 6	6 to 12	12 to 18	18 to 25	25 to 37	37 to 50	50 to 75	75 and over
To and from work	9.5	10.3	7.2	8.5	8.5	7.1	7.4	6.8	6.8	6.3
Education	4.7	4.3	3.1	3.2	2.3	2.2	2.5	2.0	1.5	2.3
Shopping	7.4	5.7	4.4	3.7	3.6	3.5	3.1	3.0	3.0	3.0
Personal business	7.4	5.8	4.3	5.8	6.4	5.3	3.7	4.1	3.2	2.8
Social	13.5	10.4	8.0	7.9	8.5	8.5	8.8	8.2	7.8	8.8

Source: 1975/76 National Travel Survey, special tabulations.

Table VII.4   Mode of travel analysed by residential density

Per cent of journeys made by residents of districts of each density

Mode of travel	Residential density: persons per hectare									
	Less than 1.25	1.25 to 2.5	2.5 to 6	6 to 12	12 to 18	18 to 25	25 to 37	37 to 50	50 to 75	75 and over
Public transport	8	10	11	10	12	10	13	15	18	22
Car	56	53	45	48	45	46	42	38	34	26
Motorcycle/moped	1	1	1	1	1	1	1	1	1	1
Cycle	5	4	3	4	3	4	3	3	2	2
Walk	30	31	40	37	38	39	41	43	45	48

Note: It is known that problems in recording and coding the data have led to some exaggeration in the 'walk' figures and some corresponding underestimate in the figures for other modes, especially public transport.

Source: 1975/76 National Travel Survey, special tabulations

Table VII.5   Car ownership in Britain analysed by household income and residential density

Per cent of households in each density and income category that own cars

Gross annual household income (1975 figures)	Residential density: persons per hectare									
	Less than 1.25	1.25 to 2.5	2.5 to 6	6 to 12	12 to 18	18 to 25	25 to 37	37 to 50	50 to 75	75 and over
Under £1500										
One or more cars	18	18	14	13	10	10	6	5	6	3
Two or more cars	*	*	*	*	*	*	*	*	*	*
£1500 to £3000										
One or more cars	69	55	50	48	48	36	41	34	30	20
Two or more cars	*	*	*	*	*	*	*	*	*	*
£3000 to £5000										
One or more cars	85	79	77	80	73	69	69	64	61	44
Two or more cars	17	12	8	7	8	7	6	3	4	2
£5000 or over										
One or more cars	95	92	89	88	90	88	82	84	81	71
Two or more cars	43	31	29	36	32	22	25	30	15	7
All income groups										
One or more cars	79	76	66	69	65	66	59	56	50	40
Two or more cars	26	23	15	17	16	14	13	10	8	5

*   Figures not given in the source document but presumably small.
Source: Mayer Hillman and Anne Walley, Walking is Transport, Policy Studies Institute, 1979. The ultimate source is the National Travel Survey, 1975/76.

VIII THE DESIGN OF RESIDENTIAL AREAS

The last chapter dealt with the relationship between town planning and road safety, where town planning was considered at the relatively abstract level of densities, the number and size of facilities and their location in relation to transport networks. Town planning at a more detailed level, almost at the level of architectural design, can also be very important in limiting the numbers of accidents and giving protection from the danger and intrusion of traffic. In residential areas, this becomes a matter of the relationship between roads, dwellings and parking spaces; the detailed design of roads, footpaths and cycleways; limitations on access, by type of vehicle or user; limitations on speed; and the physical means used to help enforce such regulations.

The importance of safety in residential areas
Table VIII.1 shows that most road accidents and casualties occur in built-up areas, i.e. on roads subject to speed limits of no more than 40 mph. The overwhelming majority of casualties to pedestrians and cyclists occur there, and a majority also of casualties, other than fatalities, to vehicle occupants. Unfortunately, it is not possible from the national statistics to say how many accidents occur in residential streets, since the Stats 19 form on which the statistics are based does not classify streets by function but only by class of road (motorway, A(M), A, B, C, unclassified). To estimate how many casualties in built-up areas occur on residential streets, it is necessary to turn to the more detailed studies which have been undertaken of particular towns, which suggest that the proportion is a quarter to a third(1). For particular kinds of casualty, the proportion is probably much higher. Thus a study of child pedestrian accidents in Hampshire in 1972 concluded that 'accidents to child pedestrians are essentially a feature of

residential areas, and particularly so in the case of young children'(2).

A slightly different way of looking at the location of accidents is by reference to the distance from the injured person's home. Some accidents quite close to home may occur in non-residential streets, for example in the local shopping centre. But in terms of policy or design, they are part of the same problem, since many of them could be avoided either by locating shops within residential areas or by ensuring that the footpaths within a residential area also connects it to the local shopping centre. The 1972 Hampshire study showed that over a quarter of the children were injured in the street in which they lived, 35 per cent within one hundred yards of home and 60 per cent within a quarter of a mile of home. A study of child pedestrian accidents in Manchester and Salford in 1969 showed very similar results: 38.5 per cent occurred on minor residential roads; 31 per cent within 100 yards of where the children lived; 73 per cent within a quarter of a mile(3). Similar breakdowns for adults are not available, but it is known that most pedestrian casualties occur on roads with which the pedestrians are familiar(4). This, together with the facts that most walking journeys are short and many injured adult pedestrians are elderly, suggests that most accidents to adult pedestrians are also local, although some of these must occur on main roads rather than on residential streets.

It has been stressed that accidents are not the only consequence of danger on the roads. It was seen in Chapter I that much of the anxiety caused by danger is focussed on children and old people as pedestrians. This is very much a matter of the local environment, as is the frustration of street life and children's play. The studies quoted in Chapter I have demonstrated the great value which people place on a good local environment, or as one of the studies put it 'the overwhelming desire to shop and live in situations free from disturbance and interference of traffic'. The same study showed how wide the gap now is between aspirations and reality. Whereas 77 per cent of the urban population would like to live in streets 'with very little traffic' (the option of living in streets with no traffic at all was not offered in the questionnaire), only 28 per cent did so; similarly, 68 per cent would like to shop in a centre with very little traffic, but only nine per cent described their local shopping centre in such terms(5).

Design and safety in new residential areas
One step in creating the desired conditions is to minimise through traffic - a policy which has been orthodox at least since the 1940s.

But this is unlikely to be sufficient in limiting the number of accidents, still less in creating conditions free from worry and intrusion. A study published in 1978 of 257 local authority housing estates of traditional design, all of which were reasonably large and relatively free from through traffic, showed that the child pedestrian accident rate there (per child per year) was about 80 per cent of that for the United Kingdom as a whole(6). It is therefore also essential to limit the danger from local traffic.

The design of new residential areas can help to separate local traffic from pedestrians and to influence traffic behaviour. The study of housing estates just mentioned showed that culs-de-sac were much safer than other streets, especially for children(7). It has been common practice in many countries for a long time to lay out new residential areas to a Radburn design, which achieves a high degree of segregation of pedestrians and vehicles while still allowing access by vehicle to all dwellings. Such areas can be between three and five times safer than non-segregated areas(8). Part of their success, and part of the reason why culs-de-sac are safer than other streets, may be due to the lower speeds which the design encourages, on some roads at least. Recently, attention has been paid in Britain to designing new estates in a way expressly intended to keep speeds low by the use of rough and changing road surfaces, narrow roads with a tortuous geometry and limited visibility, an unusual design of kerbs and some sharing of surfaces between vehicles and pedestrians. There are still relatively few such estates in Britain and no figures are available comparing their accident rates with those of estates built to a 'traditional' design. A recent study of 13 'innovative' estates showed that at nearly all points within them mean speeds were below 30 km/h and were often below 25 km/h; the report claims that these speeds are below those found in estates built to a traditional design although comparative figures are not given(9). But, notwithstanding that traffic flows were low, 56 per cent of the residents of the innovative estates studied found that road safety was a problem, mentioning particularly the lack of footpaths, excessive vehicle speeds and the difficulty of seeing cars approaching. Problems of safety were also mentioned by 78 per cent of the drivers visiting these estates(10).

On the continent, the possibilities of designing new residential areas in ways which will enforce very low driving speeds, and will generally subordinate motor vehicles to pedestrians and the environment, have been taken very much further. In the new quarter of Gouda, in Holland, for example, residential areas are planned for pedestrians and cyclists first and cars second and all motorised traffic is forced through the physical design to move at walking pace(11). But we have not seen studies showing the effects either on accidents or on anxiety.

The most effective way of preventing accidents, danger and other intrusion from traffic in residential areas would be to keep out all motor vehicles, with the fewest possible exceptions such as emergency vehicles. This would mean that car owners would not be able to drive all the way to their houses but would be obliged to park a certain distance away and to make the first or last stage of a car journey on foot. This has been accepted practice in Sweden for some time. A report Traffic in the Neighbourhood, issued in 1977 jointly by the National Board of Physical Planning and Building, the National Road Safety Office and the National Road Administration, specifies that walking distances of up to 300 metres to parking areas and 100 metres to loading zones should be accepted in new residential areas, although the possibility of vehicular access to all dwellings for emergency vehicles, furniture removal, oil delivery and vehicles serving the disabled has to be preserved(12). The effect in keeping down accidents has been shown by a Swedish university study of accidents in different districts in Gothenburg in the years 1969-72. It was found that the accident rate, per year per inhabitant, in districts where people had to walk a certain distance between dwellings and parking spaces was less than half the rate in districts laid out according to a Radburn type of design, with a high degree of segregation of vehicles and pedestrians, but nevertheless permitting parking adjacent to dwellings. The difference was especially marked for accidents to pedestrians and cyclists and accidents to children(13).

In Germany a maximum distance of 200 metres between dwellings and residents' parking is suggested(14). In the Netherlands, the principle of providing grouped parking spaces at the edge of residential districts was developed about 15 years ago, although in most circumstances 100 metres is regarded as about the maximum acceptable distance between the front door and the parking space(15).

Such ideas have not been encouraged in Britain. The official recommendation on parking provision in new housing schemes is that, except perhaps in schemes of the very highest density, parking places for residents and visitors, as well as for emergency and service vehicles, should be provided as near as possible to the dwelling(16). This requirement springs as much from a need for supervision of parked cars to prevent vandalism as from considerations of convenient access(17).

The re-design and management of existing residential areas

In existing residential areas the basic configuration of roads and buildings has to be taken as given. But streets can be closed or converted to a different use, pavements and surfaces redesigned, and regulations on access and speed introduced which such physical measures can help to enforce.

Schemes to exclude through traffic usually involve some physical changes in street design which are often intended to influence the behaviour of the remaining traffic as well; this is true, for example of the major demonstration project on urban safety that the TRRL is now conducting in five towns(18). Such action can be very effective. A scheme in the London Borough of Hackney brought about a reduction of 53 per cent in pedestrian accidents and 44 per cent in accidents of other types in the area covered by the scheme, including the perimeter roads(19).

A simple measure which scarcely counts as re-design is to install speed-control humps. After a successful programme of experiments by the TRRL on residential roads, in which it was shown that humps reduced speeds, accidents and noise and were generally approved both by residents and drivers, the Transport Act 1981 made it legal for highway authorities to install humps, subject to various conditions, on roads with a 30 mph speed limit. However, as was mentioned in Chapter III, the experiments showed that substantial numbers of residents still thought that traffic was going too fast, and that the risk of crossing the road on foot was high or quite high, even after the humps had been installed.

Schemes for treating existing streets have been more numerous and bolder in their conception in several continental countries than in Britain. The concept of a 'woonerf' was worked out in the Netherlands during the late 1960s and early 1970s, and in 1976 minimum design standards for woonerven were published by the Dutch government. As is well known, the principle of a woonerf is that space is shared by pedestrians and vehicles but pedestrians are given precedence. This precedence is established by design features which impose very low speeds indeed on vehicles. Such features include rough surfaces, 'pinch-points' which narrow the road to the width of a single vehicle, ramps at intersections, tree planting and other obstacles placed at frequent intervals. We have not seen any before-and-after studies of the effect on accidents of creating woonerven or any comparison of accident rates in them and in unconverted streets. Their popularity is attested by their rapid and widespread adoption both in the Netherlands and in other countries of northern Europe. In the Netherlands, by early 1984, less than eight years after the legislation authorising woonerven took effect, about 350 municipalities, or half the total number, had introduced some 2,700 schemes, each covering a street or group of streets(20).

We have not seen any references to the complete exclusion of traffic, including residents' own cars, from existing residential areas. It is possible that some of the continental schemes have gone that far, and there must presumably have been people living in some of the larger town centres which have been pedestrianised who would have lost the right to keep a car adjacent to their dwelling. The case for creating traffic-free streets is stronger in existing areas than in new development, since in new development the opportunities for using design to reconcile the conflict between pedestrians and vehicles are much greater. The problem is that existing rights of access and parking would be extinguished. Although a new and highly valued right would be created, that of freedom from the intrusion of traffic, to extinguish an existing right is always difficult.

Pedestrian and child pedestrian fatality rates

In addition to the statistical evidence on particular schemes that has been cited, there is probably some significance in the fact that the countries that have taken neighbourhood design most seriously tend to have the lowest pedestrian fatalities per head of the population. The Swedish example is particularly impressive. Table VIII.2 shows that for pedestrians of all ages Sweden's record is bettered only by the Netherlands; more recent figures in Road Accidents Great Britain 1982 show lower rates for Sweden than for the Netherlands(21). For children, Sweden's record is outstandingly good, with a fatality rate less than one-quarter that of the United Kingdom. Equally significant is the improvement that has taken place in Sweden in recent years. Table VIII.3 shows that the child pedestrian fatality rate is now about one-third of what it was in 1965. The fact that the fatality rate for pedestrians, and especially for children, has fallen more in Sweden than the rates for other road users again suggests that improvements in the local environment are a prime cause.

The reasons for slow progress in Britain

It has been seen that freedom from the intrusion of traffic in the residential environment, and from danger especially, is regarded as highly desirable in Britain. In addition, the British record for pedestrian safety, especially for children, is not good. One might expect that this would have led to particular attention being paid to the restriction and subordination of traffic in residential areas, but in fact progress has been slower than in several other countries, and where there has been innovation it has been less bold. The relationship between neighbourhood design and safety has not even attracted the research that its importance warrants. The authors of the study of 257 traditionally designed housing estates mentioned above remark that when their study was first planned (presumably in 1971) there was 'virtually no published information on any of these questions'.

In this field, as in others, policy has been much influenced by the idea that where a mistake on the part of a road user has led to an accident, the appropriate remedial action is to train road users so that they will avoid committing such errors in future. There seems to be a reluctance to accept the possibility that some people, including the most vulnerable, may be able to benefit very litte from propaganda and training. The fact that elderly people tend to have three times as many pedestrian accidents as other adults inspired the TRRL and the Hampshire Constabulary to undertake an investigation into their problems, with the particular object of identifying whether factors about their accidents would be appropriate for road safety propaganda. The investigation provided evidence that elderly pedestrians are more careful than others and that their difficulties stem from diminished physical abilities, which would seem to indicate that the scope for propaganda is limited, unless indeed it was designed to persuade other road users to take more care about older pedestrians. But this point is not made in the TRRL leaflet which describes the study, whose conclusion is as follows(22):

'In general the types of accident to the elderly and other adults are the same. The problem is largely one of not seeing vehicles, therefore more thorough visual scanning is required. The simplest way to achieve this would be for pedestrians to look longer and more often; particularly for nearside traffic and near junctions. Whereas the 15-60 age group are most likely to be knocked down on the nearside half of the road, the elderly are likely to be knocked down on either half. There is therefore a need for them to keep looking while crossing as well as before they start to cross'.

Similarly, a study of a campaign in Greenwich to improve children's behaviour when crossing roads near parked cars showed that it had had no statistically significant effect. But the conclusion drawn from the fact that only ten per cent of children looked both ways before crossing at the edge of a parked vehicle was that this aspect of behaviour should be given a major emphasis in publicity and teaching(23).

This is in contrast with the situation in Sweden, where the great emphasis put on designing a safe environment partly springs from studies by psychologists in the 1960s which showed that there are strict limits, which training can do little to alter, to the capability of young children to cope with traffic. In Norway too, the welfare of children has been a prime consideration, as is evident from the following extract from the report of a recent study visit to Scandinavia and the Netherlands(24):

> 'The Norwegians are showing increasing concern for the plight of the urban child who is sometimes so frightened to go outside that he misses all the joys of play and the appreciation of nature so essential to his healthy development. A redesign of housing, shopping, and amenities complexes so that a child may proceed from home to school and playground without coming into serious conflict with traffic is the most effective way of ameliorating this problem.'

The fact that pedestrianisation, whether of residential areas or town centres, is primarily the responsibility of local authorities seems to be a reason why the Department of Transport has not thought it necessary to take a very close interest in it, although the general desirability of separating pedestrians from vehicular traffic has always been stressed(25). But this seems a poor reason, especially in connection with road safety. The Road Safety Division should be concerned to promote all policies which further the cause of road safety; the emphasis it gives to each should depend only on the costs and benefits involved, regardless of whether the executive action required lies with other divisions of the Department of Transport or with local authorities, motor manufacturers or whoever. It seems likely that the neglect of anxiety and the other non-accident costs of danger on the roads, and the failure to link traffic danger with other aspects of the environmental intrusion of traffic, also help to explain the comparative neglect of road safety in the local environment. Here again, the contrast with Sweden is noteworthy, since one of the sponsors of the official guidelines Traffic in the Neighbourhood was the National Road Safety Office.

It is hard to believe, however, that problems of shared responsibility would have mattered much if the concern which citizens feel about traffic in the environment, danger especially, had been translated into concerted pressure on the Department of Transport. The main reason why this has not happened is that the people affected are not in a good position to combine and campaign. This is obviously true of the children and old people who spend so much of their time in their local environment and who are especially at risk. But it is true of their families also. There is evidence that the problems are especially acute in the poorer parts of inner urban areas, where traffic tends to be heavy, houses often give directly on to streets, and there is a shortage of private gardens and of playgrounds and similar facilities. The study of child pedestrian accidents in Manchester and Salford in 1969 mentioned above showed a very great variation, by as much as a factor of ten, in child casualty rates by district. The highest rates were in the ring surrounding the town centre(26). A TRRL study of residential districts of Swindon, Southampton, Portsmouth and Oxford showed that the child accident rate in the inner, nineteenth century areas was almost double that elsewhere and that the adult accident rate was also substantially higher(27). Residents of such areas have many other pre-occupations and often lack the time, money and skills required to organise and lobby.

Implications for the road safety effort
Safety in residential areas, or more generally in the neighbourhood, is a very important aspect of road safety. The immediate responsibility falls to local authorities, but that does not mean that the Road Safety Division of the Department of Transport, or any equivalent central government agency for road safety that might replace the RSD, should not be involved. On the contrary, it points to the need for a proper system of relationships between the central government and local authorities in the field of road safety. Recommendations for such a system are given in the next chapter; in the meanwhile, some points relevant to this particular topic may be noted.

It would help to draw attention to the problem of safety in the neighbourhood if the location of accidents was described in a more meaningfuly way in the accident statistics. The 'class of road' categories now used are of doubtful value; to categorise streets by their function would be more useful. This should not involve any more work for the police at the scene of an accident; the police would only have to record the location as they do now, and the further descriptions would be supplied at the coding stage from information held by the local authority in its computer data bank of the roads in its area. It would also be helpful for accidents involving pedestrian casualties to be described by reference to the

197

distance of the spot where they occur from the injured person's home. To supply this description would, however, involve more police time in filling in the form. Therefore it should perhaps be required only for fatal and serious pedestrian accidents.

It is suggested in Chapter IX that some of the help provided by the central government to local authorities should take the form of demonstration projects. Some such projects should cover the effects of stricter control over the behaviour, especially the speed, and the number of motor vehicles in residential areas. It was seen above that over half the residents in a sample of 13 residential estates built to an 'innovative' design still found safety to be a problem. A simple but valuable experiment would be to install speed-control humps at frequent intervals in these estates and then to repeat the surveys after about a year to see how this proportion had changed. Clearly, experiments are also needed to explore the consequences in new estates of abandoning the rule that parking must be provided within or adjacent to dwellings; such experiments would have to take account of the problem of vandalism.

However, the main problem lies in existing streets of traditional design. An experimental programme of British woonerven is needed, with especial emphasis on creating very low speeds; also experiments in creating effectively traffic-free streets. Inner city areas would be particularly suitable for such experiments. Traffic problems there are especially acute and the penalties would be relatively small, since car ownership is low, partly because there is little need for a car. This would also help to fill an important gap in the Department of Environment's programme of inner city research, which has never considered the extent to which the intrusion of traffic is a deterrent to living in the inner city(28).

This chapter also confirms the need shown in earlier chapters for due account to be taken in the road safety effort of anxiety and the other non-accident costs of road safety, as well as of the accidents themselves, and for other aspects of traffic intrusion to be considered simultaneously with road safety. It also shows the importance of being able to draw on foreign experience, for which little provision is made at present. Finally, it shows that there is an important problem in making sure that the interests of people who are less vocal and find it difficult to form pressue groups are properly taken into account; this problem is discussed in the next chapter.

References

(1) Accidents in Urban Areas, TRRL Leaflet LF 388, 1974.

(2) G. B. Grayson, The Hampshire child pedestrian accident study, TRRL Laboratory Report 668, 1975, page 4.

(3) Barbara Preston, 'Statistical Analysis of Child Pedestrian Accidents in Manchester and Salford', Accident Analysis and Prevention, Volume 4, 1972, page 326.

(4) Accidents to Elderly Pedestrians, TRRL Leaflet LF 323, 1972.

(5) Gerald Hoinville and Patricia Prescott-Clarke, Traffic Disturbance and Amenity Values. Social and Community Planning Research, 1972, diagram opposite page 9.

(6) G. T. Bennett and Jean Marland, Road accidents in traditionally designed local authority estates, TRRL Supplementary Report 394, 1978, pages 19 and 20.

(7) Ibid., pages 17, 18, 20.

(8) Traffic safety of children, OECD, 1983, page 66.

(9) Mike Jenks, 'Residential roads researched', Architects' Journal, 29 June 1983, page 46.

(10) Ibid., pages 48 and 49.

(11) H. G. Vahl, 'La ville de Gouda et l'integration de trafic', Transport, Environnement, Circulation, November-December 1977, page 20.

(12) Traffic in the neighbourhood, Report 33 part 4, the Board of Physical Planning and Building, undated, especially pages 6, 18, 29. This is an abbreviated English version of a Swedish report originally published in 1977.

(13) S. O. Gunnarson and others, Follow-up Studies of the SCAFT Guidelines 1968: Analysis of Accidents in Residential Districts with Traffic Separation, Goteborg 1969-72, Chalmers Technical University, 1973, page viii.

(14) Traffic safety in residential areas, OECD, 1979, page 38.

(15) Communication from the Dutch Ministry of Transport, February 1984.

(16) Housing Development Notes VII, Parking in New Housing Schemes, Department of the Environment, July 1977, especially figure 5, para. 1.29 and para. 1.25.

(17) Communication from Department of Transport, 1 July 1983.

(18) Urban Safety Project, TRRL Leaflet LF938, December 1982.

(19) E. Dalby, Area-wide measures in urban road safety, TRRL Supplementary Report 517, 1979, Table 3.

(20) As ref. 15.

(21) Road Accidents Great Britain 1982, Table 51.

(22) As ref. 4.

(23) C. S. Downing and Joyce Spendlove, <u>Effectiveness of a campaign to reduce accidents involving children crossing roads near parked cars</u>, TRRL Laboratory Report 986, 1981, especially page 5.

(24) J. G. Avery and P. J. Avery, 'Scandinavian and Dutch lessons in childhood road traffic accident prevention', <u>British Medical Journal</u>, Volume 285, August-September, 1982, page 621.

(25) Communication from the Department of Transport, 1 August, 1983.

(26) Barbara Preston, <u>op.cit.</u>, pages 328 and 329.

(27) <u>Road Accidents in Residential Areas</u>, TRRL Leaflet LF 650, May 1979.

(28) Telephone conversation with the Department of the Environment, October 1982.

Table VIII.1   Casualties on built-up roads as a percentage of all casualties in 1982

Type of road user	All casualties	Fatal casualties
All road users	72	60
Pedestrians	95	79
Cyclists	89	64
Riders or occupants of motor vehicles	64	36
All road users aged 0-14	86	71
Pedestrians aged 0-14	97	84
Cyclists aged 0-14	90	71

Note: The base of each percentage is the total number of casualties of that type in Great Britain.

Source: Road Accidents Great Britain 1982, Table 23

Table VIII.2   Pedestrian and child pedestrian fatal road casualty rates in OECD countries in 1979
Units: deaths per million population

All pedestrians		Pedestrians aged 0-14 years	
Country	Rate	Country	Rate
Netherlands	18.7	Sweden	9.7
Sweden	21.4	Finland	13.3
Norway	23.8	Netherlands	18.3
Japan	24.9	Spain	21.1
Denmark	28.2	Denmark	24.6
Finland	31.9	Japan	25.4
Spain	34.2	France	25.9
United States	37.4	Norway	26.3
Canada	37.6	United States	28.1
United Kingdom	39.0	United Kingdom	32.6
France	39.3	Canada	34.3
Belgium	50.4	Belgium	35.5
Switzerland	51.0	Switzerland	38.6
West Germany	51.5	West Germany	40.7
Ireland	67.4	Ireland	48.5

Source: Traffic Safety of Children, OECD, 1983, page 19.

Table VIII.3   Development of fatal road casualty rates in Sweden

Units: deaths per million population

	1965	1979	1980	1981	1982
Pedestrians aged 0-14					
Rates	30	10	12	9	11
Index, 1965=100	100	33	40	30	37
Pedestrians aged 15 and over					
Rates	42	22	16	16	17
Index, 1965=100	100	52	38	38	40
Other road users aged 0-14					
Rates	45	33	32	25	21
Index, 1965=100	100	73	71	56	47
Other road users aged 15 and over					
Rates	127	90	86	77	74
Index, 1965=100	100	71	68	61	58

Source: Swedish Road and Traffic Research Institute

IX   INSTITUTIONS

This report has looked at a number of problems within road safety where fruitful lines of attack have not been pursued, or at least not to the extent that their potential warrants.   The aim of this chapter is to suggest institutional changes which would help to correct this state of affairs.

The most important single reason why less effort has been put into road safety than it deserves and why certain promising courses of action have been regarded as non-starters, almost as illegitimate, is because of insufficient pressure from the public. This may not seem to be an institutional matter at all, and indeed it would not be if the reason for it was simply that the public was not interested in road safety.   But the evidence is that people as individuals are deeply concerned but that their concern is difficult to mobilise and is not always well informed.   These are institutional failings.

Some of the obstacles to progress discussed in previous chapters are at the theoretical level, but the reasons why poor theory is not exposed and replaced by better are also institutional. If the road safety lobby was as well organised and was backed by the same resources as the motorists' and road freight organisations, we would by now have more satisfactory accident statistics and costings and would also have developed some method of taking the non-accident costs of unsafe road conditions into account.   The fallacy of continuing to rely on training as the main method of attack on the motorcycle accident problem would have been exposed; disputes about the relationships between vehicle speeds and the number and severity of accidents would have been cleared up by proper experiments; we would have made better use of the Swedish experience on how best to reduce accidents among children and would have conducted similar studies of our own.

The next section of this chapter sets out what we see as the respective functions of the main agents involved with road safety and the relationships that ought to exist between them. We then go on to consider how well those functions are now being fulfilled and what changes would help to remove the existing weaknesses.

Functions and relations
Central road safety agency
In the following paragraphs the term 'central road safety agency' is used as if such a body were distinct from the Department of Transport. This usage is adopted for convenience and is not intended to pre-judge the question, discussed later, of whether the duties described are best carried out, as at present, by a division of the Department of Transport, or by a new and separate unit.

For the most part, a central road safety agency has to work with or through other organisations, but there are some fields in which it can it work directly, subject, of course, to Parliamentary approval. These are:

(i)   Setting the rules concerning who may drive different classes of vehicles. Some of these rules are concerned with who is eligible to apply for a driving licence and how such a licence can be obtained and may be forfeited. Otherwise, they are concerned with the circumstances in which a licence holder may not drive on such grounds as being under the influence of drink or drugs or having exceeded a set number of driving hours.

(ii)   Formulating codes of conduct for driver behaviour. Such codes may have legal force or be advisory only, like the Highway Code.

(iii)   Licensing and otherwise regulating and supervising people concerned with instructing different classes of road user.

(iv)   Organising national or regional publicity campaigns to improve road user behaviour.

(v)   Research on the values to be attached to accidents and other consequences of danger on the roads.

(vi)   Research and development generally in road safety (although some of this is likely to involve cooperation with others: for example, demonstration projects carried out jointly with local authorities).

The following fields of action will require cooperation with other central government departments.

(i)   Setting Construction and Use Regulations for road vehicles and similar specifications concerning road users' equipment. Although road safety may be the most important single consideration, noise, fumes and road damage and costs to vehicle users also have to be taken into account, so that the Department of Transport has to be involved, and possibly also the Department of the Environment, the DHSS and the Department of Industry.

(ii)   Taxation policy, including vehicle excise duty, fuel tax, company cars, road pricing. The Department of Transport, the Treasury and other financial ministries must be involved; possibly also, if more peripherally, the Department of Energy and the Department of Industry.

(iii) Investment criteria and policy on subsidies, both for road and for competing forms of transport. The Department of Transport and the Treasury are again involved.

(iv)   Policy on operators' licensing, both for bus and coach operators and for freight. The Department of Transport and the Traffic Commissioners have to be involved.

(v)   Questions of road design, lighting and street furniture. The Department of Transport has to be involved.

(vi)   Setting speed limits. This also involves the Department of Transport, the Home Office and the police.

(vii) Policy on patterns of settlement, regional planning, the locational policy of major governmental institutions. The Department of Transport, the Department of Environment and, more peripherally, the Department of Industry have to be involved, and on occasion other government departments with respect to the location of their own facilities.

(viii) Enforcement. The role of a central government road safety agency in enforcement is inevitably secondary to that of the police and the courts. The most useful way in which a central road safety agency can help them is by developing self-enforcing methods: for example, speed control through vehicle design and governors. But a central road safety agency is also involved in such activities as vehicle inspection and in putting pressure on the police and the courts, via the Home Office and the Lord Chancellor's Department, to ensure adequate and consistent policing, prosecuting and sentencing policies.

(ix)   Accident statistics. The production of good accident statistics is a very important task of a central road safety agency. It must involve the cooperation of the police, and should also involve that of the DHSS, at the data collection stage, and hence in the design of forms. The closer involvement of the DHSS in this work might lead to its also becoming more closely involved in road accident prevention as well as treatment, which would be advantageous. Other organisations with an interest in the use of the data are the Department of Transport and local authorities.

A central road safety agency also has an important part to play in supervising, encouraging and otherwise assisting local authorities in the discharge of their responsibilities for road safety and in helping to develop an effective citizens' interest in the subject. The ways in which a central agency can provide such help are described below.

Local authorities and their relationship with the central road safety agency

The scope for local authorities to take action to improve road safety is at least as great as that of central government. Apart from safety training, which does now largely fall to local authorities but could in principle be handled by a central road safety agency, working through the educational authorities and others, local authorities are inevitably involved in connection with their responsibilities for roads, transport planning, town planning and housing. Safety cannot be separated from the other considerations determining policy in those fields.

It could be argued that where local authorities have a certain road safety responsibility, central government need not be concerned. But even on the most extreme view of local autonomy, there would seem to be two essential roles for a central road safety agency. One is to ensure, through legislation, that local authorities' legal powers are adequate to allow them to discharge their responsibilities. The other is to monitor the road safety activities of local authorities in such a way that the local electorate can bring informed pressure to bear on its own local authority: this was described in Chapter IV.

However, in our view, which we think would be widely shared, central government's involvement in local road safety matters should go beyond that. Road safety is a national as well as a local issue and there must be some central body which can take a view of all the means of attack on the problem so that priorities are selected by reference to value for money, regardless of where the immediate responsibility for action lies, and so that the whole effort can be coordinated. Coordination should, however, leave room for a large degree of local autonomy and initiatives.

Another reason for central involvement is that it would be extremely wasteful for each local highway authority to undertake its own research and development programme in road safety. In addition, therefore, to making sure that local authorities' legal powers match their responsibilities, and to monitoring, the central road safety agency should help at the technical level to establish and disseminate good practice. This does not apply only to points of road safety narrowly conceived, such as developing and testing new safety-inspired techniques of road engineering. It must also involve wider issues of transport policy, such as the development and promulgation of techniques of economic appraisal which will enable a local authority to take the safety benefits into account when deciding how much subsidy to give to buses.

Finally, we believe that the central agency should operate a scheme of financial incentives which would reward local highway authorities for accident reductions in their area. The details of the scheme we recommend are given later; the point of it is to encourage local authorities to devote more attention to road safety while leaving them as free as possible in deciding how to do so. Also, such a scheme would stimulate a spirit of local competition and pride and would give local electors an inducement in their capacity as ratepayers, to add to their concern as citizens, to press for improved safety in their own areas. It would also stimulate local authorities to put pressure on the central government where appropriate. One reason might be that the central government was not doing all it should to help the local authorities carry out their own responsibilities. But, in addition, because payment would be given for all accident reductions on a local highway authority's roads, however achieved, local authorities would be given an inducement to press for reforms in areas in which central government is itself responsible, such as legislation on vehicles or on drink and driving. This would in turn help to create a bond between local authorities and citizens' groups campaigning on the same issues.

Citizens' pressure groups

In a democracy, political action ultimately depends upon the concern of the citizens, which is likely to be most effective if organised in groups. At the local level, individual citizens and local societies should be putting pressure on the officers and members of their own local authorities, both directly and through political parties and the media. A body, or bodies, to represent the citizens' interest in road safety at the national level is also required. One of its functions would be to exert pressure on a central government road safety agency, and where appropriate on the other government departments concerned, in just the same way as local groups exert pressure on their local authorities, except that the national body would have the additional function of pressing a central agency and members of Parliament for new legislation where that is required. A further function would be to represent the road safety cause in public debate in the media and to put pressure on people such as manufacturers, trade interests and the Advertising Standards Authority. The need for a pressure group to fill such a role partly depends on how active an official road safety agency is prepared to be. But even if, as we recommend, a central road safety agency campaigned much more actively and openly than the Road Safety Division does at present, there will always be a need for an unofficial body too, since it can be more outspoken in debate and can initiate ideas which it might be premature for the official organisation to launch.

A national pressure group would also be able to offer technical support and advice to local groups. So could and should a central road safety agency, but in this field too occasions will arise when it would be awkward or inappropriate for an official organisation to intervene. For example, if a local group became involved in a dispute with its local authority, an unofficial organisation might be able to offer advice when an official one would have to remain detached. A national pressure group would also be a useful channel through which local societies could learn from each other in matters of road safety, and it could help transmit and coordinate the ideas of local groups on points where national action, such as new legislation, would be required.

For citizens to become effectively involved, whether as individuals or through pressure groups, they will require some help from a central road safety agency. The most important help that this agency could give local people has already been described: to make sure that they have the information they need in order to bring rational and effective pressure to bear on their own local authorities. But much more than this could be done to stimulate an intelligent public interest in road safety. It is very hard for laymen, or for professionals either, to keep track of what is going on, especially in foreign countries, where, as has been seen, there is much interesting innovation and experiment. A central road safety agency could help by publishing a quarterly newsletter; producing films and other visual aids for groups which might have an especial interest in road safety, such as local environmental societies or women's organisations, to use at their own meetings; providing speakers for meetings, etc.

Ideally, a national pressure group in road safety should be quite independent of any government agency, just as pressure groups such as the motoring organisations are quite independent of the Department of Transport. It would generally be a constructive critic and an ally of a central road safety agency, if sometimes an awkward ally in pressing for more rapid advance than the official body might think feasible. Its influence should be particularly felt in research and development and it should command enough technical expertise in the relevant fields of engineering, economics, statistics, and public opinion research to make positive detailed suggestions on both the content and the conduct of the official research programme. Preferably it should also have the resources to undertake some limited studies of its own.

The ideal of the complete financial independence of such a body from a central road safety agency may not be attainable. If not, it would be better for some support to be given than for the organisation not to exist, and there are many precedents for financial support from government departments to pressure groups. It was mentioned in Chapter II that the Department of Transport does now give substantial support to RoSPA and also to the British Motorcycle Safety Foundation. The Department of Health and Social Security gives money to more than 200 voluntary organisations, some of which, such as Action on Smoking and Health and the Child Poverty Action Group, campaign very actively[1]. The question of financial help is raised again below.

Linking road safety with environmental issues

It has been seen in earlier chapters that there is a very close link between road safety and the intrusion of road traffic on the environment. In fact, danger on the roads can be thought of as one aspect of environmental intrusion, albeit the most important. In terms of preventive action, there is also a very close coincidence between what is necessary to make the roads safer and to protect the environment in other ways. This is especially true of those measures which involve some degree of traffic restraint through town planning, the encouragement of public transport use, taxation policy, the provision of cycling facilities and pedestrianisation. But even measures which operate principally by reducing accident rates may have environmental implications too: for example, the prohibition of powerful motorcycles and a more effective policy on speed would help to reduce noise. It is very important that the road safety effort should be organised in a way which takes account of these close links with other environmental issues.

The institutional conditions required for effective action on the environment also closely resemble those for road safety. Both central government and local authorities are involved, and pressure groups too must operate both at the national and the local level. At the local level, the very same groups and even individuals may be involved. For example, it would usually be better for road safety to be treated as one activity of the local civic society rather than to have one society concerned with safety and another with other aspects of transport planning and the physical environment. At the central level, more specialisation is necessary both in government and in the voluntary sector, but there must be very close cooperation between the specialists. That will not occur unless the institutional arrangements encourage it.

Present arrangements

To what extent does the road safety effort as now organised conform with the model that has been outlined? It should be possible to answer this question from the discussion in earlier chapters.

It has been seen that the road safety task has been conceived as how to reduce the number and severity of accidents associated with a 'given' volume and pattern of traffic. Hence, the Road Safety Division of the Department of Transport has scarcely become involved in some of the functions listed above for a central road safety agency: those which would work by modifying the travel patterns themselves. Thus, questions of taxation, subsidies, investment policy for road and rail, inner city policy and the development of new settlements have been looked at with little regard to their implications for safety.

The more traditional features of road safety policy, designed to bring down accident and casualty rates, such as driver licensing policy, vehicle design, and speed limits, are all covered in the present work of the Road Safety Division, but the message of previous chapters is that the cause of road safety has not been pressed energetically enough.

Two of the measures for which local authorities have the immediate responsibility, training road users and accident investigation and prevention through small road schemes, are concerned exclusively with safety. Training has not been discussed as a separate subject in this report, although it has been suggested that the emphasis put on teaching road users to cope with unsafe conditions has sometimes distracted attention from the more fundamental task of removing the danger. But it was clearly shown in Chapter IV that accident investigation and prevention work does not attract the attention that the high rates of return from it warrant. Otherwise road safety is one consideration to be taken into account in determining policy in various fields. It has been seen, however, that it is little regarded in public transport policy, whether on investment, subsidies or (for buses) priority schemes; that the case for treating cycling as a major mode of transport, which it would be if safe facilities were provided, has not been recognised; and that relatively little has been done to create streets and neighbourhoods which are safe for pedestrians. In short, road safety is not now given the attention by local authorities that it deserves.

One reason for this is the very weak relationship that now exists between the Department of Transport's Road Safety Division and local authorities. At times, the extreme view that was criticised above seems to hold that where the direct responsibility in some field of action lies with the local authorities, the Road Safety Division need not be concerned. Thus, as has been seen, the Road Safety Division has taken little interest in questions of safety in the neighbourhood; there is no systematic knowledge at the centre on how much local authorities are spending on accident investigation and prevention through small-scale road schemes, or even on which local authorities are well equipped to do that job. Incentive schemes are also completely lacking.

None of the longer established organisations could take on the role that has been sketched for a national pressure group for road safety without substantial changes in its present functions and perhaps in its constitution as well. The most obvious candidate is the Royal Society for the Prevention of Accidents (RoSPA). Road safety has been a major concern of RoSPA's since its foundation in 1917 and now accounts for approximately 40 per cent of its annual budget of some £2.8 million. But RoSPA's day-to-day activities in road safety are almost entirely concerned with road user training and publicity. Although it has been active in national campaigns, notably in connection with seat belts, campaigning is a low-key activity. RoSPA's constitution makes it difficult to change this, since policy is formulated by its National Road Safety Committee on which various outside organisations are represented for whom road safety is only one of several possibly conflicting concerns. Among these organisations are road user associations such as the Automobile Association, the Royal Automobile Club, the Freight Transport Association and the Road Haulage Association, none of which would be likely to support measures of traffic restraint affecting their members, although traffic restraint is an essential component of a road safety programme, while both the motorists' organisations have suggested raising the present 70 mph speed limit on motorways. The trade organisations also represented on RoSPA's National Road Safety Committee are perhaps even more likely than the road user organisations to find that safety conflicts with their other interests. They include the Motor Cycle Association of Great Britain, the Society of Motor Manufacturers and Traders and the Motor Agents' Association(2).

The activities of the Pedestrians' Association are focussed on road safety. Its original name, when it was founded in 1929, was the Pedestrians' Association for Road Safety, and that name was shortened only five years ago as a token of its wider interests. The Pedestrians' Association has a deservedly high reputation in its own area, but for it to expand to cover the whole field of road safety would involve a huge extension both of its scope and of its resources: with an annual budget of only £5,000, it now depends almost entirely on voluntary effort.

Among the other national organisations whose activities impinge on road safety are the Civic Trust, the Conservation Society, Transport 2000 and Friends of the Earth; of these, it is probably Friends of the Earth that has been most actively engaged. There should be no conflict between road safety and the other activities of any of these organisations, but it would involve a major readjustment and substantial extra funds for any of them to take it on; moreover, it would probably be better for the national body to specialise exclusively in road safety while liaising closely with ecological and environmental and transport pressure groups.

The most promising institutional development in road safety in recent years has been the foundation of PACTS (the Parliamentary Advisory Council for Transport Safety). PACTS was formally launched in July 1982 although it had been operating on an ad hoc basis for about a year before that. Membership of the General Committee of PACTS, which is in various categories, includes members of Parliament, individual outside experts, professional organisations, trade and road user associations and firms. The purposes of PACTS are(3):

'advising, briefing and keeping informed members of both Houses of Parliament, the Department of Transport, councillors, local authorities and any other individual or body or organisation whatsoever on legislation (whether proposed, prospective, mooted or actual) concerning all forms of transport safety and on all other matters whatsoever relating to transport and transport safety'.

212

Until now, PACTS has concentrated, although not exclusively, on issues concerned with legislation, partly because of their importance and partly because its resouces are limited: its annual income at present is of the order of £10,000. Clearly, PACTS is well constituted to take on many of the roles which were sketched out above for a national pressure group. It would seem, however, that some of the campaigning activities envisaged for that group might go beyond the role of 'advising, briefing, and keeping informed'. The great strength of PACTS lies in its wide and expert membership, which should ensure that its views are taken very seriously, but wide membership might also be a handicap in forming a policy on some more sensitive issues, such as speed limits, training or traffic restraint, and in circumstances which require a very quick response. Thus it would seem that even when PACTS has expanded and developed there will still be some gap at the national level.

At the local level, organisations through which the general public can bring pressure to bear on the authorities in matters of planning do now exist in the form of civic and environmental societies. Such societies have grown steadily in number and expertise over the last twenty years: there are now some 1300 registered with the Civic Trust and many others, especially at street or neighbourhood level, which are not registered. At present, however, road safety is not a major activity of such societies, except perhaps the smaller very local ones. This tends to be true even of societies which have a special interest in transport, such as the London Amenity and Transport Association, the local branches of Transport 2000, or societies which started life on account of some transport issue, for example in opposition to a proposed new road. Since road safety causes more public concern than any other intrusion of traffic, this apparent lack of interest among groups concerned with their local environment is paradoxical. In Chapter IV it was suggested that one important reason for it is that when local societies, or indeed individuals, do become involved, especially on speed limits and pedestrian crossings, they often feel themselves rebuffed by the authorities. More generally, road safety is seen as a difficult technical subject in which lay participation would not be welcomed.

If the relationship between local societies and their own local authorities is weak, their relationship with the Road Safety Division of the Department of Transport scarcely exists. This is because one of the functions that, it was suggested above, a central road safety agency should undertake, that of 'selling' road safety to citizens, is not now attempted by the Road Safety

Division, which perhaps would not regard it as appropriate. (There are publicity campaigns to make people aware of safety, and to improve their behaviour, in their capacity as road users, but that is different from helping people as citizens to take an intelligent interest in issues of safety policy.) The annual publication <u>Road Accidents Great Britain,</u> with its excellent introduction, is, however, a good foundation.

It was stated above that policy on road safety should be coordinated with policies to control the other environmental intrusions of traffic. A problem is that environmental issues are now accorded a low position in the Department of Transport's functions(4). Road vehicles are the most important source of noise in the environment (as opposed to noise in the workplace which can reach much higher levels), and noise is the most resented intrusion of road traffic after danger(5). There is, however, no monitoring of exposure to noise (to show, for example, how many people live in dwellings exposed to a given level of noise)(6) and few attempts, none since the early 1970s, have been made to find out what values people attach to the absence of noise. The studies carried out at that time were almost completely independent of the Department of Transport and were mostly to do with aircraft noise. Of course, noise is very difficult to evaluate, but that does not account for its neglect. The evaluation of travel time is equally difficult, but has attracted a great many studies. The evaluation of risk of death or injury is perhaps the most difficult topic of all, but as was mentioned in Chapter I, the Department is now undertaking research on it. In spite of the massive evidence of public concern, the Department of Transport has not regarded noise as important enough to warrant such studies. The situation is not much better in the Department of the Environment, as is illustrated by the recent abolition of the Noise Advisory Council.

Because air pollution is regarded as a health hazard, whereas noise, perhaps incorrectly, is not, there is some regular monitoring both of emissions of fumes and of air quality. However a recent Directive by the European Commission on monitoring and controlling air quality has been interpreted in the narrowest possible way, one effect of which is that places where recommended maximum levels of pollutants may be exceeded because of fumes from vehicles are unlikely to be identified(7). Traffic fumes are disliked almost as much as noise and in some situations more so(8), but attempts to evaluate this annoyance have been even fewer, although this has been officially recognised as a gap in our knowledge at least since 1968(9). The dust, dirt and visual intrusion of traffic are resented by millions of people(10) but these problems have also received little attention.

The neglect of these environmental issues is unfortunate in itself and, as has been seen, has the effect of weakening the case for those safety measures, such as traffic restraint, or more stringent Construction and Use Regulations for motorcycles, which would also bring environmental benefits.

Suggested changes

In this final section, we suggest changes in the organisation of the road safety effort to help bring it more closely into line with the model that has been sketched. With one exception, all the recommended changes could be implemented by central government, and even on that point central government could substantially assist.

Ensuring a high standing for road safety within central government

The first change required is within the machinery of central government itself. The Road Safety Division of the Department of Transport does not now have the standing or 'clout' that a central road safety agency requires. The need for such a body to have sufficient standing was recognised in the 1967 White Paper Road Safety - A Fresh Approach. The section headed 'Strengthening the organisation' argued that although the several organisations concerned with road safety had done good work, they had achieved less than they might have done 'because there has been too little coordination of effort and no clear strategy ... Just as we need a clearer approach on research and the evaluation of measures, so we need a better organisation to make sure that our attack on road safety is more systematic, better coordinated and more knowledgeable'. The focus of this improved organisation would be a new unit which was described in the following terms(11):

'15. The Government is focusing its efforts on road safety in a new Central Road Safety Unit within the Ministry of Transport. This unit will bring together a team of varied experience and will be the main link with the whole range of people working in road safety. It will develop and carry through the continuing programme of national road safety measures and give fresh impetus to local efforts, guiding, stimulating and informing them. It will be the channel through which local problems can be referred back for central study, research and resolution. In short, it will be the driving force in getting things done in road safety.
16. The new unit will work with the other organisations in road safety, rather than replace them. The National Road

215

Safety Advisory Council will balance the new emphasis on science and professionalism by informed lay opinion. In particular, it will advise on problems of human behaviour. And much necessary local action will still be possible only because of the enthusiasm of voluntary workers. Government departments have enjoyed a special relationship with the Royal Society for the Prevention of Accidents and discussions have now begun on the development of this co-operation for the future, particularly in the organisation of training and publicity where the Society has useful experience to offer. The unit will also be in touch with trade unions and trade association, and with organisations representing motorists and other road users.'

The White Paper, moreover, adopted the limited view of road safety that has been described, in terms of reducing the accidents associated with a given pattern of travel and traffic. If a central road safety agency is also to intervene in wider matters of investment, taxation, subsidy and the treatment of alternative modes, the need for it to be an organisation of high standing is all the greater. But if the changes made in 1967 did not give road safety the prestige and standing it deserves within central government, how can that be assured?

One possible step would be to create a separate govenment department for road safety. Such departments exist in Japan(12,13), Sweden and France, and in the United States the National Highway Traffic Safety Administration enjoys a fairly autonomous existence within the Department of Transportation(14). The examples of Japan and Sweden are especially impressive, since these two countries, together with Norway, have the lowest road accident fatality rates in the world(15) and have also been particularly successful in bringing down road accident deaths and death rates in recent years. In Japan, the Central Traffic Safety Measures Conference was established in the Prime Minister's office in 1970. In that year the first of two five-year plans for road safety was launched. Fatalities fell in each year from 1970, when they reached a peak of 16,765, to 1979, when they numbered 8,461; during this time the Japanese population increased by 10 per cent and the vehicle population doubled(16). In Sweden, road deaths per head of the population fell by over a third between 1963 and 1981, although the figure was already relatively low in 1963(17).

An advantage of a separate department is that there would be a Minister and senior civil servants whose reputation would stand or fall by their record in safety alone. A separate ministry might feel much less inhibited than a division within the Department of Transport about campaigning boldly for road safety, both in tackling other government departments and in carrying the message to the general public.

A problem under this arrangement would be to create links between road safety and other aspects of the protection of the environment from the nuisance of traffic. One solution would be for the new Ministry to have both functions. Another solution would be to institute a similar change within the Department of the Environment, by splitting off the functions of environmental protection into a separate government department which would become responsible for all kinds of environmental protection, taking over the existing responsibilities for road traffic from the Department of Transport, which, as has been seen, now scarcely recognises them.

There would be a great deal to be said for such an arrangement, since the problem of enhancing the standing of environmental protection within the Department of Environment is at least as hard as that of enhancing the standing of road safety within the Department of Transport. Despite its name, the major concerns of the Department of the Environment are local government finance and organisation, the provision and maintenance of government buildings and property, and housing. Except for housing, the connection of these subjects with the physical environment is tenuous. If such a department existed, its traffic division could be expected to work closely with a Ministry of Road Safety, and the two in combination should be a formidable force for improving the quality of life.

This study has not investigated environmental organisation in other countries, but our impression from previous experience is that it is common to have a government department concerned solely or mainly with problems of the physical environment. Two useful models are the Environmental Protection Agency in the United States and the Ministry of Public Health and the Environment in the Netherlands. An interesting example of the role that an environmental ministry can play in transport policy was given in Chapter V, where it was seen that in Germany the Federal Ministry of the Interior, because of its responsibilities for environmental protection, has been promoting better provision for cyclists.

Nevertheless, there is something artificial about creating a separate government department to handle road safety which is so clearly a transport problem, involving other government departments such as the DHSS and the Home Office only slightly. It would be better, if it can be done, to keep road safety within the Department of Transport but to enhance its standing there. A first step in that direction would be to free the minister in charge of road safety from responsibilities for any other matters except, because of its close functional links with safety, environmental protection. At the moment that minister's responsibilities also include the trunk road programme, local roads, the bus industry, local public transport, rural transport, privatisation of HGV testing, transport for disabled people, a Channel link and general responsibility for the Department's work in connection with the European Communities and the promotion of transport exports(18).

But would such a rearrangement be sufficient to give road safety the standing it deserves? It would seem that while the Department of Transport continues to have its present range of responsibilities, road safety is always in danger of being the poor relation. In particular, the Department's responsibility for the trunk road programme is likely to dominate others. Thus it is not only because of the size of the programme, which is bound to divert the attention of Ministers, senior civil servants and MPs from other things, but also because of its nature. In all other matters of transport policy, such as ports, airports, railways, relations with local authorities, the Department's responsibilities are regulatory and supervisory, but for trunk roads the Department itself is the investing authority. It was argued in Chapter VI that this imbalance in the Department's responsibilities largely accounted for its failure to develop common investment criteria for different modes and generally to create a better legal and fiscal framework for transport. In Chapter IV it was suggested that the present division of responsibilities for roads between the Department and local authorities also distorts local transport policy, since it splits transport spending in any one county into two budgets: one which can be spent on any transport purpose, as needs and rates of return indicate, while the other can be spent only on roads, and on a limited set of roads at that.

In reply to this, it may be said that although particular trunk road improvements usually take place within the area of a single county council, they are not primarily intended for local but for through traffic. This was the argument used by the Department of Transport when the Transport Committee of the House of Commons suggested that a review should be made of the present distribution of responsibilities for roads between the national government and local authorities(19). But it is not clear that the needs of long-distance traffic are so distinct from those of other traffic as to require a separate road-building authority, and in any case there can be very few schemes left in the trunk road programme which are primarily designed to serve longer-distance traffic or traffic going right through the county in which the road is situated. Some are urban schemes; others are short by-passes and similar quite local schemes, some of which are explicitly not intended for through traffic.

A celebrated example of one such scheme was the Aire Valley route running north-west from Bradford. A risk of the 'improvements' proposed was that they might attact some of the longer distance traffic on to that route from others where, in the community interest, it belonged. The problems in the Aire Valley were caused by local traffic going between Bradford and the smaller towns in the valley, and the possible solutions included measures such as traffic restraint and improvements to the local bus and rail services which the West Yorkshire Metropolitan County Council would have been in a position to adopt but the Department of Transport, as trunk road authoritiy, could not even consider.

Even schemes which seem at first sight to be ones of national importance may not be. The proposed Kirkhamgate-Dishforth road, which would run between the M1, where it terminates in the southern outskirts of Leeds, and the A1 to the east, sounds as if it would supply a missing link in the national road network, and it was in such terms that it was originally described by its promoters(20). But when a traffic survey was undertaken, it was found that 86 per cent of vehicle trips lay entirely within a study area which comprised only a part of West Yorkshire, and only 2.5 per cent were going right through that study area(21). The problem had much more to do with traffic and environmental conditions in south-east Leeds, properly the concern of the county council, than with serving national needs.

The Aire Valley scheme, as officially proposed by the Department of Transport, would have cost £53 million(22), and the Kirkhamgate-Dishforth scheme, including some upgrading of the A1, some £80 million(23), with the expenditure in each case being spread over several years. The total annual expenditure on transport of the West Yorkshire Metropolitan Council at the time was some £85 million, most of which, however, was spent on current items such as road maintenance and lighting, public transport support and debt charges, leaving less than £14 million for capital improvements of all kinds(24). If the money required for these two schemes had been made available to the county council for transport improvements of any kind in the county, it is inconceivable that it would have been allocated in the same way.

The distortions which arise from the present split of responsibilities for road building between the Department of Transport and county councils are, therefore, very large.

This split also causes work in administration and co-ordination that would otherwise be unnecessary. It is officially estimated that to transfer trunk roads, other than those in London and motorways, from the Department of Transport to local authorities, would save some £9.5 million a year in administration, although that sum does not allow for severance payments and other transitional costs(25).

There will always be a need for the Department of Transport to act as adjudicator in the event of a dispute between neighbouring highway authorities, and perhaps also to intervene if some county council's road plans failed to give due attention to through traffic. But such matters can be dealt with by reserve powers; they do not justify a separate 'national' road-building programme.

Thus, even if road safety is left out of account, the arguments for the Department of Transport to shed or substantially reduce its responsibilities for trunk roads are very strong. The fact that it would then become possible for a minister to be assigned almost exclusively to road safety, and that ways of improving road safety by traffic restraint and the encouragement of safer modes would be more likely to receive sympathetic consideration, only strengthens the case further. A further advantage would be to remove a source of friction between the Department of Transport and those people, such as the environmental movement and public transport pressure groups, who should be the Department's natural allies in road safety but with whom the Department is now often in conflict.

Advocacy planning
However successful the efforts to strengthen the road safety lobby, there is always likely to be an imbalance in the pressures brought to bear on the Department of Transport from outside. Those interests which can be more easily organised and have some commercial support start with an advantage over interests which are diffuse and which for other reasons too may be hard to organise. The Department should correct for this imbalance by creating an internal division whose function would be to act as advocates for these people, such as inner city residents or children, who are not easily able to represent their own interests. This division would scrutinise all departmental policy on behalf of its 'clients'; for example, it would submit replies to the Department's

consultation documents as if it were an outside organisation. If, for example, such a unit had been in existence to represent children, it is hard to believe that the long-standing problems of child pedestrian casualties, unsafe conditions for cycling and the decline of children's mobility generally would now be so bad.

A system of incentives for local authorities
The government should institute a system of financial incentives to local authorities for reductions in road casualties. Each local highway authority would automatically receive a sum of money for the reduction in road casualties in a given year, as compared with the previous year, on the roads for which it is responsible. The amount paid for each fatality, serious casualty and slight casualty saved would be a specified proportion of the value currently attached to each such casualty. It would be necessary to make allowances for changes in the local authority's responsibilities - for example, the detrunking of a road - and it might be desirable to adjust for population change, but no other adjustments for special or changing circumstances would be made.

Between 1980 and 1981 road deaths in Great Britain fell by 164, serious casualties by 1,131 and slight casualties by 2,465. At 1981 prices, the official value of a death was £132,740, of a serious casualty £5,610 and of a slight casualty £130. It was argued in Chapter I that these values are too low, but if they are accepted for the time being, the total value of the reduction in casualties between 1980 and 1981 was £28.4 million. If the incentive had been fixed at half the official value, local authorities would therefore have received a total of £14.2 million for 1981, or somewhat more if, as is the intention, the existence of the incentives had led to a greater reduction in accidents. This sum is small in relation to the total road accident 'bill' of £2,182 million for 1981, but is about what local authorities spent on road safety in that year(26). An incentive of this magnitude could therefore have a substantial impact.

What would happen if the number of road casualties rose, as indeed it did in Great Britain as a whole in 1982 as compared with 1981? It would not seem possible to charge local authorities for an increase in accidents, in the sense of making them pay into a central fund, but the equivalent sums could be carried forward as a debit against whatever payment became due in the next year. This would render the system cheatproof: there would be no incentive either to under-report accidents or to delay remedial action from one year to another. However, the effect of introducing a system of incentives, in conjunction with the other reforms suggested,

221

should be that the number of accidents would always decline from one year to the next.

The need for payment to be automatic, rather than for the local authority to have to demonstrate that reductions were due to its own efforts, arises from requirements of simplicity. But it is not necessarily a disadvantage for local authorities to be paid for reductions which arise from national rather than local action. As was seen above, this gives them a financial incentive to press for legislation or other action at a national level when progress requires it.

A similar system of incentives, based on payment by results, was launched in France in 1983. This was in connection with a national campaign to reduce road deaths by one-third in five years. Local authorities participating in the campaign are paid a certain sum for each personal injury accident saved in a given twelve-month period, as compared with the immediately preceding one. The sum per accident is 20,000 francs, or some £1,650, for accidents occurring on the main roads policed by the Gendarmerie Nationale, and 10,000 francs for those occurring on the rest of the road network. The difference in the payment reflects the fact that accidents on main roads tend to be more severe. However, in order for the local authorities to qualify for any payment at all, there must have been a reduction of at least ten per cent in road accidents in its area as a whole(27). The introduction of such a threshold is a valuable extra incentive, especially if the level of accidents is falling anyway for reasons not attributable to local authority action. Since the accident problem is less severe in Britain than in France, ten per cent would appear to be an excessive threshold here, but four per cent might be appropriate.

Even though the proposed incentive system would not be tied to the work of the county council's accident investigation and prevention unit, it was suggested in Chapter IV that in order to produce a better informed local electorate, each county should publish an annual report on the work of that unit, using common statistical techniques, accident values and accounting conventions which would be specified centrally. The payment of any incentives should be conditional upon the production of such a report. The Department of Transport should itself publish more detailed information on the accident situation within each county than is now supplied in Road Accidents Great Britain. An appropriate way to do so would be by a comparison volume to Road Accidents Great Britain which would describe the situation in individual counties, not only by tables but by articles giving details of particular successes and innovations and naming the engineers responsible.

Among other things, this would help to enhance the prestige of road safety specialists in the engineering profession. It would also be useful for this publication to describe interesting practice, innovation and research in other countries.

As an additional financial incentive, we recommend that the NHS should automatically charge local highway authorities for the medical costs of accidents occurring on their roads. Table I.6 shows that in 1982 the medical costs of road accidents amounted to £73 million. One objection which has been raised to such a charge is that it makes it seem that local authorities are culpable for the accidents which occur on their roads. But culpability in a legal or moral sense is not in question. Someone has to pay the medical costs, and it is better that they should fall on bodies such as local authorities which, if only in the longer term, can have a substantial influence in preventing the occurrence of accidents, rather than on the NHS which cannot. It is fortuitous that this does not happen already. In West Germany, because of its federal constitution, the same local authorities are responsible for both highways and hospitals; much the same was true in Britain before 1948.

The amounts paid to the NHS would not be calculated for each individual case but would be based on national averages for a casualty of the given severity. This simplified accounting would make the total amount which any county council would be asked to pay in a given year more predictable, and would maintain an incentive for the medical authorities to discharge each patient as rapidly as his or her condition permitted.

A side-advantage of this system would be to improve the quality of accident statistics. It was seen in Chapter I that the classification 'serious injury' is so broad as to be unhelpful and that it would be better to divide it into two, or alternatively to substitute the AIS scale for the present classification. Any such change would require the cooperation of the medical authorities, which is also needed in order to tackle the serious problems of under-reporting of casualties and their mis-classification in the police records and hence in the national statistics.

One possible disadvantage of this system would be that it would create a temptation for the medical authorities to classify a patient too highly in order to receive a higher payment. However, we do not regard that as a serious problem.

The proposed change would require some adjustment in the Rate Support Grant to compensate local authorities for their new responsibilities. This should not be of a kind or degree which would nullify the financial incentive to local authorities to reduce road accidents.

In our view, this would be a simple and valuable institutional reform. It would reinforce the system of payments for accident reductions and would make it more likely that money received by local authorities under that scheme would be reinvested in road safety.

Involving citizens at the local level

The reforms that have been suggested in the relationship between the central government and local authorities would also remove most of the obstacles that now deter people from taking an informed interest in road safety in their own areas. As well as the facts, they would be given an extra incentive. There would still be room, however, for the Road Safety Division to take a more active educational role by providing material, speakers for meetings and so on, as suggested above.

The relationship between citizens and local authorities would also improve if local authorities were to take a more sympathetic view on the points where disagreement tends to arise. We are not suggesting that they should modify otherwise sound policies simply for the sake of public relations. The implication of Chapter III is that on speed the layman's intuition is right and the experts have been wrong: the requirement is not to raise 'unrealistic' speed limits but to lower the limits and to enforce them. General pedestrian policy has not been considered in this study, but there is ample reason to suggest that it has been neglected and that the present system of priorities as between motor vehicles and pedestrians grossly favours the vehicles. It was seen in Chapter IV that tension can arise between engineers and local people about small-scale engineering schemes. This is partly because the criteria used by the engineers and local people about small-scale engineering schemes. This is partly because the criteria used by the engineers are too narrow: they are interested only in saving accidents, whereas local people may be interested in the relief of anxiety as well or they may wish to allow their children to play in the streets. Where the disagreement turns on a point of budget allocation, in that the engineers might agree that some action would be desirable, but they have better schemes on their list, perhaps it would be removed by increasing the budget for accident investigation and prevention so that more schemes could be included. There is plenty of room to do so by transferring funds from other items with lower rates of return in a local authority's transport budget: an increase in the total of transport expenditure is not required.

A national pressure group

There remains the problem of filling the present gap in the national organisations. The first priority is to strengthen PACTS. It was argued above that another smaller and less formal group would also be desirable, which ideally should be a new group concerned only with road safety, though working closely both with PACTS and with the existing environmental and similar pressure groups. The problem, either in building up PACTS or in starting anything new is, of course, to find the funds.

It might be awkward for the Department of Transport to provide funds for outside groups one of whose principal functions would be to bring pressure on the Department, and perhaps equally awkward for the outside groups to receive the funds without jeopardising their independence or giving the appearance of doing so. Nevertheless, as has been seen, there are precedents for such support. It might be easier for the Department to give money for particular purposes, such as making educational films, or keeping a record of interesting innovation in other countries, rather than to give general support. The relationship would then become that of customer and contractor. The DHSS would also be a suitable source of funds, since road safety can be regarded as preventive medicine.

Outside government, the problem is that there is little commercial interest in road safety, at least if safety is thought of in the traditional narrow way. If it is conceived more widely, as we have argued it should be, then the public transport industry and its suppliers also have an interest, and that of the bicycle industry is even stronger and more direct. In America, the Insurance Institute for Highway Safety and its offshoot the Highway Loss Data Institute, whose work we quoted in Chapter III in connection with on-vehicle speed control, are supported by the insurance industry. But apart from those sections or industry to which road safety is of especially concern, it should have a wider appeal to any firms which sponsor outside activities or support charity, especially once it is realised how large the prize is and how easily it could be grasped.

References

(1)   House of Commons Hansard, 20 December 1982, Columns 356 to 360.

(2)   RoSPA Report and Accounts 1981/82, supplemented by other documents and correspondence.

(3) Parliamentary Advisory Council for Transport Safety, Chairmen's Report for 1982/83.

(4) In a recent paper by the Director of Statistics of the Department of Transport (E.J. Thompson 'Transport Statistics Overview', Transport Statistics Conference, November 16th 1983, published by IMAC Research on behalf of the Standing Committee of Statistics Users, 1983), environmental protection is mentioned only in the context of marine pollution. The first paragraph of Annex A to this paper reads as follows:

'The main functions of the Department of Transport (DTp) are:
(a) development and management of the national road system;
(b) sponsorship and regulation of, and financial assistance to, inland and surface public transport; and sponsorship and regulation of road haulage;
(c) sponsorship and regulation of the shipping and ports industries; sponsorship of the civil aviation industry and, mainly through the Civil Aviation Authority, its regulation on safety and economic grounds;
(d) allocation of resources and guidance to local authorities for their transport functions;
(e) conduct of international relations and negotiation in respect of international civil aviation and shipping;
(f) road safety, including regulation and licensing of vehicles and drivers, and marine safety, including the coastguard; and
(g) prevention of pollution of the sea by ships and cleaning up pollution of the sea caused by ships and oil installations.'

(5) Jean Morton-Williams, Barry Hedges, Evelyn Fernando, Road Traffic and the Environment, Social and Community Planning Research, 1972, especially page 63.

(6) A survey for this purpose was conducted on a once-off basis in 1972 and 1973 and is reported in a TRRL report published in 1977: D.G. Harland and P.G. Abbott, Noise and Road Traffic outside Homes in England, TRRL Laboratory Report 770. It showed (page 10 and Figure 2) that seven per cent of the population experienced a noise level which would entitle them to compensation if it had arisen as a result of building a new road. This survey is unlikely to be an accurate guide to the present situation: on the one hand, individual vehicles probably emit less noise than they did; on the other hand

traffic has increased and motorcycle traffic has more than doubled.

(7) Directive No.80/779/EEC, Official Journal 30.8.80, is concerned with air pollution both as a health hazard and as an environmental nuisance (see Article 1), but the Department of the Environment's circular on this Directive (Clean Air, Department of the Environment Circular 11/81, para. 20) mentions only health. The Directive states that measuring stations 'must be located at sites where pollution is thought to be greatest and where the measured concentrations are representative of local conditions' (Article 6). The official British response to this is that 'it is recognised that this Article is open to a variety of interpretations but the UK Government understanding of such terms as 'representative' and 'local' is in the context of the general atmosphere in a town or conurbation, or significant parts thereof, and not in the context of very local, relatively small spatial scale, situations disproportionately influenced by a single or small number of sources' (Progress on implementation of the EC Directive on air quality limit values for sulphur dioxide and suspended particles, Warren Springs Laboratory, December 1982, para. 3.2). Since pollution from motor vehicles tends to be heavily concentrated near busy roads, places where it exceeds the recommended levels are unlikely to be revealed by methods of measurement designed to represent a town or large district.

(8) As ref. 5.

(9) Road track costs, a report by the Ministry of Transport, HMSO, 1968, especially Annex 12, 'The evaluation of accident costs and loss of amenity due to vehicle noise and fumes'.

(10) As ref. 5.

(11) Road Safety - A Fresh Approach, Ministry of Transport, HMSO, 1967.

(12) Japanese Government White Paper on Transportation Safety, May 1982.

(13) Bernard Mamontoff, 'La securite routiere au Japon', Transport, Environnement, Circulation, No.38, January-February 1980.

(14) Information on Sweden, the United States and France is taken from two reports prepared for the Delegation a la Securite Routiere, attached to the Prime Minister's office in France, in 1973. They are L'organisation de la securite routiere dans cinq pays etrangers and La securite routiere en France, comparaison de l'organisation francaise avec celles de cinq pays etrangers.

(15) Road Accidents Great Britain 1982, Table 51.

(16) Japanese Government White Paper on Transportation Safety, op.cit., Tables 1, 3 and 7. The fatality figures quoted are not directly comparable with British figures since they relate only to deaths occurring within 24 hours of the accident, but this difference is allowed for in the international comparisons shown in ref. 15.

(17) See ref. 15 and corresponding figures from the 1964 edition of Road Accidents.

(18) Ministerial responsibilities in the new Department of Transport, Department of Transport Press Notice No.195, 15 June 1983.

(19) 'Government Observations on the First Report of the Committee, Session 1980-81 (The Roads Programme)', House of Commons Third Special Report from the Transport Committee Session 1980-81, HMSO, April 1981. The relevant passage reads as follows:

'The reasons which led to the establishment of the trunk road system are still valid. The country needs a national road network to serve long-distance through traffic. While such roads also serve local traffic, their main purpose goes beyond the area and interest of any individual local highway authority. While taking account of local circumstances, especially in detailed design, improvements to the system must be based on a national view of needs and priorities'.

(20) Yorkshire to the North-East. We need your views. Consultation paper issued by the Department of the Environment. Undated but early 1970s.

(21) Strategic Corridors, Traffic and Economic Assessments, 1978 Review: Summary Report, report for the North Eastern Road Construction Unit on the Kirkhamgate-Dishforth scheme by Jamieson MacKay and Partners, 1978.

(22) Documents from the Airedale Route Public Inquiry, 1980.

(23) Documents from the Kirkhamgate-Dishforth Public Inquiry, 1981.

(24) Highways and Transportation Statistics, based on estimates for 1980-81, Society of County Treasurers and County Surveyors' Society, May 1980.

(25) Report of the Working Party on the Future of the Trunk Road System, National Annual Consultative Meeting, NACM (83)2, Department of Transport, 1983, Chapter 5.

(26) See Transport Statistics Great Britain, 1971-1981, Table 1.18. According to this table, local authorities spent £13 million on

'road safety etc.' in 1981/82, but as explained in Chapter IV there may well be some expenditure contributing to greater safety itemised under other headings.

(27) <u>Objectif 10%</u>, Delegation Interministerielle de la Securite Routiere, Paris, 1983.

APPENDIX NOTES ON THE STUDIES REQUIRED TO REVEAL THE EXTENT AND IMPORTANCE OF UNSAFE CONDITIONS ON THE ROADS.

Chapter I showed that the present accident statistics and 'costings' understate the extent and importance of unsafe road conditions. Mention has been made in other chapters of ways in which small changes in the accident records could improve the description of accidents. This Appendix makes some suggestions, although only in outline, for providing better information on accidents, their costs, and the other harmful consequences of unsafe road conditions.

Records of accidents and casualties
Records based on STATS 19
Accident statistics are derived from the STATS 19 form filled in by the police. Although the scope and detail of this record is inevitably limited by practical considerations of the time that the police can spend on form filling when an accident occurs, some changes are possible, especially with the cooperation of the NHS and the Driver and Vehicle Licensing Centre at Swansea. The system of payments to the NHS described in Chapter IX would require some simple records to be kept which could also be used to amplify the information given on the STATS 19 form. The computerisation of the DVLC records makes it very easy to obtain details of any driver or vehicle involved in an accident: there should be no problem about doing so in a way which protects the anonymity of the individual licence holder. We suggest the following changes and additions.

1. The definition of death in a road accident should be changed so as to include both anyone who dies within 30 days of the accident, as at present, and anyone whose death occurs after that time but is clearly a consequence of the accident. It is accepted that the application of this definition will sometimes involve medical judgement, whereas the present definition has the advantage that its application is automatic. The present definition will also have to be retained, at least for some time, for purposes of showing trends and making comparisons with other countries.

2. The category of serious casualty (and hence serious accident) should be divided into two or more by reference to the AIS classifications.

3.   The classification of particular casualties by degree of severity should be made as far as possible by hospital staff rather than by the police.

4.   The police should record the name and driver number shown on the driving licence of each driver, including motorcyclists, involved in an accident, such that further details from the DVLC can be entered on the STATS 19 form of the driver's age and sex, the type of licence held and the length of time for which it has been held. In addition, for motorcyclists it would be valuable to record whether or not the rider had undergone training at an approved centre, although to do so would require some changes in the present DVLC records.

5.   The police should also record the number on the licence plate of each vehicle involved so that information about its make, model, age and engine size can be entered on the form from DVLC records.

6.   The function of the road on which an accident occurs (e.g. purely residential, shopping street etc.) should be entered on the form at the coding stage. This would involve looking up the grid reference, or other description of location provided by the police, in some computerised data bank held by the local authority.

7.   For the more serious pedestrian accidents, the police should where possible record the distance of the accident site from the injured pedestrian's home. 'Home' would have to be defined as place of temporary residence in the case of people visiting or on holiday.

Monitoring hospital records
Chapter I described how hospital records used to check the information in the STATS 19 forms had shown that this information was incomplete, in that some casualties from road accidents had not been included at all, and was also sometimes inaccurate, in that the severity of the injury was often misdescribed, usually by way of understatement. It is likely that these problems would remain, if somewhat reduced, even if more use were made of hospital records in completing the STATS 19 forms. Therefore it is desirable for there to be a continuous monitoring, based on the records of a small number of hospitals, of the STATS 19 information. Although the detailed tables in Road Accidents Great

Britain would have to be based on the original uncorrected information, the results of the monitoring could be used to adjust the national statistics of casualties and costs and also to adjust the calculation of the benefits obtained or expected from particular safety measures.

Household survey

A regular household survey to monitor road accidents and casualties is required both as a check on the STATS 19 information and to supply details of accidents which are excluded by definition from the STATS 19 records.

Monitoring hospital records does not constitute a complete check on the information derived from the STATS 19 form because some injuries are not treated in hospital. In addition, hospital records may not always reveal that the patient's injury occurred in a road accident. For example, if there is some delay between the occurrence of the accident and the decision to seek treatment, or if the patient is originally treated for certain injuries but then has to seek more treatment because other symptoms emerge, the fact that the injury resulted from a road accident might not be recorded.

Accidents which are excluded by definition from the STATS 19 form include those that occur off the public highway, those that involve pedestrians but no vehicles (as when someone trips on a pavement), and those which involve vehicle damage but no personal injury. The household survey should include such accidents and could also obtain information about household pets killed or injured in road accidents. If possible, it should also establish the numbers of people involved in some capacity other than that of victim, for example as a close relation of a killed or seriously injured person or as a witness to an accident

It might be necessary to supplement a household survey with a survey of people living in residential institutions, especially so as to ensure a proper coverage of old people.

Travel surveys

STATS 19 data on casualties by type and characteristics of road user become still more useful if they can be converted into casualty and accident rates. To do so, data on the distance travelled by particular classes of traveller are required. Traffic counts are insufficient sources of such data because they cannot provide much detail about road users and their vehicles. The National Travel Survey is a good source but should be conducted more frequently and on a larger scale. For motorcyclists, even an enlarged NTS might not produce a sample large enough to allow detailed breakdowns; it might therefore be desirable to supplement the NTS by a continuous travel survey of motorcyclists based on a sample drawn from DVLC records.

The costs of casualties and accidents
In order to establish more accurate costs for casualties and accidents, it is first necessary to list the various people and other economic agents who are affected by them, or rather the various capacities in which people are affected, since any particular person may be affected in more than one capacity. It seems to us that the absence of such a list accounts for some of the apparent omissions of items of cost noted in Chapter I. We suggest the following list of people and effects.

1. <u>People killed</u>
    (i)   Curtailment of life.
    (ii)   If death is not immediate, the effects for injured people also apply.

    Curtailment of life is partly allowed for in the present costing system under the 'lost output' heading, since this is measured by income, some of which would have been enjoyed by the dead person. It is also allowed for under the 'pain, grief and suffering' heading, although this heading is a complete misnomer with respect to people who die immediately; also, for the reasons given in Chapter I, there is no reason to accept the present figures even as approximations.

2. <u>People injured</u>
    (i)   Pain and shock.
    (ii)   Curtailment of activities due to disability.
    (iii) Loss of income.
    (iv)   Temporary disruptions, possibly involving extra expense (e.g. in hiring home helps).

    Item (iii) is covered under the 'lost output' heading, although, as noted in Chapter I, a substantial loss of income may have consequences in altered life styles etc. (for example if it becomes necessary to move to a smaller house perhaps in a different neighbourhood) which are not adequately allowed for by the nominal loss. Item (i) is allowed for under 'pain, grief and suffering', but again there is no theoretical basis for

233

the figures and no reason to suppose that they are even approximately right numerically. Items (ii) and (iv) do not seem to be covered.

3. Relatives and friends (emotional dependants)
   (i)   Feelings of bereavement and similar feelings of loss associated with the severe injury or disability of a loved person.
   (ii) For children who lose a parent or parents, loss of parental guidance and moral support. This may apply in some cases of severe injury as well as death.
   (iii) Loss of shared activities.
   (iv) Possible long-term burden of nursing or similar care.
   (v)   Temporary disruption of having to rearrange activities, visit hospitals etc.

Except for the 'grief' element of 'pain, grief and suffering,' these effects are not now considered.

4. People whose actions may have helped to cause the accident
   (i)   Remorse and guilt.
   (ii) Possible financial losses through having to pay compensation.
   (iii) Disruption (filling in forms, attending court etc.)

This class of affected person seems not to be recognised at present. Item (ii) should be included only if there is a corresponding adjustment elsewhere; otherwise there will be double counting, except insofar as there may be legal fees or other transaction costs.

5. Witnesses of the accident
   (i)   Shock and emotional distress.
   (ii) Temporary disruption of activities by having to help police or insurance companies, attending court etc.

This class of affected person is also not recognised at present.

6. People who lose household pets
   (i)   Shock and grief.

This category of person is excluded by definition.

7. Financial dependants of the dead or injured person
    (i)   Loss of income.

    This is covered under 'lost output', but the same caveat applies as for item 2(iii).

8. People dependent on the dead or injured person for unpaid 'production'
    Unpaid production may take the form of cooking, housework, etc. which is allowed for under the present system only in the case of non-working housewives, or of help to neighbours, work in voluntary groups etc. which is not allowed for at all.

9. Employers and the economy generally
    (i)   Loss of 'surplus'.

    The present heading 'lost output' should allow for this, but as it is estimated by reference only to the costs of employing someone, in practice it does not.

10. People who suffer damage to vehicles or other property
    (i)   Costs of repairs or replacements.
    (ii)   Transaction costs (dealing with insurance companies etc.).
    (iii) Temporary disruption (hire of replacement vehicles and similar expenses; lost time).

    Only item (i) seems to be covered in the present costings.

11. Police and the NHS
    These costs are now allowed for, although it was noted in Chapter I that to take salaries and other costs of provision as an estimate of the value of the work which the police and medical staff concerned would otherwise have been able to do is likely to produce an understatement at a time of excess demand for their services.

12. Insurance companies
    (i)   Costs of administration.

    This item is now allowed for; we know of no reason to doubt that the present costings are approximately accurate.

13. Road users not directly involved
    (i)   Cost of delays and diversions because of congestion on road closures following an accident.

Not allowed for at present.

We would have thought that it would be possible to improve the estimates of 'lost output' (items 2(iii), 7(i) and 9(i) fairly easily by drawing on existing calculations of value added for various industries; however, this topic lies outside our own field. The studies now in hand of the valuations people place on differences in accident risks should allow items 1(i) and 2(ii) to be evaluated. It would be necessary to adjust the lost output figure, part of which now relates to 1(i), in order to avoid double-counting; this would mean reverting to the former practice of offsetting what would have been the future consumption of someone who is killed against what would have been his future production. There may be problems too in knowing to what extent a person's evaluation of risk allows for the other unpleasant consequences to himself of becoming a casualty and, indeed, the losses to other people such as his dependants and perhaps even his employer.

For most of the other effects in the list, which are not now covered, or not adequately so, it is too soon to talk of evaluation: not enough is known about what the effects are. There is a need for follow-up studies of all those affected by an accident to find out more about the consequences. Such studies would fall roughly into two groups: those that would be concerned to ascertain the short-term disruptive effects; and for fatalities and the more severe serious injuries, those that would deal with the psychological impact and with the longer term adjustments that the victims and their financial and emotional dependants are obliged to make. The first step would be a number of exploratory interviews, preferably conducted by psychologists, for which great sensitivity would be needed.

Non-accident costs
Unsafe conditions on the roads distort travel patterns. People who in safe conditions would walk or cycle may forego their journeys or make them by other means. Other people may be obliged to act as escorts for them and sometimes as chauffeurs. It may also be that motorists choose their routes partly to avoid what they perceive to be more dangerous or stressful roads. When travel is still made by the means that would have been chosen in safe conditions, it may be a cause of anxiety and stress to the travellers themselves or to

others on their behalf. Unsafe conditions also frustrate other activities such as children's play and other forms of street life and casual social contact. To the extent that such activities still occur, they may be, once more, a source of anxiety both to the participants and to others.

Evidence was given in Chapter I that these effects are both widespread and resented, but more up-to-date and systematic studies of them are required.

Traffic safety in the neighbourhood

A great many of the issues can be grouped together under the heading 'traffic safety in the neighbourhood'. Children and the old are the people least likely to be able to look after themselves in traffic; their activities tend to be very local.

A simple and useful survey would be to list the various problems and to ask people whether each was of concern to them and if so whether they regarded it as major or minor.

A more difficult and detailed study would be to compare the behaviour, and the degree of stated satisfaction or dissatisfaction, of people living in neighbourhoods where traffic is more or less of a problem. How much do old people get about? At what age are children allowed to walk or bicycle to school? How much do they participate in street play? How does the incidence of worry among parents vary? It was seen in Chapter VIII that some other countries have tackled safety in the neighbourhood much more boldly than Britain; in spite of the problems of cultural differences, it might therefore be useful to attempt inter-country comparisons. The most useful studies of all might be before-and-after comparisons in streets and areas where substantial changes are introduced, including the creation of traffic-free neighbourhoods.

Studies of people who have recently moved house, or are contemplating doing so, should throw useful light on the importance of safety either as a motive for moving or as a consideration influencing the choice of where to look when a move is made for other reasons, such as a change of job. Among other things, such people would be in a good position to rank neighbourhood safety against the other considerations which they have to take into account when looking for accommodation, and they might even be able to attach a money value to it. Estate agents should have a shrewd idea of the wishes and priorities of house-hunters; surveys among them would also be useful. It would be especially useful to explore the issue of traffic safety in the context of the flight from the inner city.

There is also a whole range of market research techniques, some of them already used in the surveys cited in Chapter I, which can be used to ascertain the relative priority which people attach to safety. The technique of asking people to state what their priorities would be if they were house-hunting appears especially promising.

Walking and cycling on journeys outside the neighbourhood
Walking should not be thought of as a mode of transport suited only for journeys within a residential area or to the local schools and shops. It can serve longer journeys, including journeys to work. Cycling can be used for journeys of several miles. But the attractions of both modes are very dependent upon the conditions. The extent to which unsafe conditions now inhibit walking and cycling is best ascertained by comparisons of safe and unsafe towns, but there are substantial problems in measuring safety, in finding towns which exhibit different degrees of safety, and in controlling for other factors influencing choice, such as traffic fumes or the price and quality of public transport.

Perhaps these problems can be solved only in the context of large-scale demonstration projects to make selected towns, or large districts of cities, safe and attractive for pedestrians and cyclists. In the meantime, it may be possible to find pairs of towns which are roughly comparable with respect to size, density and layout but which happen to provide a very different standard of service for pedestrians and cyclists. It was seen in Chapter V that several continental towns have made especial efforts to accommodate cyclists. Comparisons of the share of journeys made by cycle, within purpose and distance categories, in such towns and in British towns of a similar size would be useful. Similar comparisons could in principle be made for walking, but whether or not suitable towns could be found, i.e. towns where, either by historical accident or because of more recent acts of policy, walking is especially safe and attractive, is a question that has not been examined in this study. Waldman's statistical analysis of the factors accounting for variations in the propensity to cycle to work should be repeated with more recent data, and if possible extended to journeys for other purposes; the possibility of carrying out a similar analysis for walking should also be investigated.

To evaluate the costs of frustrated walking or cycling, or in other words the benefits that would flow from changes that would allow more people to walk and cycle for short and medium-distance journeys, is difficult. Conventional analysis based only on changes in travel time and expenditure is unlikely to represent the position of those who are now frustrated pedestrians and cyclists. The pleasure of walking and cycling, the health benefits to be derived therefrom; the flexibility in being able to come and go when one pleases, in the case of those who now use public transport, or in not having to worry about parking, in the case of motorists; the further flexibility of being able to modify the route or stop off on the way: all these may be as important as travel time and expenditure. In addition, the effect on other road users of a transfer to walking and cycling would have to be considered. A modest but essential first step would be attitudinal surveys both among people who now walk and cycle, and among others who claim that they would do so in better conditions, to ascertain how they see and rank the various advantages.

Long-distance travel

There is no doubt that long-distance motoring can be a source of stress to drivers and of anxiety to others on their behalf. Social surveys are required to establish how many motorists and lorry drivers claim to be affected, how seriously they regard it, and whether it affects their travel behaviour at all, for example in the choice of mode or route. Similar surveys on anxiety should be conducted among the wives and families of the drivers concerned; this inquiry should also cover the relatives of motorcyclists.

Such surveys might throw some light on the more difficult question of what the relationship is between stress and anxiety and the actual degree of risk involved, since it might be possible to examine how answers varied according to the roads usually driven on and the traffic, weather and lighting conditions. But the experiments with speed limits and enforcement recommended in Chapter III would provide better opportunities to explore this relationship.

1810